Form and Content in Revived Cornish

Reviews and essays in criticism of Kernowek Kemyn

by

Michael Everson
Craig Weatherhill
Ray Chubb
Bernard Deacon
Nicholas Williams

evertype
2007

Published by / *Dyllys gans* Evertype, Cnoc Sceichín, Leac an Anfa, Cathair na Mart, Co. Mhaigh Eo, Éire / *Wordhen*. *www.evertype.com*.

First edition 2007. Reprinted with corrections January 2011.
Kensa dyllans 2007. Daspryntys gans ewnansow Genver 2011.

Editor / *Penscrefer*: Michael Everson.

ISBN-10 1-904808-10-7
ISBN-13 978-1-904808-10-7

Typeset in Palatino by Michael Everson.
Olsettys yn Palatino gans Michael Everson.

Cover / *Cudhlen*: Michael Everson

Printed by / *Pryntys gans* LightningSource.

CONTENTS

FOREWORD

Kernowek Kemyn, a form of spelling currently promoted by the Cornish Language Board, has been subject to sustained criticism for nearly two decades since its inception.

The present collection of essays takes its title from my observation in a 1999 review of Ken George's *Gerlyver Kres*, that there were only two things wrong with that dictionary: its form and its content. The form and content of the Cornish Language Board's publications continue to invite criticism and have inspired this volume.

The essays begin with a review of recent Cornish Language Board typography, including the second edition of Ken George's *Gerlyver Kres*, the New Testament in Kernowek Kemyn, George's *Gerlyvrik*, and the recent and controversial "preliminary edition" of *Bywnans Ke*. This is followed by a reprint of my review of the first edition of George's *Gerlyver Kres*, as it is referred to in the first article.

Craig Weatherhill, Cornwall's foremost expert on place-names, provides the next two articles, both reviews of Cornish Language Board publications, *Place Names in Cornwall* and *The Formation of Cornish Place Names*.

Ray Chubb and Craig Weatherhill collaborated on a short paper in which they provide an analysis of the similarity of Revived Cornish orthographic forms to traditional spellings of Cornish place-names.

Bernard Deacon provides two insightful articles, the first on the values expressed in Kernowek Kemyn rhetoric, and the second on the aims and methods of the Cornish Language Board.

Finally, Nicholas Williams reviews *An Testament Nowydh* edited by Keith Syed and published by the Cornish Language Board.

This is a volume of criticism. Those we criticize may attempt to accuse us of trying to discredit the Cornish Language Board because we publish books which "compete" with them. We believe, however, that our reviews and analyses are verifiably fair. We believe that quality speaks for itself.

Michael Everson
Westport, February 2007

RECENT TYPOGRAPHY IN KERNOWEK KEMYN

Michael Everson

INTRODUCTION

In this article I will discuss recent typography in Kernowek Kemyn, beginning with the second edition of the *Gerlyver Kres*. My review of the first edition of that dictionary appeared in 1999 in *Cornish Studies Seven* and is reprinted immediately following the present article for the convenience of readers who may wish to refer to it.

Good typography is, to someone trained in it, a quiet pleasure. Bad typography is painful as a bad pun, but without the secret enjoyment. It just hurts. *Why, oh why*, the typographer asks when seeing an example of bad typography, *did they not know better?*

Many readers will never notice good typography; it is invisible. They may not really notice bad typography either—but it will nevertheless interfere with their use of the badly typeset material. A poor font or font-size will make the reader squint and hesitate. Unusual typographic or editorial conventions will give a reader pause until he or she figures them out or becomes inured to them.

But typography is not rocket science. Training in typography is helpful, and there are many books about typography which can help in the absence of a teacher. But even those things are not really necessary. If you are putting a book together, and if you want it to look good, you need do no more than get a number of copies of similar books *and simply look at them*. Some will be better than others, and you will be able to tell by examination and reflection. If you *pay attention* to what other authors and publishers have done, you will be able to ask yourself "How can I make my dictionary (or novel, or grammar, or newsletter, or invitation) look like a *real* dictionary (or novel, or grammar, or newsletter, or invitation)?" And then you can use your computer to help you to achieve the look that you want, or you can seek the advice of someone who could help you to achieve it.

Unfortunately, the promulgators of Kernowek Kemyn who have run the Cornish Language Board for the past two decades do not seem to have considered the need to strive for excellence in presentation. Even when I pointed out specific problems in my review of the first edition of the *Gerlyver Kres*, its author and editor decided to take little notice.

The result was that the second edition offered little improvement over the first. Let us begin with a look at the *Gerlyver Kres*.

GEORGE'S *GERLYVER KRES*, SECOND EDITION

In 2000, a year after my review of the *Gerlyver Kres* appeared in *Cornish Studies Seven*, the second edition of Ken George's dictionary appeared. George had read the review, and in his foreword to the second edition he endeavoured to dismiss it thus:

> M. Everson* has criticized *Gerlyver Kres* on superficial grounds, but as the publisher of a different dictionary of Cornish, he can hardly be regarded as impartial. He considers the following to be unconventional:
> (a)   the use of different fonts for Cornish and English;
> (b)   using + (instead of -) for indicating "add-on" plural endings;
> (c)   using angle brackets for distinguishing homographs[.]
> The editor of *Gerlyver Kres* regards all of these features as improvements.

It seems a little insolent to dismiss a careful review as "superficial". Was I an "impartial" reviewer? Well, no. No reviewer is "impartial". Did I write an unfavourable review with some strange notion that I could influence the sales of either the *Gerlyver Kres* or of Nicholas Williams' *English-Cornish Dictionary*? Hardly. I doubt that sales of either dictionary are much influenced by reviews in *Cornish Studies*. I wrote a review of the dictionary because dictionaries deserve review. I wrote an unfavourable review because in very many ways the dictionary was bad. I wrote a review pointing out what was bad, thinking that in doing so I might be able to encourage better typography in the Cornish Revival.

My hopes were dashed. But the Cornish Language Board, in the hands of the promulgators of Kernowek Kemyn, seem not to understand book publishing at all. George's foreword begins by saying "This is essentially a reprint of the first edition, but since a new ISBN has been assigned, it must be described as a new edition". Well... no. When a book is simply reprinted, it is not assigned a new ISBN number. When a book is printed with changes, even "minor corrections" as it states on the copyright page, then it *is* a new edition, and *therefore* it is assigned a new ISBN. Goodness knows how the Cornish Language Board manages its publications. The first edition of the *Gerlyver Kres* had the ISBN 0-907064-87-6. The second edition's ISBN is 0-907064-79-5. Most publishers assign their books numbers from 00 to 99. Perhaps the Cornish Language Board is counting backwards.

---

*Modern editorial practice favours writing out names in full.

George apologizes for the first edition not having very much front matter because they were "restricted" to 320 pages. Such a restriction is based only on the cost of printing the book, but we will look at the new front matter below. First, though, let us look at the "superficial" criticisms I made in my review of the dictionary.

1. The design in terms of font choice and font size within each entry is ugly and irritating.
2. The design in terms of font choice and font size with each entry is *different* in the Cornish-English half and the English-Cornish half of the dictionary. This is unprecedented in bilingual dictionary design.
3. The plus sign is used to indicate additive plural suffixes and the hyphen is used to indicate suppletive plural suffixes. So we have *ger, +yow* for *geryow* but *triger, -oryon* for *trigoryon*.
4. References glossing homophones are given in <angle brackets> and are not separated from the headword by a space. This information is redundant, as the first word in the definitions gives exactly the same information.
5. A bug in conversion from database to dictionary text results in Cornish headwords beginning with a hyphen not being listed in bold (-iv, -oleth, -vann, -ya instead of **-iv, -oleth, -vann, -ya**).
6. "GERLYVER KRES ... Kernewek - Sawsnek" and "GERLYVER KRES ... Sawsnek - Kernewek" appear as headers on every page instead of the useful guidewords one usually expects.
7. "Dr Ken George" and "mis-Hedra 1998" appear as footers on every page.
8. Even-numbered page numbers in the Cornish-English part are inset 66% into the footer instead of being centred as other page numbers are.
9. The front matter was not properly proofed. "never-endingtask" is run-on, as is "asonderstondya". The terms "English-Cornish" and "Cornish-English" are written with "space en-dash space" ("English – Cornish") where a hyphen would suffice. The dust jacket contains the spelling error "signicance".

Now let us look at George's response to those criticisms.

1. "The editor of *Gerlyver Kres* regards [the use of different fonts for Cornish and English] as [an improvement]." An improvement on what? To be fair, I must admit that "ugly and irritating" is not really the constructive criticism it might have been. But it was not "the use of different fonts" which I objected to. It was the specific mix of fonts and sizes and weights which I considered to be indicative of poor design choice. Is this element of the design of the *Gerlyver Kres* really an "improvement" on two centuries of bilingual dictionary design? Go into a decent bookshop and look at a dozen good bilingual dictionaries from

known publishers like Oxford or Harrap. Is the *Gerlyver Kres* really more legible and usable than they are?

2. George did not address this complaint. Of all of the things which I complained about, this is the one I would most have liked to have seen addressed. Having the two halves of the dictionary look so different does not enhance legibility or usability in any way: quite the opposite. It is bad design, and neither excuse nor rationale can be offered for it.

3. "The editor of *Gerlyver Kres* regards [using + (instead of -) for indicating "add-on" plural endings] as [an improvement]." An improvement on what? On Nance? On generations of Latin or Greek dictionaries? Is there some special pedagogic utility to this convention? Does it figure in some significant way in George's database and software? Is it a secret? And we have *kelli, kelliow*; ought we not expect *kelli, +ow*?

4. "The editor of *Gerlyver Kres* regards [using angle brackets for distinguishing homographs {sic}] as [an improvement]." An improvement on what? On the normal lexicographic tradition of using superscript numbers to show mark homophonic headwords? These glosses are redundant, and while they may be helpful to the compiler of the dictionary, they are worthless to the end user—particularly those "glosses" such as <AV>, <CJ>, <CN>, <FN>, <IJ>, <MN>, <PV>, and <VP>, which are not explained in the front matter. We have **kons**<causeway> alongside **kons**<FN>. Is this the "Feminine Noun" *par excellence*? Or is this an error for **kons**<vagina>? Ah! Compare **kalgh**<lime> and **kalgh**<MN> (for **kalgh**<penis>). But no… compare also **kosk**<sleep> and **kosk**<FN> (for **kosk**<admonishment>). No, there's no discernible pattern. No sense to these undefined abbreviations. And what excuse is there for not separating these glosses from the headword by a space? I fail to understand this "improvement" and my criticism of it stands.

5. George did not address this error.

6. George addressed this by replacing the headers with guidewords, but he has done so inconsistently. In the Cornish-English part, the first and last word on each page are both given next to each other, separated by "space hyphen space" flush left above the left-hand column on left-hand pages, and flush right above the right-hand column on right-hand pages. In the English-Cornish part, the first word on each page is given flush left above the left-hand column of each page, and the last word on each page is given flush right above the right-hand column of each page.

7. George addressed this error by deleting all of these footers.

8. George addressed this error and the foliation is correct.

9. The front matter was altered and expanded. There appears to be some sort of space inserted to break up "never-endingtask" on page ii, but it is a hair space or non-breaking space, evidently, as it is thinner than the other spaces on the line. The run-on "asonderstondya" on page iv was

broken up, but just two lines above that we have the run-on "the*Gerlyver Meur*". The run-on "of*Gerlyver Kres*" appears on page xiv. Again on page ii the terms "English-Cornish" and "Cornish-English" are written with "space en-dash space" ("English – Cornish") where hyphen is wanted. Indeed the punctuation used produces a syntactic error. Both "space en-dash space" and "em-dash" are equivalent in European English and those punctuation conventions are used to show a parenthetical insertion. The following three sentences are equivalent:

> "New software has been written by the editor to produce English (Cornish as well as Cornish) English dictionaries." (with parentheses)
> "New software has been written by the editor to produce English—Cornish as well as Cornish—English dictionaries." (with em-dash)
> "New software has been written by the editor to produce English – Cornish as well as Cornish – English dictionaries." (as the *Gerlyver Kres* has it)

The editor needs to use hyphens, so that the sense is clear:

> "New software has been written by the editor to produce English-Cornish as well as Cornish-English dictionaries."

The dust jacket no longer contains the spelling error "signicance" or the phrase in question, which was appropriate to the announcement of the first edition. However, the dust jacket now claims that "The Gerlyver Kres is the first bilingual dictionary of Cornish to be published." This is not really true. Nance's Cornish-English and English-Cornish dictionaries have been available in a single volume for a very long time now.

And there is more to be said about the new front matter. When one looks at the way the text is typeset, one notices that the common typist convention of adding two spaces after the full stop. This convention was developed in the days of lead-type composition to assist compositors in identifying sentence ends from typescript. No well-trained compositor would insert additional space after a full stop, however. Yet throughout the front matter, it appears that two spaces follow the semicolons and three or four spaces follow the full stops.

In the new section "Layout" the first paragraph is indented twice as far as all of the other paragraphs. It appears that George is copying the formatting I used in my review of his own book to describe the fonts and font-sizes used. He runs-on "inLarge Arial", though, and calling it "large" isn't as specific as naming the point size.

The new section "Spelling and Pronunciation" has much to offer the critic, and I am tempted to write a good deal about the content of these eight pages, though I aim to endeavour to confine myself to *form* here, rather than *content*. On page vii George makes a number of grumpy allegations about "N. Williams".* These are given between parentheses and attention is drawn to them by setting them in italic type. All three of them are written incorrectly, with the full stop outside the closing parenthesis where it ought to have been inside it.

On page ix George lists the phonemic value of <e> as /ɛ/, giving its phonetic value as [ɛ̩]; he does not discuss why he gives the vertical bar diacritic below the vowel. In the International Phonetic Alphabet, the vertical bar diacritic indicates syllabicity and is not applied to vowels. On the same page he lists the phonemic value of <o> as /ɔ/, giving its phonetic value as [O:] when long and [O] when short. This is presumably a font error for [ɔ:] and [ɔ]. In the last sentence of the same section he describes the sound "when mid-length" as "between [O:] and [O]" where the length mark crashes into the first vowel as I have reproduced here. In any case, why did he not write [ɔ·], since in the next sentence he lists [o:] and [o·] as forms of his <oe>? He says that [o] unrounded when unstressed is [ɤ], but it is odd that he says that this is similar to [ʌ], since [ʌ] is the unrounded version of a different phoneme, that is [ɔ]. At the bottom of this page and on the next there are again typographical spacing problems with the vowels [i:] and /œ/ and /ʎ/ and [ə] crashing into their preceding punctuation as I have shown here.

Of the discussion of consonants on pages x–xi I have little to say in terms of typography. However, one may write geminate consonants [p:] as easily as [pp]. Where the hypothetical geminate <mm> is discussed, George suggests that it is pronounced as a "doubled [m], as *mm* in English *Mummy*". I know of no dialect of English in which this word is pronounced ['mʌm:ɪ] rather than ['mʌmɪ].

Typographic conventions are ignored on page xiii. George mentions words "spelled with <-e> and pronounced [-ɛ]" and words "spelled with <-a> and pronounced [-a]" He must mean "spelled with final -*e* and pronounced [ɛ]" and words "spelled with final -*a* and pronounced [a]". The hyphens do not belong inside either the angle brackets or square brackets.

A new section entitled "Technical" has been added; I assume George means "Technical information". The section tells us just how old the computer language George uses to write his dictionary is; he tells us how many source files he has; he tells us that they are in ASCII format rather than in Unicode format (which may help explain his problems with character sets); he gives us the names of three programs he uses to

---

*Modern editorial practice favours writing out names in full.

manipulate the data, so that we may blame "GLSK3" for applying the codes denoting the font and type-size used in the book. As the font formatting is automatic, it seems that the Cornish Language Board should insist that those codes be changed so that the output would be pleasant to the eye and consistent with accepted practice in lexicography.

It is a pity that George did not consider the advice given in my review of the first edition of his dictionary more carefully.

THE CORNISH LANGUAGE BOARD'S *AN TESTAMENT NOWYDH*

There will doubtless be complaint that I criticize the typography of the Cornish Language Board's edition, since I edited and typeset Nicholas Williams' *Testament Noweth agan Arluth ha Savyour Jesu Cryst*, published in 2003. In this case, certainly, our edition was available for scrutiny and criticism before the Cornish Language Board's edition was, and I am content to let the reader make up his or her own mind as to whether what I say below is fair or not. I will not discuss the content of *An Testament Nowydh*; Williams has done so far better than I could in the last article in this volume.

For some reason the words "Kernewek Kemmyn" appear immediately above the ISBN on the copyright page. I cannot think of any reason for this to be so.

The overall appearance of the text of the *An Testament Nowydh* is not very satisfying. The text is set out across the page, rather than in two columns as is more usual with Biblical translations printed in books of this size. The verse numbers are not superscripted, but rather are printed in the same point size and weight as the text itself and thus appear to be an essential part of the text, rather than merely an aid to the reader. On reflection I found that I could make a guess as to why this was done. The editors made the choice to translate the footnotes given in the English-language versions they consulted (for instance, the note to Luke 2:14 "Henn yw, on bolonjedh da a Dhyw. War-lergh re a'n dornskrifow *hag y'n bys kres, bolonjedh da dhe dus*" which refers to the manuscript reading; this is similar to the *New English Bible*'s "*Some witnesses read* and on earth his peace, his favour towards men." Since the editors were using a word-processor's footnote function to link these notes to the text, superscript numbers in the text are used to call out the footnotes, and were not available for verse numbering. This is not the right way to handle Biblical typesetting.

The chapter number of each book is given as a drop capital, which is fine. But it is missing at Matthew 1:1. Most of these drop capital numbers are flush right, as expected, but at Galatians 1:1 the drop capital is indented and indeed superscripted somewhat. Many of the drop capital numbers are followed by a space to separate them from the text and aid reading, but not in Philippians 1, 2, or 3. In Colossians 1:1 the third line of text, "dhiworth Dyw agan Tas", does not run underneath the drop capital number as expected. A second line of text is missing at 2 Timothy 2:1. For the books of Philemon, 2 John, 3 John, and Judas, each of which has only one chapter, the editors of *An Testament Nowydh* do not give a drop capital number but simply a verse number. (In Williams' *Testament Noweth* I do use a drop capital number; this is consistent with the practice I found in other New Testaments.) At Acts 8:1 the drop capital number looks bad because the editors have inserted the heading in the middle of a verse.

Regarding the headings themselves, Williams points out below (page 124) that the editors of *An Testament Nowydh* have translated them from headings in the *New English Bible*, the *New International Version*, and *Today's English Version*. In the *New English Bible* and the *New International Version*, the headings are printed discreetly in an inconspicuous italic, and in my opinion, if one is going to editorially insert such headings into the text, they should be discreet and unnoticeable. In the *Today's English Version*, however, the headings are printed in a bold font. This practice has been followed by the editors of *An Testament Nowydh*. Unfortunately, they have also chosen to print quotations from the Old Testament in the text of the New Testament in bold. This means that the headings, which are extraneous to the text, are given a prominence which they do not merit; they are made to appear to be as important as the citations from the Hebrew scriptures in the text itself.

A new book does not always begin on a new page. The gospel of Mark, for example, begins half-way down the right-hand side of the page with the end of the gospel of Matthew above it and opposite. Revelation begins almost three-quarters of the way down the right-hand side of the page, with the epistle of Jude taking up the rest of the page above and the page opposite. A new book should always begin on a new page.

The wrong point size has been used for the digit 7 at Acts 28:7 and as a result the leading is disturbed. The same thing has happened with the word *Mes* 'But' at the beginning of Galatians 2:14.

Transliteration of Greek seems to perplex the editors. The names *Alfeus* and *Thaddeus* appear at Matthew 10:3 and footnotes are given to indicate that their readings are "*Alfe-us*" and "*Thadde-us*". Are readers

of Kernowek Kemyn really in danger of pronouncing ['alfœz] or
['θad:œz]? A note to Matthew 10:28 says that the Greek is "*Gehenna*"
and at Matthew 11:23 it is "*Hades*" though the actual forms in the text
are γέεννη and Ἅιδου. At Luke 20:24 the note says that the Greek is
"*denarion*", but that is a transliteration; the Greek is δηνάριον. The list of
names of currencies in the table of measures and maps on page 420 also
gives Greek words in the Latin alphabet.

The editors chose to use single quotation marks for quotations and
double quotation marks for quotations within quotations. In English-
language typography, this is often a matter of taste, and there is certainly
a strong tradition in Britain of following this convention. In my own
experience typesetting Cornish, Irish, and Scottish Gaelic, I have found
that the use of double quotation marks for quotations and single
quotation marks for quotations within quotations is better for legibility,
because double quotation marks are more easily distinguished from the
apostrophe, which occurs very frequently in these languages.

An Testament Nowydh is set in Times, which is terribly pedestrian for
such a work of literature. Again, this is a matter of taste.

GEORGE'S *GERLYVRIK*

Many of the criticisms of the *Gerlyver Kres* apply to the *Gerlyvrik*. Some
things unique to it may be noted. In the front matter, instead of using
proper arrows → to show the change of consonants in mutation, em-
dash and greater-than sign are used —>; on page 10 the one between *d*
and *dh* is mistakenly set in bold, although all the others (except the
three illustrating the mixed mutation on page 12) are in plain type.

Typesetting in a small format is challenging, but some attempt
should have been made to hyphenate manually.

In both the Cornish-English and English-Cornish halves of the
dictionary, each headword is written in what George claims is the
International Phonetic Alphabet. The usual stress marks are used, as in
Kernowek Kemyn *dynnerghi* [dɪnˈerɦi] 'welcome'. I am not sure why
George believes that <gh> is voiced as [ɦ] here. In the front matter he
states that intervocalic <gh> is pronounced [ɦ] "like the *h* in *aha*". But
the *h* in English *aha* is not voiced, at least not phonemically: there is no
difference between [aˈhaː] and [aˈɦaː]. I would write UCR *dynerhy* as
[dɪˈnerhi]; despite the etymological origin **do-ind-arc-i-* (compare
Middle Welsh *denneirch*), the syllabification is surely *dy-ner-hy*, not *dyn-
er-hy*, so George should write [dɪˈnerɦi], not [dɪnˈerɦi].

9

There is no explanation given for the use of a stress mark in the transcription of every monosyllabic word, as in *penn* ['penn] (UCR *pen* [pe^dn] or [pɛn]). This is contrary to normal IPA practice.

Although George transcribed *e* as [ɛ̩] in the *Gerlyver Kres*, in the front matter of the *Gerlyvrik* he writes [ɛ̜], with the left-half ring diacritic. In the International Phonetic Alphabet, the left-half ring diacritic denotes a "less-rounded" pronunciation. I am not sure how "rounded" George believes [ɛ] to be that it needs such a diacritic, but in the main body of the dictionary he uses neither [ɛ̜] nor [ɛ], but [e], which is a different vowel from [ɛ]. Even more strangely, George again transcribes *o* as [O] (which is not an IPA character), and then notes that [ɔ] is used for it in the body of the dictionary. The only phonetic uses I can find for [O] are non-IPA: Pike and Smalley suggested it might be used for a voiceless vowel [o̥] (as in Cheyenne); in Chomsky and Halley [O] is used informally to represent the vocalic nucleus that is realized as [ɔ] when lax and [ow] when tense; and Crothers used it for a mid-back rounded vowel ([ɵ]?).

Here as in the *Gerlyver Kres*, George writes the following for *o*: long stressed [oː], mid stressed [o·], short stressed [ʏ]; here he also writes unstressed *o* also [ʏ]. Then again he notes that [ʌ] is used for [ʏ] in the body of the dictionary. Why the change in signs? The whole use of IPA in the body of the dictionary is rather odd in any case. Is it really necessary, if Kernowek Kemyn is phonemic?

In the front matter, the name of the language is written in small-caps as KERNEWEK KEMMYN. There is no real reason this should be done. It reminds me of branding, as though it were "Kernewek Kemmyn™".

GEORGE'S "PRELIMINARY EDITION" OF *BEWNANS KE*

It is difficult to find the heart to review this monograph. As I write this, Graham Thomas and Nicholas Williams' scholarly edition of *Bewnans Ke* has been printed and awaits its launch in about a fortnight. I first began to typeset that volume in August 2003. Work was sporadic, of course, since much time had to be taken by both Thomas and Williams to proof intermediate drafts of the 576-page book. When it becomes available, readers will be able to judge the typesetting for themselves.

I feel I have to say this because there just isn't a single nice thing I can say about the typography of George's "preliminary edition", called *Bywnans Ke* in Kernowek Kemyn. A baroque typographic awfulness pervades the book from beginning to end.

The cover of the book dates it to "mis Ebryl 2006". On the title page it is "mis Gortheren 2006".

In the front matter, the title **Bywnans Ke** is given, thus, in **Arial Bold**, with the title in Middle Cornish given as Beunans Ke, thus, in Bookman Old Style. "Kernewek Kemmyn™" is given as *Kernewek Kemmyn*, thus, in *Times Bold Italic* throughout the front matter. The front matter also describes this practice by naming the fonts ("The text in *Kernewek Kemmyn* is in Arial: roman [*leg.* Arial Roman] for Cornish words"). This perverse practice derives, as far as I can see, from my own review of the *Gerlyver Kres* in 1999 where I used the convention *in criticism* to point out the bad typography in that book. I never intended that George should take it up as part of his editorial repertoire, though he has used it in the front matter of the second edition of the *Gerlyver Kres*, in the *Gerlyvrik*, and here.

Microsoft Word's ugly automatic superscripts are used in ordinals like "16th". In decent typography "16th" suffices, or if superscription is wanted, it should be balanced as in "16th".

Two spaces follow colons and semicolons, and three or four spaces follow full stops, throughout.

George describes a manuscript abbreviation "consisting of a super-script semicircle with a dot at its centre … frequently used, usually but not always to denote <n>; this is indicated in the printed text by ^." This is an unprecedented method of editing manuscript abbreviations. George invents his own method of foliation, and cites in the front matter "BK39.62–BK39.68" (by which he means stanza 434 or lines 3235–3242):

> An duk an gevith pur wyer / rag e laver ol an tyr / A thowr hombyr the Scotland / ha mi^s a^ geva horsus / lerd in Kint ha hengystus / in termyn mortygernus, / whe^ he was king in this la^d.

The actual reading of *Scotland* in the text should have been "*Scotla^d*" according to George's convention, and for *lerd* read *berd* (for *'berdh*). In his edited text at the same stanza George has inserted a line from the margin into the middle where it does not belong:

> An duk an gevith pur wyer / rag e laver ol an tyr / A thowr hombyr the Scotland / ha mi^s a^ geva horsus / **Mortigernus King of this [la]nd** / lerd in Kint ha hengystus / in termyn mortygernus, / whe^ he was king in this la^d.

The addition is puzzling. It is inserted into the stanza after line "BK39.65" (line 3238) but not given a line number, not even "BK39.651" (line 3238a). Here I give the uncorrected text, in the two ways one

11

would ordinarily find it presented if one wished to preserve an indication of the manuscript abbreviations:

> An duk an gevith pur wyer / rag e laver ol an tyr / A thowr hombyr the Scotland / ha mins an geva horsus / berd in Kint ha hengystus / In termyn mortygernus / when he was king in this land

> An duk an gevith pur wyer / rag e laver ol an tyr / A thowr hombyr the Scotlãd / ha mĩs ã geva horsus / berd in Kint ha hengystus / In termyn mortygernus / whẽ he was king in this lãd

It is hard to determine why George engages in such adventurism in devising editorial conventions. The traditional italicized letter or letter with tilde is easier to read than the ASCII circumflex. And such novelty pervades the presentation of the text itself. George marks every line with his idiosyncratic numbering system. He indicates rhyme patterns and evidently syllable counts above each stanza. There is no discussion of this, though one may guess that *aabccb* differs from *aaBccB* if the capital letters indicate polysyllabic rhyme.

Perhaps George is unfamiliar with traditional scholarly editing practice. Why not simply examine Norris' or Stokes' editions? Perhaps he thinks his innovations to be "improvements". I don't fathom it.

Typographic errors happen. I make them myself. Design is often a matter of taste. But recent typography in Kernowek Kemyn shows nothing but unapologetic amateurism in design and execution. It is regrettable that the Cornish Revival should suffer from such low standards.

REFERENCES

Cornish Language Board. 2004. *An Testament Nowydh.* [Saltash]: Cornish Language Board. ISBN 1-902917-33-2

George, Ken. 2000. *Gerlyver Kernewek Kemmyn: an Gerlyver Kres. Kernewek-Sowsnek Sowsnek-Kernewek. Cornish-English English-Cornish dictionary.* [Saltash]: Kesva an Taves Kernewek. ISBN 0-907064-79-5

George, Ken. 2005. *Gerlyvrik Kernewek-Sowsnek & Sowsnek-Kernewek: Cornish-English & English-Cornish mini-dictionary.* Callington: Kesva an Taves Kernewek; Fouenant: Yoran Embanner. ISBN 1-902917-43-X, 2-914855-11-7

George, Ken. 2006. *Bywnans Ke.* Pareusys gans Ken George. [Saltash]: Kesva an Taves Kernewek. ISBN 1-902917-57-X

International Phonetic Association. 1999. *Handbook of the International Phonetic Association: a guide to the use of the International Phonetic Alphabet.* Cambridge: Cambridge University Press.

Pullum, Geoffrey K. & William A. Ladusaw. 1996. *Phonetic symbol guide.* 2nd ed. Chicago: University of Chicago Press. ISBN 0-226-68536-5

"AN EVENT OF GREAT SIGNICANCE" [sic]: REVIEW OF GEORGE'S *GERLYVER KRES**

Michael Everson

Ken George, *Gerlyver Kernewek Kemmyn: an Gerlyver Kres. Kernewek-Sowsnek Sowsnek-Kernewek. Cornish-English English-Cornish dictionary*, 1998, 320 pp. [Bosprenn]: Kesva an Taves Kernewek. ISBN 0 907064 87 6, £14.99

INTRODUCTION

The publication of a new dictionary for a Celtic language is generally a cause for celebration. Ken George's new dictionary, appearing five years after his *Gerlyver Meur*, is rather a disappointment, as it is defective in two essential features: its form and its content.

FORM

Producing a dictionary is a formidable task: unlike most other books, a dictionary contains a very large number of paragraphs ("entries"), each of which must adhere closely to the chosen style, and be as stylistically perfect as possible. Given the emphasis George places on computer-aided linguistics, one would expect a high degree of precision in the presentation of entries in his dictionary.

Precise they are; readable and attractive they are not. I find the typography of the *Gerlyver Kres* to be ugly and irritating, reflecting rather slipshod design parameters. In Part One, Cornish headwords are presented in **12-point Helvetica Bold**, with grammatical notes in *10-point Times Italic*, and English definitions in 10-point Times Plain. Within an entry, Cornish subentries are presented in **10-point Helvetica Bold**. References glossing "homographs" (the usual word in lexicographical practice is *homophones*) are given in <angle brackets> (which are normally used in linguistics to represent orthographic entities, rather than semantic ones); these are, inexplicably, not separated from the headword by a space.

Turning to Part Two, the English-Cornish half of the dictionary, one would expect that the same conventions would be applied. They are not. In Part Two, English headwords are given in **12-point Times**

* First published in *Cornish Studies*. Second series: Seven. 1999. Exeter: University of Exeter Press. Pp. 64–87. ISBN 0-85989-644-7, ISSN 1352-271X

Bold (not **12-point Helvetica Bold**), and Cornish definitions in **10-point Helvetica Bold** (not 10-point Times Plain). Grammatical notes are still given in *10-point Times Italic*, and sub-articles in 10-point Times Plain. In some entries, additional comments are given in 9-point Times Plain with **9-point Helvetica Bold**. A bug in the conversion from database to dictionary text resulted in headwords beginning with a hyphen being set in plain text instead of bold (-iv, -oleth, -vann, -ya, instead of the expected **-iv, -oleth, -vann, -ya**).

This typography gives a totally different colour to the text of the two halves of the dictionary. The inconsistency is quite unacceptable, being confusing to the user, and without precedent in bilingual dictionary design. It appears to be the result of some kind of automated text-dump without sufficient attention to stylistic harmonization. It makes the dictionary hard to use. It draws the attention of the user to the typography, which is a cardinal sin in typesetting: the best typography is *always*, in lexicography at least, invisible.

In the entries, the plus sign is used to indicate a plural suffix added to the root (*ger, +yow* for *geryow*); the hyphen is used with plurals when some letters of the root are replaced (*triger, -oryon* for *trigoryon*). This convention was also used in George's 1993 *Gerlyver Meur*. I cannot see that it has anything in particular to recommend it; at least in 12-point Helvetica Bold, the plus sign appears *very* large and black, leaping off the page at the reader. Nance did not find it necessary to make use of such a convention: he wrote *ger, -yow* for *geryow*, and *tryger, -goryon* for *trygoryon*. The practice is also unknown in Breton and Welsh dictionaries. It is possible that George may make some use of the +/- distinction in his database for purposes irrelevant to users of the *Gerlyver Kres*.

Let us take some sample entries, presented in actual size: first from George's dictionary. I chose this example only because it had showed all three of the features criticized above: varying sizes and faces of type, glosses in brackets attached to the headwords, and the use of the plus sign before the plural ending. I chose these examples before I looked at the equivalent entries in Nance's *Cornish-English Dictionary*.

> **les**<plant> *m.* **+yow** plant, wort; **les an gog** marigold; **les densek** dandelion
> **les**<profit> *m.* profit, advantage, benefit; **dhe les** *adj.* useful, interesting, worthwhile
> **les**<width> *m.* width, breadth

Notice that no plural ending is given for the second and third entries, though they are nouns (this makes those entries dependent upon the first one), and that the <glosses> are completely redundant, as the first word in the definitions gives *exactly* the same information. Compare Nance:

> lēs, *m.*, breadth, width; landyard of 18 feet square, D. "lace": *trelles* (*trylles*), three times the width O.M. 393; *l. tyr* (*lace teere*), a "lace" of ground (Carew MS., 1599, Hearne's *Curious Discourses*).
>
> lēs, *m.*, profit, advantage, behoof, interest, use, good, benefit, *hydh* Aelfric; to serve, be of use (of things): *nyns-yu dhe l.*, it is of no use; *myr dh'y l.*, watch over his interests; *oll rag agan l.* for the good of us all; **les-kemyn*, commonwealth; *ef a-drel dhyso dhe l.*, it will turn out profitable for thee; C.W. 739.
>
> †les, -les, *m.*, plant, -wort (in old compounds): see losowen, made from pl., losow.
>
> †les-an-gōk (C. Voc. *lesengoc*), *m.*, marigold, *solsaeve* Aelfric, lit. "cuckoo-flower"; see cōk.

A great deal more information is given in Nance than in George.

In fairness to George, however, note that the plural is not given clearly for Nance's entries at all. I am not sure what to think about the fact that Nance gives lēs for 'breadth' and 'profit' but les for 'plant' while George gives only les. Either George considers the latter to have the same vowel length as former, or he has forgotten to respell it less in his orthography. The point size is considerably smaller (8.5-point type on 8-point leading where George has 12- and 10-point type on 10.5 point leading); it is well to observe that George's dictionary would be far shorter than it is, were it set like Nance's.

> les<plant> *m.* +yow plant, wort; les an gog marigold; les densek dandelion
> les<profit> *m.* profit, advantage, benefit; dhe les *adj.* useful, interesting, worthwhile
> les<width> *m.* width, breadth

And that means quantifiably shorter. Nance's English-Cornish letter L runs to 199.5 column centimetres and his Cornish-English letter N runs to 120.5 column centimetres. George's English-Cornish L runs to 216.5 column centimetres (8 per cent longer than Nance) and his Cornish-English letter N runs to 84.5 column centimetres (30 per cent shorter than Nance). But setting George at the same size as Nance would yield something like 149 column centimetres for L and 58 column centimetres for N, 25 per cent and 48 per cent shorter than Nance's L and N respectively. The *Gerlyver Kres* has about 200 pages of material in it page for page compared with Nance, though its typographical padding brings it to over 300 pages.

I was stunned by the headers and the footers of the dictionary. "GERLYVER KRES ... Kernewek - Sawsnek" and "GERLYVER KRES ... Sawsnek - Kernewek" appear, pointlessly, atop every page instead of the useful guide words one normally expects in a dictionary. The footers remind us that "Dr Ken George" finalized the text of his dictionary in "mis-Hedra 1998" on each page. People often use their wordprocessors to put this kind of information on draft documents, but one does not expect it to survive the publication process. Some uncorrected error resulted in the even-numbered page numbers in the Cornish-English half of the dictionary being inset 66 per cent into the footer, instead of being centred as are all the other page numbers in the dictionary.

The English in the two pages of front matter appears not to have been proofed: "never-endingtask" on page 2 should have been "never-ending task". For "asonderstondya" on page 3 read "as onderstondya". The terms "English-Cornish" and "Cornish-English" are written with "space en-dash space" ("English – Cornish") where a simple hyphen would have sufficed. The dust jacket proudly announces that the publication of this dictionary "is an event of great signcance [sic] in the development of the language".

Typographically, this dictionary is a disaster. It looks as though it were prepared by people who neither cared for, nor understood the noble art of lexicography.

CONTENT

The title of the dictionary is difficult to ascertain, as the book has a number of titles. On the title page: *Gerlyver Kernewek Kemmyn: An Gerlyver Kres. Kernewek-Sowsnek Sowsnek-Kernewek. Cornish-English English-Cornish dictionary*; on the spine and dust jacket: *The New Standard Cornish Dictionary. An Gerlyver Kres. Cornish-English English-Cornish*. If George thinks we shall consider 'Gerlyver Kernewek Kemmyn' to be an acceptable translation equivalent for 'The New Standard Cornish Dictionary', he should think again. 'New Standard Cornish Dictionary' in Cornish is 'Gerlyver Savonek Noweth a'n Tavas Kernowek'. "An Gerlyver Kres" could also mean 'the Middle Dictionary', 'the Dictionary of Faith', or 'the Dictionary of Peace'. What does the author intend us to understand? Just that this dictionary is smaller than the *Gerlyver Meur* of 1993? The learner of Cornish will certainly be confused.

The front matter comprises just two pages, which is a bit scant.

The list of abbreviations omits symbols such as <AV>, <CN>, <IJ>, etc., although these appear with some frequency. The information contained in these codes is redundantly entered in the dictionary, and it is often possible to decipher them. My objection is that the user of a dictionary should not be presented with such material nor required to perform decipherment. Consider:

> **as-** *pref.* re-
> **-as<-ful>** *suff.* **-asow** -ful
> **-as<VN>** *v.* (VN ending)
> **-as<33>** *v.* (3rd sg. pret. ending)
> **es<PV>** *v.* thou wast
> **ha<IJ>** *int.* ha
> **ow<-ing>** *ptl.* -ing
> **ow<my>** *adj.* my
> **-ow** *suff.* (pl. ending)

One can guess VN to be "verbal noun", and suppose PV to be "personal verb" (or something), but I won't hazard a guess at decoding "33". Is there a 30, 31, 32? Note that for *-as* VN is given not only in brackets, but also in the definition—though VN does not appear in the list of abbreviations. Neither does *sg.* or *pret.* or *ptl.* or *pl.*—though *plur.* does. The list also gives *int.* "interjection", though *interj.* is more usual in dictionaries in opposition to *intr.* "intransitive". Redundant or not, it looks as though in generating the dictionary from the database, the information was exported from the same field as the glosses which also appear within brackets. A database structured so that grammatical information and glosses appear to be in the same field is certainly something to wonder about.

I suppose if one is going to go to the trouble to gloss *es* as 'thou wast' instead of 'you were', one should also give 'thou wert'.

Non-penultimate stress is not indicated in the *Gerlyver Kres*. Non-penultimate stress is unpredictable; it must be indicated in a Cornish dictionary. Nance used the middle dot to indicate this. Does George not use it because his database and his comparison programs are unable to handle headwords so marked? That would be one explanation for not showing stress in the headwords. Otherwise, there is no excuse. Either way the dictionary is faulty. The dust jacket states that it is "an essential volume for beginner and scholar alike", but this fault alone reduces the dictionary's usefulness for either.

Regarding the coverage of the dictionary, the blurb on the dust jacket claims: "This New Standard Dictionary contains all known words of the traditional language, except the English borrowings for which there are perfectly good Cornish alternatives, plus the [sic] new words for the 21st. [sic] century." The front matter, however, asserts that "the master-files include practically all the words found in traditional Cornish, and many more words introduced into Cornish in the 20th century, especially by R. Morton Nance." Why exactly do the "master-files", the basis for all of George's work, not include *exhaustively* all the words found in the corpus of traditional Cornish? Exactly what percentage has not been included, and why?

In any case, neither claim is true. An assertion that a dictionary contains "all known words" is extravagant and easily checked. But let us look just at the loanwords which George finds offensive. Taking a list of 513 borrowed verbs ending in -*a* and -*ya* found in *Pascon agan Arluth*, *Origo Mundi, Passio Christi, Resurrexio Domini, Beunans Meriasek*, John Tregear's *Homilies, Sacrament an Altar*, and *Creation of the World*, and we must first note that 191 of these (37 per cent) are *only* found in Tregear's texts and can't be expected to be found in Nance 1938. Of the 322 words remaining, 48 (15 per cent) are missing from Nance as headwords in the dictionary. I have not checked the provenance of these 48 words. Some may also have been unavailable to him; some may be erroneous omissions. One does not suspect Nance to have withheld Cornish words from publication.

In George's dictionary, of these 513 words borrowed into traditional Cornish, 270 (53 per cent) do not appear as headwords in the *Gerlyver Meur*. One could be tempted to believe the front matter's claim, which explains that "[s]ome of the words in the traditional corpus, such as *onderstandya*, [which] have not found favour with Cornish speakers" have therefore been omitted, but an investigation of the loanwords included and omitted makes one wonder what criteria George used in order to make his determination of which words Cornish speakers liked and which they did not. Of the 191 words from Tregear unavailable to Nance, but available to George, 143 (75 per cent) have been omitted by George. Why omit *glorifya* when *glori* and *gloryus* are included as headwords? Why omit *rebellya* but not *rebellyans*? Why omit *kreatya* when *kreador* is included? Under the English headword **creator**, *furvyer, gwrier*, and *kreador* are given, while under **create**, only *gwruthyl*

18

is cited. Why are *furvya* and *kreatya* omitted under the verb? English admits the synonyms *'form'*, *'make'*, and *'create'*. Surely Cornish may also be as rich. Why include *confessya, ordena*, and *marya*, but not *confyrmya*? Why is *comondya* (found in *Origo Mundi, Beunans Meriasek,* John Tregear's *Homilies, Sacrament an Altar,* and *Creation of the World*) omitted, but *comendya* (found only in *Beunans Meriasek*) included? Why is *remembra* omitted in favour of *perthi kov* 'bear in mind' when it is found frequently in *Beunans Meriasek,* John Tregear's *Homilies, Sacrament an Altar,* and *Creation of the World? Perthi kov* cannot be used in a phrase such as *remember vy dhe'th whor* 'remember me to your sister'.

Nance's 1955 English-Cornish dictionary recognized the importance of Tregear, remarking that his homilies gave "by far the longest run of Cornish prose". Tregear's Cornish must be considered to be authentic, regardless of the proportion of loanwords it contains; and what loanwords it does contain must be considered to be authentic Cornish. Traditional Cornish of all periods contains loanwords from other languages.

The front matter states that some of the doubtful borrowings are "included in the English-Cornish section (printed in light print) because no suitable alternatives have yet been found for them" and asks readers with ideas for such alternatives to inform the editor. Possibly this is an excuse for the questionable typography. In any case, paging through the English-Cornish section, I found 21 such doubtful words. I give them below, with traditional Cornish sources in parentheses.

> **contentious** kavillek (OM 2784), **controversy** kontroversita (TH 19, 37, 38), **domineer** lordya (CW 456), **hobby-horse** hobihors (BM 1061), **implore** konjorya (PC 1321), **inheritance** eritons (BM 2452, TH 41), **installation** installashyon (*recte* Kernowek Kemyn *stallashyon* BM 3017), **interlude** ynterlud (Nance < Lhuyd *antarlick*), **justify** justifia (TH 9 x 2), **perfume** perfumya (possibly an error for *perfumyas* TH 21a 'performed' *perfumya* 'to perform' TH 51a, cf. *performya* TH 52 with the same sense), **persecute** persekutya (TH 22), **pertain** pertaynya (TH 10 x 2, 22, 26a, 43), **petition** petyshyon (BM 4300), **precept** presept (TH 10), **pronounce** prononsya (TH 54), **protest** protestya (SA 64a), **radish** redigenn (*redic* OCV), **second** (**2nd**) sekond (OM 17, BM 2198, CW 51, CW 80, TH x 16), **suppress** suppressya (TH 28a, 42, 42a), **swerve** swarvya (TH 18a, 38), **usurp** usurpya (TH 31a).

I do not know what objections George has to *kavillek* or *redigenn*. But the rest of these are perfectly authentic. All of these words come from traditional Cornish texts, so it is hard to see why they are so disfavoured. Nevertheless, hiding problematic words in "light type" is not how one should elicit comment on them. One should publish an article discussing them, or, if such doubtful words must appear in the dictionary, one should place them all together in an annex for easy access and discussion.

It would appear that George's dictionary is intended to solidify in some way the authority of George's orthography by offering the Cornish market a replacement for Nance's dictionaries. In terms of the lexicon presented, however, he has failed to do so. I took for comparison the letter L (chosen at random) in the English-Cornish half and the letter N (also chosen at random) in the English-Cornish half of both books. Allowing for certain editorial differences in arranging headwords and subheadwords, and for possible errors on my part made during the attempt to locate words in the two different orthographies, I found the following.

Out of a total number of 261 English headwords, Nance has 84 headwords which George omits:

labial, laboratory, laburnum, lad, laden, Lammas, languid, languish, languor, lapse, larch, lass, lassitude, latten, latter, launch, launder, lavatory, lavender, lavish, lea, league, leal, leaven, leavings, lechery, ledge, leer, lees, legate, legislate, leisure, lenient, lest, lethargic, leveret, Leviathan, Levite, lexicon, liar, libel, lilac, limber, limbo, limp, linden, linger, linseed, lint, lintel, lissom, litany, literal, lithe, loafer, loath, locomotive, locust, lodge, logan-berry, logan rock, loll, loneliness, loquacious, lounge, lovely, lozenge, lubber, lucid, lucrative, ludicrous, lug, lugworm, lullaby, lullay, lumber, lunacy, lurch, lurid, lustre, lusty, lute, lying-in, lymph.

Out of a total number of 342 English headwords, George has 70 English headwords which Nance does not; 11 of these begin with *long-*:

laceration, lacking, lamp-chill, lamp-post, lamp-wick, lancet, landing, land-surveyor, langoustine, lapse-rate, lardy, large-footed, laryngitis, lathe, latitudinal, Launceston, laurels, law clerk, lawn-mower, lay-by, leading, lead pencil, lectionary, ledger, left-overs, leniently, leper-hospital, letter-box, ley, ley-land, liaise, liaison, LibDem, life-style, light-bulb, liken, lime-juice, limp, limpid, limpidity, line-drawing, linguistics, Liskeard, lisper, litigation, litter-bin, liver-fluke, locate, Lombardy, long-beaked, long-distance, long-eared, longitude, longitudinal, long-lasting, long-limbed, long-muzzled, long-nosed skate, long-sight, long-standing, long-stone, long-tongued, Looe, lorry, Lostwithiel, loudspeaker, lowering, Loyalist, luggage-rack, luminosity.

One cannot say anything against the publication of Cornish words for useful terms like *laryngitis, lawnmower, ledger, leftovers…* but one must ask why useful words like *laboratory, lavatory, languish, lavender, launch, launder, league, ledge, legislate, leisure,* and *lethargic* do not appear as headwords.

Out of a total number of 168 Cornish headwords, Nance has 27 headwords which George omits:

> *na fors, namma, nappa, nāsya, nasyon, na-vē, navyth, na-whāth* ('nevertheless'; George glosses 'not yet'), *neb-ür, nedha, negesa, negeth, negh, neghy, nep-dēn, nep-part, nep-plas, nep-pow, nep-tra, nessa, nomber, nowedhyans, nowedhynsy, nowyjyans, nowys, noys, nȳthowa.*

Out of a total number of 165 Cornish headwords, George has 52 English headwords which Nance does not:

> *nadh, nadha, naturel, nawmen, naw-ugens, nebreydh, negysya, negysydh, nerthegeth, nerv, nervenn, nervus, neskar, nester, -neth, neusynn, neuvell, neuvella, neuvelladow, neuvwisk, neuvyer, neves, nevesek, nevra, -ni, nijys, nivel, niverenn, niverieth, niveronieth, niverus, niwlgorn, niwllaw, niwl-ster, niwlwias, Normanek, north-west, noskan, noswara, noswikor, noswikorek, noswikorieth, notenn, noter, notyans, nowedhys, nowydhadow, nowydhses, Noy, nuk, nuklerek.*

In all fairness to George, it has to be said that the additions in his Cornish headwords are good ones, and the omissions from Nance are not particularly alarming. All the *nep* words are more or less predictable compounds. They are still worth listing in a dictionary, however.

In general, though, I find the wordlist in the English-Cornish part to be quite weak. Its selection seems rather *ad-hoc*; I think that a learner, for instance, would find this dictionary rather frustrating to use due to its omissions. No mention is made of dictionaries or works presumably consulted (such as English, Welsh, Breton, or other Cornish dictionaries) in selecting the headwords.

George has been recognized by many Cornish speakers as an authority on spelling. This recognition, merited or not, does not confer upon him authority in lexicography. The lexical content of the *Gerlyver Kres*, especially in terms of its exclusion of loanwords found in traditional Cornish, calls into question the scope of his "master-files".

KERNOWEK KEMYN

I do not like Common Cornish (Kernowek Kemyn), but my criticisms on the form and content of the *Gerlyver Kres* stand on their own merits regardless of the spelling used. Nevertheless, the fact that the dictionary *is* a dictionary of Kernowek Kemyn calls the whole enterprise into serious question.

The front matter states that the Kernowek Kemyn "orthography was criticized by N. Williams in his book *Cornish Today*, but his criticisms are largely unfounded, as shown by Paul Dunbar and the present editor in their reply *Kernewek Kemmyn: Cornish for the 21st Century*."

It is understandable that George might consider Dunbar and George (KKC21) to be an adequate response to the criticisms made by Williams in *Cornish Today* (CT), but few Cornish speakers and even fewer Cornish scholars would take that dialogue seriously.

In *Cornish Today*, Williams presented a cogent analysis of the Cornish language situation as he saw it: Unified Cornish (Kernewek Unyes) as an orthography with some failings, Modern Cornish (Curnoack Nowedga) as an orthography with too many ambiguities and too many differences from Medieval Cornish, Breton, and Welsh to be practical, and Common Cornish (Kernowek Kemyn) as an orthography derived from unsuccessful respelling of traditional Cornish orthographic forms on the basis of a mistaken phonemic theory. Dunbar and George try to show that Williams is wrong, but one is so put off by the sniggering schoolboy tone of the discourse that in the end one prefers to reject the work *in toto*. It cannot be taken to be a serious reply to Williams' criticisms.*

In any case, it is important to note that many of the arguments in Dunbar and George's book are based on George's proprietary "master-files" and graphemic analysis algorithms. Since these files are not in the public domain, one does not know either how complete they are or whether they are trustworthy.

George's arguments for a phonemic orthography for Cornish are questionable for a number of reasons.

(1) George's phonemic analysis has always been suspect. Williams, as early as 1987, showed that George's introduction of the *dj*/*tj* distinction was erroneous, and George withdrew it in 1989. Williams has shown quite clearly that George's understanding of

---

*Nevertheless Williams has responded to it in *Towards Authentic Cornish* (Evertype 2006).

Cornish vocalic length is mistaken, though George says that he does not believe him.

(2) The whole nature of the Kernowek Kemyn reform is based on George's assertion that phonemic orthographies are better than historical ones based on quasi-phonemic and other traditional conventions (he gives the usual tiresome complaint about English orthography, which was dealt with far more comprehensively by Axel Wijk decades ago (Wijk 1959). George maintains that it is difficult to implement phonemic reform where the size of the populations using competing orthographic practices is large. But this is not true to the facts. Reforms in many languages occur quite regularly, for very large populations. Languages with millions of speakers like Norwegian *bokmål* and *nynorsk* routinely implement reforms. Other languages have successfully implemented complete revisions of their orthographies: Azerbaijani changed officially from the Cyrillic alphabet to the Latin in 1992; when Irish Gaelic shifted from Gaelic script to Roman this was done in conjunction with spelling simplifications in the 1940s and 1950s.

(3) George posits that because the population of Cornish speakers is small it did no harm to introduce a radically different system as opposed to making simple corrections of the existing system, regardless of the merits of the system. I disagree: the harm done has been considerable.

(4) George maintains that real and proportionally significant grass-roots consensus had been achieved with regard to Kernowek Kemyn when the Cornish Language Board adopted it in 1987; this is not the case, as the continuing language debate attests.

Kernowek Kemyn was a sociolinguistic disaster. It split the Cornish Revival in two. It encouraged Richard Gendall into further splitting the community with his Modern Cornish. (Gendall, it must be remembered, is acknowledged by Nance for reversing the *Cornish-English Dictionary* of 1939 which became the basis for Nance's 1955 *English-Cornish Dictionary*.) Williams' approach, based on his genuine concern for the future of the Revival, was to go back to first principles and suggest corrections to the errors in Unified Cornish. Unified Cornish Revised (Williams 1997), as Williams himself admits, will not be the last word in that process—but it is the best way forward. Unified Cornish Revised was made in the spirit of the Norwegian orthographic reforms—an incremental step towards perfecting the orthography, correcting known errors in Nance's orthography. Future revisions will be taken on their merits with true consensus of academic and non-academic experts alike.

CONCLUSION

The *Gerlyver Kres* is certainly no substitute for Nance's 1938 and 1955 dictionaries, as it omits much which can only be found in them. Its claims to comprehensiveness are unfounded. Its appearance at this time does little to advance the Cornish language revival, not least because it is presented in the experimental orthography known as Common Cornish (Kernowek Kemyn), a form that has experienced sustained criticism from Celtic scholars and must be regarded as flawed.

REFERENCES

BM = Whitley Stokes (ed.), *Beunans Meriasek: the life of St Meriasek, Bishop and confessor, a Cornish drama* (London: Trübner and Co. 1872)

CT = Nicholas Williams, *Cornish Today: an examination of the revived language*, first and second editions (Sutton Coldfield: Kernewek dre Lyther 1995)

CT3 = Nicholas Williams, *Cornish Today: an examination of the revived language*, third edition (Westport: Evertype 2006, ISBN 978-1-904808-07-7)

CW = Whitley Stokes (ed.), *Gwreans an Bys: the Creation of the World*, (London: Williams & Norgate 1864 [reprinted Kessinger Publishing 1987, ISBN 0-7661-8009-3])

KKC21 = *Kernewek Kemmyn: Cornish for the Twenty-First Century*, Paul Dunbar and Ken George ([s.l.], Cornish Language Board 1997) ISBN 0-907064-71-X

OCV = "Old Cornish Vocabulary" [quoted from Norris 1859 ii: 311-435 and Campanile 1974]

OM = "Origo Mundi" in Norris (1859) i: 1-219

Nance 1952 = R. Morton Nance, *An English-Cornish Dictionary* (Marazion 1952) [reprinted 1978]

Nance 1955 = R. Morton Nance, *A Cornish-English Dictionary* (Marazion 1955) [reprinted 1978]

Norris 1859 = Edwin Norris, *The Ancient Cornish Drama* i-ii (London [reprinted New York/London: Benjamin Blom 1968])

PC = "Passio Domini Nostri Jhesu Christi" in Norris 1859 i 221-479

TH = John Tregear, *Homelyes xiii in Cornysche* (British Library Additional MS 46, 397) [text from a cyclostyled text published by Christopher Bice ([s.l.] 1969)]

Wijk 1959 = Axel Wijk, *Regularized English: An Investigation into the English Spelling Reform Problem with a New, Detailed Plan for a Possible Solution*. (Acta Universitatis Stockholmiensis: Stockholm Studies in English; 7) Stockholm: Almqvist & Wiksell, 1959.

Williams 1997 = Nicholas Williams, *Clappya Kernowek: an introduction to Unified Cornish Revised* (Agan Tavas, Portreath 1997, ISBN 1-901409-01-5)

"THE BEST CORNISH FORM OF CORNISH PLACE-NAMES": REVIEW OF THE CORNISH LANGUAGE BOARD'S *PLACE-NAMES IN CORNWALL*

Craig Weatherhill

Ken George, Pol Hodge, Julyan Holmes, Graham Sandercock, 1996, *Place-Names in Cornwall, Henwyn-Tylleryow yn Kernow: A preliminary list of recommended Cornish language forms of place-names in Cornwall* (A background to Cornish, an occasional series; 1), 1996, 20pp. [Saltash]: Kesva an Taves Kernewek, The Cornish Language Board. ISBN 0 907064 62 0. £1.75.

INTRODUCTION

In 1996, the Cornish Language Board commenced the production of a series of inexpensive booklets, of which the first was *Place-Names in Cornwall*. This was a preliminary list of recommended Cornish language versions (in this case, spelt according to the Kernowek Kemyn system adopted by the Board in 1987) of place-names throughout the Duchy. It also recommends readers to obtain further information or background details of these place-names through the Board's Place-Name database.

The booklet's introduction mentions *"research into place names over many years"* and adds that: *"For Cornish speakers, it is appropriate that they should use, wherever possible the best Cornish version of Cornish place names. That is the purpose of this document"*.

Examination of the recommended forms, however, show that many of them are not the best Cornish versions and, in several cases, the necessary research has been inadequately undertaken for such an exercise into a difficult and sensitive subject.

Too many names have been misinterpreted or misrepresented and, in my own view, the Board has not taken into consideration the fact that place-name research is not a wholly linguistic exercise, but at least to an equal extent, an historical one that deserves full consideration and respect. For example, toponyms retaining an Old Cornish form (e.g. **Penquite, Trenant, Bodieve**) are frequently found in areas of East Cornwall where they were adopted into English before undergoing the assibilation process of Middle Cornish and no evidence currently exists

25

to suggest that assibilation was ever applied. Is it right, then, for a purely linguistic body to manufacture a history which did not occur by offering those same names as (using the Kemyn spelling of the booklet): **Pennkoes; Trenans** and **Bosyuv**? True, there are examples where medieval assibilation is found in the historically recorded forms place-names that currently display an Old Cornish form (e.g. **Liskeard**: *Lyskerrys* 1375). In such cases, the fact that assibilation historically occurred is proven and, therefore, it can be used without detriment or against historic principles.

We can add to this complaint the fact that Kernowek Kemyn (and, indeed, revived Cornish in general), then goes on to ignore a further historical development in place-name history: the occurrence of Late Cornish features, particularly in West Cornwall. These include written pre-occlusion and features where <s> and even <y> are replaced by <j>.

Translating place-names that derive from English or Norman French into Cornish is a matter for discussion. If the site had a known earlier or alternative Cornish name, then no problem arises. However, if the place-name had no known Cornish alternative, is it acceptable to—again—manufacture a history that never occurred? I have no doubt that discussion into this particular aspect of the study will run for some time to come. Arguments have been made that a similar practice takes place in Wales but not always. Some Welsh place-names of English origin do not have Welsh alternatives, ancient or modern. In any event, should we simply imitate the practice of others at the cost of historical integrity?

The Cornish Language Board, not only in its present Kemyn persona but also under its previous Unified Cornish identity, has already made the mistake introducing into its recommended and established place-name forms elements that did not exist in historical record. The outstanding example of this is its use of the element *Aber-* to denote "estuary, river mouth". Although commonly found, with that meaning, in Wales and less frequently in Brittany, not a single Cornish place-name can be shown to contain this element. The only record of its use anywhere in Cornish is in the Old Cornish Vocabulary where it is glossed as: "confluence, whirlpool, gulf".

Granted that the use of the word to rename **Falmouth** as *Aberfal* and **Plymouth** as *Aberplym(m)* has been practised for more than half a century but should such a glaring error be condoned by perpetuating it? Cornish has two words for "estuary": *logh*, which normally denotes one that retains deep water at all tides or a ria; and *heyl*[1] for those that display extensive flats of sand or mud at low water. In the case of **Falmouth**, the historical name of the river tends to be *Fala*, so a constructed name such as *Loghfala* might be rather more appropriate. Better still (and bearing in mind that Falmouth did not have a Cornish name), historical origins might be considered. The development of Falmouth as the town and port of that name occurred in the 17th century, following the granting of a Charter to Sir Peter Killigrew by Charles II. The seat of the Killigrews, whose estates covered much of the land upon which Falmouth developed, was Arwenack House. To establish a Cornish name for Falmouth that is firmly anchored in history and linked with its development, *Arwennek* (or *ar Wennek*) would be far more appropriate.

The Board's booklet also misunderstands the use of an epithet in those place-names that include a saint's name and, in the cases of **St Columb Major** and **Minor**, ignores the recorded Cornish names of those settlements by preferring to translate the current English name. The use (or omission) of the "saint" epithet in these place-names has been fully explained by Nicholas Williams ("'Saint' in Cornish", *Writings on Revived Cornish*, Evertype, 2006).

A further fault to be found in the booklet is a failure to note that *eglos*, "church" rarely causes lenition to the following element (out of scores of historical examples only two lenited examples have been found, both of them late in date and probably erroneous).

It is neither the purpose nor the intent of this critique to denigrate the Cornish Language Board, but to point out inaccuracies and in some cases (e.g. **Torpoint**) absurdities that only serve to undermine credibility at a time when the foundation of all that we do and achieve in the field of Cornish needs to be as firm as the proverbial rock. In the list below, KK denotes the place-name form recommended in the booklet by the Cornish Language Board (CLB).

ANALYSIS

Albaston (KK: Trevalba): an Old English (OE) name with no known Cornish alternative. The CLB assumed translation: "Alba's farm/settlement", is incorrect, as shown by its early forms such as *Alveveston c.* 1296; *Aliveston, Alptone* 1303; *Alpiston* 1337; *Alpeston*

---

1   Examinations of the historic forms of all place-names containing *heyl* show that the correct spelling of this word should be *heyl* and not *hayl* as given in many current dictionaries.

1337, 1341. Its true meaning is obscure, although Svensson translates it as "solitary stone" < OE *anlipigan stan*.

Bathpool (KK: Pollbath): this C15 Eng. name, with no known Cornish alternative, means "bathing pool". One has to question the CLB's choice of the Eng. word *bath* in its recommended Cornish form and why it rejected the established Cornish term for such a feature: *pollen dus* (cf. **Pullandese**, coastal name, St Just).

Bocaddon (KK: Boskaswynn): one of many East Cornwall toponyms which is not recorded in an assibilated Middle Cornish form. For the sake of historical integrity, it should remain in Old Cornish form. None of the available examples give <-y-> as the last vowel, <-e-> being most commonly found (cf. *Bodkadwen* 1315), otherwise it is <-o->.

Bodmin (KK: Bosvenegh): assumptions that this name translates as "monks' dwelling" are not borne out by the early place-name forms which rather suggest *bos* + *menehy* (i.e. "church land dwelling"), cf. *Botmenei* C9; *Bothmenia* 1177; *Bodmynye* 1265; *Bodminie* 1342. Historical record does show that, in this case, OC *bod* assibilated to MC *bos*. The better choice would, therefore, be *Bosvenehy* (for lenition cf. *Bosvenna* 1584).

Bojewyan (KK: Bosuyon): 14 out of the 19 available historic forms of this name give an ending in <-an>, in contrast to just 3 with <-on> (the remainder being <-weyn> and <-oun>. The overwhelming evidence would, therefore, support *Bosuyan*. As the final vowel is traditionally schwa, one would have expected the KK system to insist upon doubling the final consonant.

Boskednan (KK: Boskennon): the CLB assumes the final element to be a personal name and this may well be correct. However, as Williams points out, *kenyn*, "ransoms, wild garlic", is a distinct possibility, as is Pool's *kenen*, "reeds". The topography supports both alternatives. As there is a distinct element of uncertainty here, one can only go with the available historic forms, only one of which shows <-o-> as the final vowel. The available forms are as follows: *Boskennen* 1310, 1371; *Boskennan* 1313, 1483, 1570, 1597; *Boskennon, Boscennen* 1327; *Boskenan* 1457; *Boskednan* 1609, 1623. (**Boskinning,** less than 2 miles away, has almost identical historic forms). Again, traditional pronunciation reduces the final vowel to schwa which would lead the Kemyn system to apply doubling of the final consonant. This has not been applied.

Botus Fleming (KK: Bosflumyes): a preserved OC name which has no record of undergoing medieval assibilation. The second element is a Norman French personal name and to assibilate its final letter not only damages the integrity of Cornish linguistic history but that of Norman French as well.

Braddock (KK: Brodhek): the CLB states that this name is of obscure derivation but nonetheless applies <-dh-> when the evidence, confirmed by provection to Eng. <-dd-> rather suggests an original unvoiced <-th-> or <-d->. Examination of the 17 available historic spellings strongly suggests that this is indeed OE *brad ac*, "broad oak"; the <-th-> forms probably representing a Middle Cornish adaptation of an English name. All other forms (10 of them) show <-d->, with just one <-dh-> (almost certainly not representing the voiced <-dh-> of Cornish), this being *Brodhoke* 1342.

Bray Shop (KK: Shoppa Bre): this is a C18 English name, "Bray's shop". There can be no certainty that the personal surname originated as Cornish *bre*, "hill" and, therefore, should not be assumed. According to the Penguin Dictionary of Surnames (2nd ed. 1978), Bray can derive from OE (with the meaning "brow"); from Celtic e.g. Cornish *bre*, "hill" or from Old French with the possible meaning "mud". In this locality, the Cornish derivation is the more likely but it cannot simply be assumed.

Brazzacott (KK: Chibrosya): the selection of the CLB's second element, and its description as "a non-Celtic personal name", are inexplicable. In fact, this element is an OE compound containing a Cornish personal name, the name being derived from *Brassinga cot*, "cottage of Bras's people/family", *Bras*, in the form of a noun, can, in such a personal name, be translated as"big (man)".

Breage (KK: Eglosvreg): as mentioned earlier, *eglos*, "church" does not cause lenition, cf. both its established Cornish names *Eglosbrek* and *Eglospenbro*, which share 11 historic forms, none of which show lenition.

Brighton (KK: Trewolow): perhaps one of the CLB's more ill-advised choices. This C19 Eng. settlement (no recorded Cornish alternative) might well have been named after Brighton, Sussex. If so—and on present evidence we cannot be sure—that name is OE *Beorhthelmes tun*, "Beorhthelm's farm/settlement" (*Bristelmestune* 1086) and certainly not "bright farm".

Budock Water (KK: Dowr Budhek): here, the CLB's choice betrays a lack of research. This is an Eng. name given to a stream and then a

C19 settlement which developed during that century around a farm called **Roseglos**. A historically solid choice would, therefore have been *Ros Eglos*.

Bugle (KK: Karnrosveur): this choice has been applied to the wrong place. Bugle developed in the C19 around a public house of that name. There was no previous settlement on the site. The CLB's choice is the likely derivation of **Carnsmerry** (*carn* + *ros* + *vuer*), a separate settlement lying a quarter mile to the south and named after a topographical feature since destroyed by china-clay quarrying (**Rosevear** and **Rosevean** lie half a mile to the east). Carnsmerry is not Bugle and, therefore the name should not be transferred to it. One wonders what the CLB would make of **London Apprentice**, also named after a public house which, in turn, took its name from a popular folk song.

Burlawn (KK: Boslowen): this name is the same as **Burlorne** close by. Historic forms are ambiguous, with seven supporting OC *bod* + *elowen*, "elm" and others favouring OC *bod* + *lowen*, "happy, joyful". I tend to favour the former, if only in the light of the oldest form *Bodolowen* 1243 which shows a pronounced vowel after *bod*. None of the available historic forms show a definite medieval assibilation of *bod* (two give *Both-*, perhaps hinting at the beginnings of a softening process), which should not, therefore, be introduced.

Callington (KK: Kelliwik): The CLB claims, in its introduction to this booklet, that its work is based upon that of Oliver Padel. Clearly, in this case, it is not done so and has preferred to perpetuate a common but modern myth. Padel and others have conclusively shown that Callington is not the *Kelliwic* of the Mabinogion, nor the C9 estate of *Caellwic* and can never have been derived from either of those names. Callington is purely OE, *calwan* + *tun*, "farm in the Calu (a district name meaning "bare hill")". All its earliest known forms, from 1086 to 1285, consistently support this OE derivation.

Calstock (KK: Kalstok): related to the above entry this name is OE *calwan stoc*, "outlying farm in the Calu". The CLB choice is not a Cornish translation but a respelling of the Eng. name. This is not its usual practice.

Camborne (KK: Kammbronn): the insistence upon this spelling is fast becoming an old chestnut. The CLB assumes the "crooked hill" translation (which, in such a compound should have invited *-vron*) but, in reality, the meaning is uncertain. The complete list of available historic forms is: *Cambron c.* 1100, *c.* 1230, 1252, 1280, 1302,

1305, 1329, 1342, 1427, 1497, 1504, 1603, 1616, *c.* 1700, 1816; *Camberon* 1182; *Kameron* 1252; *Cambroun* 1302, 1311, 1333, 1355; *Camberoun* 1308; *Camron* 1403; *Cambrone* 1426, 1580; *Camborne* 1431, *c.* 1570, 1591, 1628, 1692, *c.* 1720; *Camburn* 1576, 1591; *Camburne* 1576; *Camborn* 1580; *Camburne, Cambourn* 1584. From these it can immediately be seen that the CLB's choice of **Kammbronn** is utterly unrepresentative. Possible translations of the name include the assumed "crooked hill", "swingle-tree" and "dog-leg", the latter perhaps referring to the course of a road or stream. With so much uncertainty, surely the safest practice would be to adhere to the most commonly found spelling, *Cambron*, which occurs over a period of seven centuries.

Canonstown (KK: Tre an Chenon): a C16 Eng. name for a settlement named after an unidentified churchman. It has no Cornish name. *Chenon*, although used in BM, is not a Cornish word but a Middle English adoption from Norman French and retaining the <ch> for /k/ convention as commonly found, for example, in Domesday. The CLB's rendition contains an unnecessary definite article that does not feature in the Eng. original.

Canworthy Water (KK: Boskarn): the original name of this place appears to have been Cornish *carn*, "tor", to which was later added the OE element *worðig*, "enclosure, enclosed settlement", a meaning inadequately translated by the use of Cornish *bos*, "dwelling". The Cornish name of this location is therefore *Carn*. Inconsistency in the CLB's system is shown here by the fact that **Water** (i.e. stream) has not been translated into Cornish, as in **Budock Water** above, but omitted entirely.

Carland Cross (KK: Krows Korlann): criticism of this presentation is twofold. Firstly *crows* is never traditionally used to denote a crossroads (there being no recorded wayside cross to otherwise account for it), in addition to which the "Cross" element of the name was only added to it in the mid C20 by either the Ordnance Survey or the Highways Department. Secondly, and bearing in mind the CLB's stated notice of Padel's work, the derivation of **Carland** is uncertain. As yet, no mention of the name prior to 1813 has been found and, in that year, it appears as *Cowland.*, Eng. "cow land", corrupted in 1842 to *Carland*. There is no evidence to support the assumption that Cornish *corlan*, "cemetery", is involved despite there being a notable group of Bronze Age barrows here.

Carn Brea (KK: Karnbre): *carn*, in the meaning of "tor, outcrop" is a distinct element in its own right and traditional convention separates the element from the qualifier, e.g. Carn Kenidjack, Carn Galva, etc. There can be no justification for joining the two to form a compound as the CLB has done here. *Carn Bre*, by far the better representation, simply translates as "hill tor" and is not, as some suggest, a tautology.

Carnhell Green (KK: Pras Karnell): this toponym was consistently *Carnhel* until 1813 when the Ordnance Survey added Eng. "Green". This word is therefore not an element of the original name and, in any case, would have been far better translated as *glasen*, "greensward", than by the use of *pras*, "meadow". The CLB also seriously errs in its representation of *Carnhell*, which is *carn + hel*, "hall tor".

Cawsand (KK: Porthbugh): another Eng. name with no Cornish alternative, this has become subject to a peculiar and unprecedented trend in the CLB's list: the use of *porth*, "cove, landing place" to translate Eng. *sand*, instead of using the direct translation *treth*.

Chacewater (KK: Dowr an Chas): a C17 English name, without Cornish alternatives and which does not feature the definite article as included by the CLB. *Chas* cannot be accepted as Cornish, being Middle Eng. borrowed from Middle French. *Helgh* might have been preferable.

Chilsworthy (KK: Boschyl): an exclusively OE name without a known Cornish choice. As detailed in **Canworthy Water** above, *bos* does not translate OE *worðig* and it is questionable whether *Chyl* suffices to represent the OE personal name *Cïol*, which contains a diphthong.

Colan (KK: Kolan): here the CLB has failed to find the recorded Cornish name *Plewe-Golen* 1501 and demonstrates inconsistency in its representation of saints' names. Elsewhere in its list, the CLB wrongly introduces (or translates directly from the English version of the toponym) *Sen* before the saint's name.

Constantine (KK: Lanngostentin): 98% of all historical examples of *Lan-* names use <n>, not <nn>. For the weakness of this application of the Kemyn system see *Lanivet* below.

Coppathorne (KK: An Spernenn): the CLB's choice, translating as "the thorn tree" is inadequate as the OE name, for which no Cornish alternative is known, is *coppandan þorn*, "pollarded thorn tree".

Cotehele (KK: Koesheyl): Nicholas Williams has explained elsewhere why the KK <oe> phoneme is erroneous in this word. **Cotehele** is a name that has no record of appearing in assibilated Middle Cornish and, in order to avoid inventing history, its Old Cornish form should be retained.

Crackington Haven (KK: Porthkrag): Padel has shown that the original Cornish place-name is *craken/crakyn*, alternatively "sandstone" or "little crag". <krag> is therefore insufficient.

Crantock (KK: Lanngorrow): early forms of this name give *Langorroc*, *Langorroch* (1086), the subsequent <-ou>, <-u> and <-ow> forms being corrupt. *Corroc* is an acceptable pet form of the saint's name *Carantoc* and would have the correct choice here.

Crowan (KK: Egloskrowenn): early forms of the saint's name agree *Crewen(na)* and, therefore the historic first vowel should be adopted. Again inconsistency is shown by the CLB not providing the female saint's name with an -*a* suffix, as it does in the case of **Creed** (KK: Krida) and by not applying lenition to the saint's name after *Eglos-* as it does in most other *Eglos-* place-names. Here, both choices are, in fact, correct.

Dobwalls (KK: Fos an Mogh): here, the CLB prefers to translate the lone appearance of this C17 Eng. name (*Hogswall* 1607), which may be corrupt. Three other historic examples give the Eng. personal name *Dobbe* + *walls*. Note that the second element in all three of these examples is plural.

Drift (KK: An Drev): on current maps, the place shown as Drift is, in fact, Lower Drift, formerly Drift Vean (*Drefbyghan* 1262). Higher Drift still exists in its own right. The CLB's choice is, therefore, incorrect and due to insufficient research.

Duloe (KK: Dewlogh): the CLB's choice is a fair one, the earliest mention of the name being *Dulo* 1283. However, the churchtown was also *Lankyp* (1286), an abbreviated form of *Langyby*, "St Kybi's church site".

East Taphouse (KK: Diwotti Est): this C17 Eng. name has no historic Cornish alternative. *Dewotty* is not genuinely Cornish but a modern borrowing from Welsh which should be discarded in favour of *tavarn*, which is attested in Cornish texts.

Eastcott (KK: Chi an Est): another OE name with no known Cornish alternative. Again the CLB inserts an unnecessary definite article which does not feature in the original.

Escalls (KK: Askall): there is no historic record of this name to support the CLB's inexplicable version. The full available list of historic forms is as follows: *Heskels* 1280, 1481; *Eskeles* 1281; *Eskels* 1296, 1302, 1329, 1335, 1350; *Iskals* 1580; *Scalls* 1584; *Escols* 1880. None of these has the *A-* initial adopted by the CLB and all feature a final *-s*, omitted by the CLB whose choice is wholly unacceptable. The translation offered by Pool (1985), "sedge cliff" (< *hesk* + *als*) is doubtful; a more feasible meaning being "place of thistles" (< **eskel* + *-ys*).

Falmouth (KK: Aberfal): see introductory piece above.

Flushing (KK: Nanskersi): in this instance, the CLB has considered only a late and probably corrupt form of the Cornish alternative of this late, Dutch-influenced name (< the Dutch port of **Vlissingen**). An earlier and more complete form is *Nankersis* (1590) and, therefore, the original Cornish name is **Nanskersys*.

Fowey (KK: Fowydh): this is a river name, transferred to the town in the C13, and is *faw*, "beeches" + the river name suffix *-y* (the *-ath* suffix appears only in two C17 examples—as *Foath*—and is probably incorrect). Here, the CLB has chosen to ignore or discard the original name of the church and settlement, *Langorthow*, **Langordhow* (*Langorthou* 1310).

Fraddon (spelt **Fraddan** by the CLB) **(KK: Frodan)**: the CLB's policy is to modernize all Old Cornish place-name survivals but, in this case, shows inconsistency by retaining the Old Cornish hard consonant. Its chosen form in fact replicates the commonest spelling of the name (1321-1511) and is therefore authentic. This toponym is unusual in retaining its Old Cornish form so far west (no historic form of its name shows medieval assibilation); the *frod-* element, "stream, current", becoming *fros, froze* further west, e.g. *Froze Lavur* (coastal name), St Just, *Froze Muzzam* (coastal name), Sennen/St Levan.

Freathy (KK: Frethi): this location takes its name from a local family, recorded as *Fridia* (1327) and *Fredea* (1428). The place-name itself was *Vridie* 1286 and *Freathy* 1699. From the records of the family name, it is evident that the final *-e* of the 1286 example was pronounced and, therefore, the CLB's choice here is in error. In addition to this, the Kemyn system normally prefers an archaic i affection and one would, therefore have expected **Frydia*.

Georgia (KK: Gorga): the CLB's final *-a* is erroneous, the name being derived from *gor-ge*, "low/ruinous hedge" despite the *Gorga* historic forms from the C17.

Germoe (KK Germow): the saint's name is *Germoch* (*c.* 1186) or *Germogh* (1283-1347) and should, therefore, have been correctly rendered as *Germogh*. Like **Colan** above, the CLB has here abandoned its normal practice of prefixing all saints' names with *Sen*.

Godolphin Cross (KK: Krows Woldolghan): as at **Carland Cross** above, the CLB has taken the unprecedented and incorrect step of applying *crows* to denote a crossroads (no wayside cross is involved here). In doing so, it has merely adopted and translated the modern Eng. practice of abbreviating "crossroads" to "cross". The name **Godolphin** has caused many problems of translation despite the existence of no less than 27 different historic spellings (**godolghan*, "mound" is a modern invention and does not exist). The most likely derivation of the name, and an appropriate one for the site, is suggested by forms such as *Wotholca* 1166; and *Godholkan c.* 1210, "tin-stream" < *godh + olcan*.

Gorran Haven (KK: Porthyust): It is extremely rare to find examples of this saint's name given in Cornish with its initial Y/J. The common practice was to omit the initial entirely (e.g. *Kilguthe East, Venton East, Porthuste, Lanuste*, the *Usticke* family name and the nickname *Santusters*). The CLB, however, opts to apply the exception rather than the rule.

Great Bosullow (KK: Boswolow Veur): the KK form fails to reflect the historic name of this settlement, the modern form contracting the original *bos*, "dwelling" + a lost place-name **Chywolow* (e.g. *Boschiwolou* 1301). **Great Bosullow** was *Bosuoylah wartha* 1313, *Bossowolo-meour* 1517. **Meur* should be applied rather than **Vuer*.

Gunnislake (KK: Lynngonna): the place-name derives from an OE personal name **Gunna* + OE *lacu*, "stream". The Cornish word *lyn*, "pool", does not translate *lacu*.

Gweek (KK: Gwig): out of 11 available historic spellings, only two include a final <-g>: *Gweege c.* 1700 and *Guague* 1704, both very late and therefore unreliable. They are also much later than the *c.* 1500 date that KK quotes as its basis date. All other forms give <-k>.

Gwinear (KK: Sen Gwynnyer): there is neither precedent nor necessity for the CLB to add <Sen> and to do so is to imitate Eng. convention. With Celtic or apostolic and angelic saints, the Cornish convention is not to prefix their names with "saint", particularly in place-names (Williams 1999).

Gwithian (KK: Sen Goedhyan): again, <Sen> is superfluous and contrary to Cornish practice. There is also no apparent justification for the <-oe-> vowel.

Halsetown (KK: Trehals): this settlement was founded *c.* 1830 by James Halse on a greenfield site. There is no evidence to suggest that Halse ever spelt his own surname <Hals> and, in fact, his family name descends from the *de Als* family, whose name originated from the place-name **Alsia** , St Buryan (*Als* 1266).

Helford (KK: Pennkestel): historically, the **Helford** toponym, with variations in spelling, is consistent from 1230 onwards. Not until 1732 do we find *Helford alias Penkestle* and then only once (the separate settlement of **Kestle** lies half a mile inland). This provides only thin evidence for the CLB's assumption. The original name appears to have been *Heyl* to which was added the Eng. *ford* (cf. *Hayleford* 1318), most likely referring to the creek beside which it stands rather than the river (estuary) which, historically was *Mahonyer, Monhonyer* C13; *Mawonieck, Mawoniek* C14. The correct form and translation of this name has yet to be determined.

Helland (KK: Hellan): bearing in mind the "correctness" insisted upon by the KK system, this choice is surprising. The name is a compound of Cornish *hen,* "old, ancient" + *lan,* "early church enclosure and one would have expected the CLB's rendition to have been **Henlann.*

Hessenford (KK: Rys an Gwraghes): although the CLB has interpreted the Eng. name correctly (OE *haegtsena ford,* "hags' ford"), it again inserts an unnecessary definite article that does not feature in the original. The KK preference for <y> over <e> in words such as *res, segh, enys, kensa, bledhen* (an archaism several centuries older than KK's *c.* 1500 base date) has recently been questioned by Hodge (Hodge 2005)

High Street (KK: Stretughel): In this C18 Eng. name, "high" does not refer to altitude but to importance, i.e. "principal street". <ughel> is, therefore, entirely the wrong word to apply here. The settlement did not have a known Cornish name.

Indian Queens (KK: Krows Karworgi): this is one of the CLB's most inexplicable inventions. **Indian Queens** is a settlement founded in the late C18 and early C19 around a post house and public house called, in 1780, *The Queen's Head,* then *The Indian Queens* (1802) and *Indian Queen* (*c.* 1870). The crossroads called **Carworgie Cross** is located at St Columb Road and **Carworgie** itself is an entirely separate settlement, respectively half a mile and a mile to the north west of Indian Queens. Again, the CLB wrongly applies *crows* to a crossroads and there can be no justification for what appears to be a complete flight of fancy on its part.

Jacobstow (KK: Lannjago): from an historian's point of view, the use of Cornish *lan* to translate OE *stow,* "place, assembly place, holy place", is disturbing. A *lan* is a particular type of site, important in archaeology and recognized as an ecclesiastical enclosure (often a reused pre-Christian earthwork) of the Early Celtic Church. To apply *lan* to a different type of site, an early English *stow*, invites unwelcome confusion and a good example of why it is wiser to leave alone toponyms of non-Cornish origin, particularly where they cannot be accurately translated into Cornish.

Kea (KK: Sen Ke): once again, a superfluous addition of <Sen> that contrasts with traditional Cornish practice.

Kehelland (KK: Kellihellan): as with **Helland** above, the CLB lapses on its insistence upon "correctness" within the KK system, as the name derives from Cornish *kelly*, "grove, copse" + the compound *henlan*, "disused / abandoned early church enclosure".

Kelly Bray (KK: Kellivre): this has been inadequately researched by the CLB, its second element not being *bre*, "hill", but *bregh*, "dappled" (*Kellibregh c.* 1286).

Kilkhampton (KK: Tregylgh): the earliest known form of this name, and evidently the Cornish original, is *Kelk c.* 839 < *kelgh*, "circle". OE *tun*, "farm, settlement" is a later addition and, therefore, the CLB has concentrated upon the English place-name and not the Cornish one.

Kingsand (KK: Porthmyghtern): another C17 Eng. name with no known Cornish alternative. As with Cawsand above, Cornish *porth* does not translate Eng. sand. The use of *myghtern* misleadingly suggests that the place is named after a monarch when, in fact, it is named after the King family.

Laneast (KK: Lannast): this name invites further discussion. The spelling *Lanast* occurs in 1076, *c.* 1170, *c.* 1200 and 1373, after which it becomes *Lanayst* 1226, 1311, 1342, 1464; *Laniast* 1291; *Lanayste* 1413; *Laneyst* 1428, 1437; *Lanneste* 1548; *Lannest* 1554 and *Lan-easte* 1584. Most of these suggest that the second vowel has a lengthened quality. The element concerned is probably a personal name, the original form of which is not known, and it would be best to utilize the C13, C14 or C15 *-ayst* or the C15 *-eyst*.

Lanivet (KK: Lannives): this rendition by the CLB shows the weakness of using the KK system to represent place-names. To use the strict convention of its system, this place-name is Cornish *lann*, "early church enclosure" + *nives*, "pagan sacred grove", which would give a triple <n> as *Lannnives*. In this example, therefore, the CLB has no choice but to discard its orthographical convention to avoid such an absurdity but the effect of this is to imply that the second element is *ives*. These difficulties would not arise if traditional Cornish orthography was utilized. The use of <i> is also erroneous, in that it implies /iː/, a pronunciation that has never applied to this name, and generally became /e/ from *c.* 1300 (Cornish *neves*, Old Cornish *neved*, derives from British *nemeton*). Historic forms of this toponym, from 1298, generally show /e/. Here, the assibilated form favoured by the CLB is historically correct, as shown by the 1301 form *Lanneves*.

Latchley (KK: Kelligors): the CLB has mistranslated this OE name, which is *leacc leah*, "boggy clearing/glade/meadow". *Kelly* is entirely the wrong word here for the following reason: in early OE, *leah* did indeed mean "wood, grove" but, by the time Anglo-Saxons settled in East Cornwall, its meaning had altered to "clearing, glade, meadow". This will apply to all place-names in Cornwall containing OE *leah*.

Leedstown (KK: Trelids): this C19 settlement, on a spot which had no known Cornish name (other than possible field names) or previous settlement, was founded by the Duke of Leeds. To thus respell the name of an English town in order to satisfy the conventions of a modern, theoretical spelling system is a patent absurdity.

Ley (KK: Kelli): see **Latchley** above for an explanation of why *kelly* is the incorrect word to translate OE *leah*.

Lezant (KK: Lannsans): this name preserves an Old Cornish final consonant that never historically assibilated and, for that reason, the CLB choice is incorrect.

Liskeard (KK: Lyskerrys): the name **Liskeard** requires close examination. The CLB choice is not incorrect as its recommended spelling is found *c.* 1375. However, its qualifying element has never been satisfactorily translated, its earliest form (*Lis Cerruyt c.* 1010) suggesting a personal name **Kerwyd*, assibilating in 1375 before reverting to the Old Cornish final). The word might also be an Old Cornish form of Middle Cornish *kerwys*, "stags". The first vowel of this element varies from *c.* 1010 to 1239, showing <e> and <a>. After 1239, it settles to <e> and <i/y>, although the occasional <a> also appears. On balance, however, <e> is by far the most commonly featured vowel.

Lizard (KK: Lysardh): here, the CLB makes the assumption that this name is Cornish, but this is far from certain. If Cornish, it would translate as "high-place court/administrative centre/ruin". It does feature in Domesday as a "manor" (more realistically an estate) but one hide, 4 wild mares, 3 cattle, 20 pigs and 60 sheep hardly constitutes an administrative centre. Additionally, in this notably flat-topped landscape, where is the place that could be identified as the "high place"? Old Cornish *ard* would also, this far west, have assibilated to Middle Cornish **ardh* and even to Late Cornish *are* but, apart from examples of *-ardh* in the early C14, such historic development is lacking. It is possible, even probable, that the name is either an English or French mariners' name (as, for example, **Cape Cornwall** [Eng.] and **The Brisons** [French]). Common spellings from the earliest references are identical with Middle French *lesard*, "lizard", and may be a likening of the long, regular shape of the peninsula as viewed from sea being likened to a lizard's tail.

Luckett (KK Chilova): the KK rendition of the OE personal name *Leofa* is scarcely appropriate with regard to the diphthong contained in the OE name (**Luckett** is OE *Leofan cot*, "Leofa's cottage"). Also, the CLB chooses <v> to represent the <f> of the personal name but inconsistently retains <f> in **Lannstefan* (for **Launceston**).

Madron (KK: Eglosvadern): *eglos*, "church", does not traditionally cause lenition and, accordingly, the CLB should correct this to the historically attested *Eglosmadern*.

Malpas (KK: Kammdrog): the French place-name translates as "bad step" but the CLB's choice of **kamm*, "step", is confusing as it coincides with a word spelt identically in the KK system meaning "bend, curve".

Marahamchurch (KK: Eglosvarwenn): the CLB again employs unhistorical lenition after *eglos*. Also, the choice of the final vowel is arguable as early forms of the saint's name give <y> as often as <e>. To add to the confusion, the Domesday forms give <o>. However, as Cornish *gwyn*, "white, fair, holy", might be involved here, a feminine form of this verb, *gwen*, is frequently recorded in place-name records.

Markwell (KK: Fentenvargh): an example of poor research by the CLB. The name is not Cornish *margh*, "horse" or personal name *Margh*, but the OE name *Aelmarch* (possibly a hybrid OE-Celtic name) as attested by *Aelmarches wylle* 1018.

Mawgan (KK: Sen Mowgan): the CLB adds <Sen> superfluously as explained above. There seems little justification for <ow> when 8 historic forms give <aw>, <au> against a single example of <ow>. Again CLB research has been lacking, the Cornish place-name *Pluvogan* being attested from 1523.

Menheniot (KK: Mahunyes): early forms of this name strongly favour <-hyn->, rather than the CLB's choice of <-hun->, which fails to appear in any of the 34 available historic forms of the name. There is also no historical justification for the CLB to assibilate the final consonant, other than the occurrence of *-th* 1327, 1342, 1371, and *-the* 1317, in which case *Mahynyeth* might be justified.

Merrymeet (KK: Merimet): a C17 Eng. name, a contraction of "merry meeting (place)". In this instance, the CLB does not attempt a Cornish translation but, instead, offers a strange rendition of the English.

Merther (KK: Eglosverther): As borne out by all historic forms, lenition is not historically employed in this name and has been wrongly introduced only by the CLB's decision. *Eglosmerther* is the correct rendition.

Minions (KK: Menyon):this name suffers from a dearth of historical forms: only *Minniens* 1613 and *Minions* 1897 being currently available. Its meaning, and even its language, remains unknown. Notwithstanding, the CLB has ignored the final <-s> common to both examples and has apparently assumed a hitherto unknown plural form of *men*, "stone", despite the fact that <e> does not feature as a first vowel in either of the historic forms.

Mitchell (KK: Toll an Voren): the place-name is OE *maedes holh*, "maid's hollow" and does not contain the definite article that the CLB has needlessly introduced. "Hollow" would be better translated as *pans*; the CLB's current translation resulting in a rather unfortunate innuendo.

Mithian (KK: Mydhyen): although <-en> occurs in the earliest form of this name, the subsequent 9 historic forms consistently contain <-an>.

Morval (KK: Morval): this name requires further study to ascertain its language. The 1290 form, *Moruell*, suggests it is OE *mor wielle*, "marsh stream/spring". Historic forms of the name give the final vowel as <e> and <a> equally, so that even this is uncertain.

Morwenstow (KK: Lannvorwenna): as explained under **Jacobstow** above, the Cornish word *lan* is unsuitable to translate OE *stow*.

Mount Edgcumbe (KK: Menydh Pennkomm): a C16 Eng. name containing the Eng. family name *Edgcumbe*. It seems absurd to translate these family names into Cornish.

Mount Hawke (KK: Menydh Hok): a C19 Eng. name with no known Cornish precedent and again containing an Eng. family name. The observations under **Mount Edgcumbe** above apply here.

Mousehole (KK: Porthynys): I am far from alone in criticizing the KK respelling of *enys*, "island" to make it identical with Welsh. In words such as this /i/ became /e/ *c.* 1300, only reverting to /i/ *c.* 1700 under the influence of the Eng. vowel shift that affected "English" to become "Inglish". For a system with a base date of *c.* 1500, only /e/ would be correct in this context. The traditional pronunciation of *enys* as "ai-nez" by Sennen fishermen should also be studied. The final vowel tends to become schwa, so that an historically accurate (and attested) spelling of the word would be *enes*, keeping it distinct from Welsh *ynys* and Breton *enez*.

Muchlarnick (KK: Lannerghmeur): *lanergh* is sufficient to represent this toponym as it was evidently the original name before the addition of Middle Eng. *micel*, "great".

Mullion (KK: Eglosvelyan): I again refer to my previous references to the lack of historical lenition after *eglos*. Although various recorded spellings have tended to introduce a <-y-> to the saint's name, the original saint is certainly *Melan* and a historically accurate rendition of this place-name would be *Eglosmelan* in spite of the various recorded forms that introduce <y> in to the saint's name.

Newbridge (KK: Hal an Taken): the Penwith **Newbridge**, a C19 replacement name, has an earlier Cornish one. Historical forms suggest the last element of this to be *tegen*, "jewel, pretty one", evidently the former name of the river.

Newquay (KK: Tewynn Pleustri): the CLB has closely followed Padel here but, in doing so, has introduced an unknown word in Cornish. Padel (1988) suggests a Breton cognate *pleustriñ*, "to work, busy oneself". He doubts that *porth*, "cove, landing place" could have contracted to *p'* or *por'* as early as 1308 but we have, for example, *Porquin* (1201) for **Portquin** a century earlier. Nor does Padel believe that *lystry*, "ships" is involved, averring that the vowel is <u> in the early forms. However, we have the following forms: *Towenplystre* 1530; *Towanvlister* 1562; *Towenblyster* 1574; *Towan Blistra* 1755, *c.* 1840, 1906 and *Towan Blystra* 1770, 1838 and, for support, the existence of a rock north of the harbour named *Listrey* (*id. c.* 1830). The jury remains out on this name; however, the original name of the settlement was simply **Towan**: appearing as *Tewyn* and similar from 1289 and 1813. The problem, however, is that the CLB has adopted

Padel's tentative suggestion and treated it as fact. In cases like this, and in order to avoid this kind of dilemma, the only realistic course is to select a suitable historically recorded form and, as the meaning is not certain, retain the original spelling of that form.

North Hill (KK: Bre Gledh): again, the CLB's recommended name betrays insufficient research. Eng. "hill" does not occur in the name, therefore the use of *bre* is incorrect. The place-name was simply *Henle* 1238, with Eng. "north" added later to distinguish it from South Hill. *Henle* is OE *hean leah*, "high clearing".

North Petherwin (KK: Paderwynn Gledh): the name saint, **Patern**, was masculine and yet *Gledh* is lenited as though it follows a feminine proper noun. One wonders why the saint is not referred to as *Padernwyn(n)*, "holy Patern".

North Tamerton (KK: Tre war Tamer): the original name of this settlement was *Tamer*, after the river, with OE *tun* added later. The CLB's <Tre war> is unnecessary and merely translates the Eng. name rather than recreate the Cornish one.

Otterham (KK: Prasdowrgi): *pras*, "meadow" is not an adequate word to translate OE *hamm*, "enclosure; land hemmed in by water, marsh or higher ground; land within a river bend; river meadow; promontory". It is often difficult to determine whether this OE element is *hamm* or *ham*, "homestead, village, estate" and either could apply here (note that there is no appreciable river bend here and the site lies close to the river's source, so the latter is the more likely word). The <Otter-> part of the name is, in fact, a contraction of OE *oter ea*, "otter water", for which the CLB has not made full provision.

Pelynt (KK: Plunennys): there is no evidence from the 13 available historic forms of the name to suggest that medieval assibilation ever occurred, every one ending with <-t> or <-te>.

Perranporth (KK: Porth Pyran): there are various observations to make here. Firstly, the saint's name is, in the majority of historical place-name forms containing it, rendered as *Peran*, forms with /i/ being the exception rather than the rule. Secondly, the name is an English coinage: a poor C19 concoction that reverses the normal word order. The only *Porth Peran* that exists in historical record is Perran Sands, Perranuthnoe. As in my suggestions regarding Falmouth, rather than simply adopt the English coinage it is best to seek out historical origins. In Perranporth's case, the manorial centre of *Tywarnhayle* actually lay in the centre of the town and as this name has all but disappeared from the modern maps, it is appropriate to adopt.

(N.B. It is a particular feature of Cornish manorial place-names that they retain the Old Cornish form <Ty->, e.g. Tywarnhayle, Tywardreath, Degembris, Tybesta, Tehidy, rather as though such a feature denoted status. It is recommended that <Ty-> be retained in this use in revived Cornish).

Perranzabuloe (KK: Pyran yn Treth): historic forms consistently give *Peran Treth* (with just one <*in treth*> from 1425). The CLB's insertion of <yn> is therefore unnecessary. Generally, *Peran Treth* refers to Penhale Sands while Perranzabuloe itself is, historically, *Lanberan*. The present place-name was, in fact, transferred from the site of the second church when that was overwhelmed by encroaching sand-dunes and it was that site which was the historical *Lanberan*.

Phillack (KK: Felek): once again, the CLB has (correctly) moved away from its usual practice of inserting <Sen> before a saint's name. However, this saint (Felicitas) variously appears as *Felok, Felyce, Felak* and *Felocke*, none of which contains <-ek>. In its choice, the CLB has discarded the earlier Cornish name of the settlement: *Egglosheil c.* 1170; *Eglasheil* C12, *Egloshayle c.* 1500, 1659, 1842.

Playing Place (KK: Plen an Gwari): This is a C19 Eng. name with no known Cornish predecessor. In 1813, it was *Kea Playing Place* and, to distinguish it from other Plen an Gwary place-names, it might be appropriate (if a little unwieldy) to render this name as *Plen an Gwary Ke*.

Polyphant (KK: Pollefans): once again, the KK convention of doubling consonants after a short vowel creates difficulties and forces the system to adapt in order to avoid a triple L (see also **Lanivet** above). The second element, OC *lefant*, did not undergo Middle Cornish assibilation and this historical fact should be observed.

Polzeath (KK: Pollsygh): the KK use of /i/ where, historically the vowel is /e/ has been questioned by Hodge (2005) and is not borne out by the historic forms of the place-name.

Ponsanooth (KK: Pons an Woedh): further study is required to ascertain whether the final element of this name is "goose" or "watercourse". Historic forms show <oeth> once and <woth> four times from 1555 to 1620.

Port Isaac (KK: Porthusek): as *porth* has a habit of losing <-th> in place-names and colloquial speech (e.g. Par, Pelistry), one wonders why the KK system did not opt for **pordh*. However, it is the second element of this name which is in doubt. Padel suggests an assumed adjective—otherwise unknown—*usek*, "place of chaff", but the more usual suggestion, *ysek*, "place of corn, corn-rich" remains (in my own view) alive. Historic forms give: *-usek* 1337; *-issek c.* 1540; *-esyke, eseke c.* 1550; *-ysack* 1566; *-yseke* 1576; *-ezick, -izick, -issick* 1584.

Porthcurno (KK: Porthkernow): *Kernow*, "Cornwall" is emphatically not contained in this name. Instead, it is a word **cornow*, most likely a plural of *corn*, "horn" and perhaps a reference to the peculiar rock formations that surround the cove. Historic forms give: *Porth Cornowe* 1580; *Porthe Cornewe* 1580, 1582; *Port-Curno, Port Curnoe* 1584; *Port-Curnoe c.* 1605; *Porcarnow* 1839. In this instance, the CLB has decided to perpetuate a myth rather than follow Padel's sound advice.

Porthoustock (KK: Porthewstek): the second element of this name requires clarification. Historically, we have *-ustech, -eustek c.* 1250, 1360; *-ustok c.* 1500; *-ewstock* 1529; *-owstock* 1543; *-oustock* 1699. It may be the family name Ustick(e), "of St Just" and, if so, *-ustek* would be correct (see **Gorran Haven** and **St Just**).

Portwrinkle (KK: Porthwikkel): this name has to be considered alongside that of nearby **Trewrickle**, the historic forms of Port-wrinkle being late (C17 onwards), corrupt and singularly unhelpful. The second element of both is undoubtedly the same, the inland site being *-wikkel c.* 1190; *wikkill* 1348; *-wykkil* 1349 and *-wykkell* 1410. This would appear to be a diminutive or adjectival form of *gwyk*, "forest settlement", presumably **gwykel*. The two place-names are therefore likely to be **Trewykel* and **Porthgwykel*. Assuming that the CLB is aware of this probable derivation then its preferred system shows inconsistency in the light of their choice regarding **Gweek** (above) which, if rigidly applied, would give **Porthgwigel*.

Poughill (KK: Fentenvoekka): here the CLB has misinterpreted the OE name which does not contain either Puck or the Cornish *bucca*, but is OE *pocca wielle*, "frog spring/stream" (*Pochewelle* 1227, *Pochewille* 1269).

Praa Sands (KK: Porthgwragh): historic place forms do not give *porth*, but *pol* (*Polwragh* 1331 is the only clear form available).

Probus (KK: Lannbroboes): the <-oe-> vowel is unjustified and has been assumed from the unreliable Domesday forms *Lanbrebois, Lanbrabois*. *Lanbrobes* 1302 is a far better model and, traditionally, the final vowel approaches schwa.

Rame (KK: Hordh): it is highly unlikely that Rame means "ram" as the CLB assumes without taking notice of Padel, even though we have the (late) name for **Rame Head**, *Pendenhar c.* 1680. Padel believes it more likely to be Old High German *rama*, "(at the) barrier" (or an OE equivalent if one exists).

Redmoor (KK: Halrudh): the CLB wrongly translates this Eng. name as "red marsh" when, in fact, it is OE *hreod mor*, "reed marsh".

Relubbus (KK: Ryslowbes): none of the ten historic forms of this name justifies the CLB's version of the second element given between 1249 and 1613 as -(g)*lubith*; -*lehoubes*; -*lobus*; -*lubbas* and -*lobis*. The incorrect use of <rys> for <res> is explained above.

Ruan Minor (KK: Ruan Vyghan): the form *Ruan Vean* is late, not appearing until 1549, but an earlier Cornish form is recorded: *Rumon in Woen* 1319. This also contains the correct form of the saint's name, apparently missed by the CLB's research.

St Agnes (KK: Breanek): in compiling its list, the CLB has uniquely decided to break with normal convention which would locate names beginning with <St> at the beginning of S, as though they were spelt fully as <Saint>. With regard to this place-name, the CLB has followed Padel (1988) who states that it is not: " *'pointed hill'* ... *for the forms do not allow a derivation from* bannek, *'pointed'"*. The forms *Brievennoc* 1201; *Brevannek* 1261, 1342, 1415; *Brevannec* 1314, 1327; *Breivannek* 1345 and *Brevannek wartha/ woles* 1386, once thought to refer to St Agnes, actually belong to a site in St Hilary.

St Austell (KK: Sen Ostell): as before, the use of<Sen> is superfluous and incorrect. The authentic Cornish form of the name occurs as *Austol c.* 1150. The CLB's decision creates a precedent in altering <Au-> to <O->, presumably to correlate with traditional pronunciation that its members normally decry as "dialect". Elsewhere, the KK system replaces traditional <au> with <ow> as, for example, in its rendition of **Mawgan** and **Mawnan**.

St Breward (KK: Sen Branwalather): the CLB has here misrepresented the saint, who was actually *Bruered* or *Bruvered* according to the early recorded forms. Again, the use of <Sen> is incorrect.

St Buryan (KK: Eglosveryan): as outlined in the foreword, the CLB has incorrectly applied lenition and, by doing so, invites confusion with Veryan. Historic forms of the name do show a single rare lenited form from C15, *Eglosveryan*, but only two such lenitions after *eglos* are known throughout Cornwall. Both are late in date and probably a result of hypercorrection. Four other recorded forms for this name exhibit no lenition.

St Clement (KK: Sen Klemens): the 1464 form *Clemens* shows the true Cornish form of this toponym, again showing that the use of <Sen> is incorrect.

St Clether (KK: Sen Kleder): in this case, the CLB steps outside its own practice by retaining the unassibilated OC form of the saint's name. Again <Sen> should be omitted.

St Columb Major (KK: Sen Kolomm Veur): the CLB has chosen to translate the Eng. form of this name. It has either decided to discard the recorded Cornish form *Plewgolom* 1543, or it has not done the necessary research. The lenition of <Veur> can be argued about: the gender of the saint was, in early medieval times regarded as female and later as male.

St Columb Minor (KK: Sen Kolomm Vyghan): taking *Plewgolom* into account for the above, this toponym would be simply **Colom*, supported by the form *Colom* 1742.

St Day (KK: Sen Day): as this is a foreign saint, <Sen> is applicable here (as in *Sent Eler c.* 1680 for St Hilary). However, historic forms give <Dey> for the saint's name.

St Dennis (KK: Tredhinas): there is no necessity to prefix the unprecedented <Tre-> when **Dynas* is wholly adequate. There may be an argument for **Dyn Mylyek*: the Domesday estate of *Dimilihoc* (modern **Domellick**) may have been named after the hill fort within which St Dennis church stands. However, this will require further research.

St Gennys (KK: Sen Gwynnys): again <Sen> is an incorrect addition and historic forms of the saint's name give <-as> rather than <-ys>.

St Hilary (KK: Bronnlowena): here, the CLB has inexplicably opted for choosing a name based upon that of a farm adjoining the churchtown, Barlowenath (*Bronlowena* 1548) but which cannot be demonstrated as having been an alternative name for it. The *St Eler* of *John of Chyanhor* (c. 1680) gives a perfectly acceptable form, <Sen> being appropriate, the name saint being Bishop Hilarius of Poitiers.

St Ive (KK: Sen Iv): there may be a case here for rendering the saint's name as **Yvon*, following *S. Yvone* 1201, 1256; *S. Hyvon* 1258; *S. Ivon* 1291, 1327, 1342. He does not appear to have been a Celtic saint and, therefore, the use of <Sen> might in this case be justified.

St Just in Penwith (KK: Lannyust): my reasons for criticizing this are given under **Gorran Haven** above. Although we do have *Pluyust*

C16, dozens of other historic place-name examples omit the initial of the saint's name. Nor was it pronounced, as shown by the traditional nickname "Santusters". The only *lan* form recorded is *Lanuste* 1396.

St Kew Highway (KK: Fordh Lanndogho): this toponym dates only from C17 when it first appears as merely *Highway*. If, in the first place, Cornicizing the name is deemed necessary, then perhaps it is more advisable to consider the original.

St Lawrence (KK: Sen Lorens): the CLB has again introduced an unprecedented vowel to represent the <-aw-, -au-> of the name (it utilizes <-o-> in **St Austell** but <-ow-> in **Mawgan** and **Mawnan**) and, in fact, reflects only the modern Eng. pronunciation of the name. <Sen> is superfluous as shown by the 1380 form *Laurens*.

St Levan (KK: Sen Selevan): again <Sen> is incorrect, historic forms showing *Selevan* 1480, 1523, 1545, 1580; *Sellevan* 1580; *Slevan* 1610. The final vowel is schwa, normally represented by the KK system as <e>.

St Mabyn (KK: Sen Mabon): as a Celtic saint <Sen> should again be discarded. The real question here is the value of the vowel in the final syllable. Historic forms give <e> in 4 examples, <a> in another 4, <o> twice, <y> twice and <ou> once. <o>, as chosen by the CLB, may well be correct as the saint's name is given in the C10 list as *Mabon* (usually represented as female).

St Mawes (KK: Lannvowsedh): Historic forms of the saint's name give, in some instances, a hard ending, e.g. *Mawdyt* 1433; in others it is dropped (*Seynt Mausa* 1467). The *lan* forms adopt the latter without exception and in no historically recorded form does a final <th> or <dh> appear. The stressed vowel of the saint's name, taking all historic forms into account, is in 14 cases <au>; <aw> occurs 8 times; <ou> 3 times; <a> once and the CLB's preferred <ow> just once. The overwhelming evidence, therefore, favours <au>. Taking the total evidence into account, the most authentic form of this name would appear to be *Lanvausa*.

St Mawgan (KK: Sen Mowgan): as before, <Sen> is surplus to requirements and should be discarded. Again, the CLB has selected an entirely unrepresentative vowel to replace the historic <au>, <aw>, which also unjustifiably alters the traditional pronunciation. (NB. There may be a case for arguing that *Lanherno* may be an acceptable alternative but this requires further study).

St Minver (KK: Sen Menvra): the saint's name here is historically *Menfred(e)* or *Menvred(e)*, only becoming *Mynfre*, etc., in occasional instances. Most forms retain the final consonant. Various forms show that <Sen> is unnecessary and, therefore, a more representative choice would have been *Menvred*.

St Stephen in Brannel (KK: Eglosstefan): in St Stephen names, the normally rigid KK system seems to break down, insisting upon <f> instead of the <v> usually employed. The CLB has made its choice from a single (1578) instance of *Eglostephen*, even though there are eight examples of an alternative, given as: *Eglosselans* 1297; *Eglosshellans* 1293; *Eglossellans* 1336, 1380; *Eglosellans* c. 1350; *Egloshellans* 1379; *Egloshellens* 1838; *Egloshellings* C19 (*eglos* + probable personal name **Helans/Helant*).

St Tudy (KK: Eglostudi): the saint's name, as evidenced by early forms, is *Tudic*. This name should, therefore, be presented as *Eglostudek* or *Eglostudyk*.

St Winnow (KK: Sen Gwynnow): the CLB's choice reflects only the modern form of the original saint's name which was **(G)winnoc* (e.g. *S. Winnoc* 1181). A strong case, therefore, can be made for representing this name as *Gwynnek*, <Sen> being unnecessary and incorrect as explained above.

Saltash (KK: Essa): <Essa> is nothing more than a stylized version of OE *aesc*, "ash tree", although it is found c. 1230. If the CLB's policy is to translate all Eng. names into Cornish, one must ask why it did not favour **Onnen*.

Sandplace (KK: Tewesva): there is no such word as *tewes* in Cornish (being a modern invention by Nance) and, despite analogy with Welsh *tywod*, its use here is historically unjustified.

Sennen (KK: Sen Senan): as explained above, the use of <Sen> does not accord with traditional practice and should be discarded. Early historical references to *S. Senan* refer to the dedication of the church and not to the settlement name. For further confirmation, q.v. **Sennen Cove**, *Porthsenan* in 1370 and 1461, not **Porth Sen Senan*.

Shop (KK: Shoppa Parkyn): the 1748 form gives the personal name as *Parken*, not **Parkyn*.

Sithney (KK: Sen Sydhni): once again, the CLB's use of <Sen> is incorrect. In addition, the CLB appears to have discarded the Cornish name of the settlement (now transferred to the churchtown farm as **Marsinney**), recorded from 1140 to 1376 as *Merthersythny* or *Merthersytheny*.

South Hill (KK: Bre Dheghow): insufficient research has been carried out by the CLB, as in North Hill above. The OE name is *suð hean leah*, "southern high clearing". Eng. "hill" is not involved in the name.

South Petherwin (KK: Paderwynn Dheghow): see **North Petherwin** and **South Hill** above. The lenition of **dyghow** also appears to be incorrect.

South Wheatley (KK: Kelliwynn Dheghow): in this OE name, from *hwitan leah*, the second element would, by the date of the first Anglo-Saxon settlement in East Cornwall, have had the meaning "clearing/glade", not the earlier meaning of "grove/wood". The use of *kelly* is therefore incorrect.

Stithians (KK: Sen Stydhyans): the final <-s> is a late addition to the saint's name, not appearing until 1524. It should therefore be discarded. As before, <Sen> is superfluous and does not feature in six historic references. All examples prior to 1569 show that the first vowel is <e>; the CLB's <y> is mistaken.

Stoke Climsland (KK: Eglosclym): in this instance, the CLB's rendition is utterly baffling, particularly its inclusion of *eglos*. OE *stoc* translates as: "place, outlying farmstead, secondary/dependent settlement", difficult to render in Cornish unless the pertinent meaning can be ascertained. "Church" is nowhere involved. The whole name means: "the *stoc* within the manor of Climsland"; the latter name translating as "land belonging to a man called *Clym". The whole would not only be difficult to put into Cornish but to do so would produce an ungainly result. This example is an excellent illustration of why it is best to leave place-names of non-Cornish origin alone, unless a genuine Cornish alternative exists.

Stratton (KK: Strasnedh): this name did not evolve beyond its Old Cornish form and, therefore, the first element should be left as <strad> in order to fully respect its history rather than invent one that never occurred. The early river name appears as *Neht, Neet* and a softened form *Neth*, showing that the final is /θ/, not /ð/.

Talskiddy (KK: Talskisi): according to the CLB's key, it does not consider this name to be Cornish. Padel, however, considers it to be *tal*, "brow" + an unrecorded Cornish word corresponding to Breton *skidiñ*, "to clear land", or perhaps a plural form of Middle Cornish *scues*, "shadow" in an Old Cornish form. The historic forms give: *Talschedy, Talskydy* 1297; *Talskedy* 1300, 1376; *Talskidy* 1310; *Talskythy* 1332; *Talskithy* 1358. In view of the uncertainty, the only practical course is to find a representative choice from these.

Tideford (KK: Rysteusi): the CLB correctly translates this as "ford on the River Tiddy". However, the river name did not evolve beyond its Old Cornish form, which should therefore be preserved. No historic form of the river name gives <eu>, historic spellings being *Tudi* 1018; *Tody* 1216, 1260, 1300, 1317; *Tudy, Tedy* 1395; *Tuddy, Tuddye* 1613; *Tyddie* 1613, 1618. It has been explained elsewhere in this paper why <rys> is incorrect and should be replaced by <res>.

Tintagel Castle (KK: Dyndagell): there is no certainty that this name is Cornish and, in my view, the evidence leans heavily towards it being of Norman-French origin. There is no mention of the name prior to Geoffrey of Monmouth (*c.* 1137) and the soft j of the name is difficult to reconcile with the /g/ of the assumed Cornish **tagell*. A similar Norman-French name applies to a Channel Islands site: *Tintageu*, earlier *Tente d'Agel*, Sark, apparently "stronghold of the devil". On the balance of evidence offered by Professor Charles Thomas, the likely Cornish name of the site prior to the Norman period was *Purocoronavis* (for *Durocornovio*) c700 (c400), "fortress of the Cornovii" which in revived Cornish would be rendered as **Dyn Kernowyon*. I would suggest that this becomes the adopted name (and would doubtless upset the site's current manager, "English" Heritage).

Torpoint (KK: Penntor): arguably the CLB's most unfortunate offering. It is several decades old but apparent "establishment" does not excuse the failure to correct it. The Eng. place-name does not contain "tor", this element being a contraction of OE *steort*, "tail, promontory", to which was added the tautologous Eng. word "point" (*Stertpoynt* 1608). The change of one letter to form **Pentyr* might suffice to correct the error.

Townshend (KK: Penn an Dre): Townshend was founded in the C19 and named after an Eng. family (after a local landowning St Aubyn had married a Townsend). To thus alter an Eng. family name to a toponym in Cornish is as inappropriate as referring to John Major as "Jowan Bras". The site has no alternative Cornish name, was founded after the demise of the language in this area and should simply be referred to by its authentic name (spelt *Townsend* in 1867).

Tregadillett (KK: Tregadyles): a further OC name, no form of which features Middle Cornish assibilation, and should not be provided with a false history.

Tregole (KK: Tregowl): historic forms from C14 and C15 suggest that the qualifying element is disyllabic: *Tregowel, Tregewel* 1306; *Treguwal*

1319; *Tregewyl* 1346; *Tregowele* 1425. Although the meaning is unclear, *tre* + *gew-el*, "enclosed place" is a distinct possibility.

Tregony (KK: Trerigni): as Padel points out, the original form of this name's second element—a personal name—is fraught with problems. The earliest mention (1049) gives *Rigoni* and Domesday (1086) has *Rigani*, but, to explain the modern stress on the first element, Padel considers that an unknown name, **Rigni* or the like, might account for it. However, we have no record of how the name was pronounced in the past and stress might well have shifted at some point (as is unfortunately happening with many Cornish place-names today), perhaps under the influence of the Norman French speech of the dominant Pomery family during the Middle Ages. Padel himself states that: "*there is little justification for a personal name of the form* *Rigni" (a point ignored by the CLB) and, therefore it should be discarded, perhaps in favour of the early form.

Trelights (KK: Treleghrys): historic forms consistently begin the final syllable with <t>: *-tos* twice; *-tres* 3 times and *-tees* once. The name is certainly *tref-*, "farm, settlement", followed by a compound of *legh*, "slab" + an uncertain word that might be *treys*, "feet" (giving *leghtreys*, "feet-slab" i.e. "pavement"). In view of the uncertainty, it is best not to apply assumption, as the CLB has done here, but to offer one of the historic forms unaltered: I would suggest *Treleghtres* 1426.

Trelowarren (KK: Trelowaren): from the earliest records, the second element of this name appears to be a personal name **Lewaren(t)*, where <ew> and <eu> are consistently found. No available form gives <ow> until modern times and its use is therefore incorrect.

Tremail (KK: Trevel): the personal name contained in this toponym is OC *Mael*, better represented as **Mayl* (*Tremayl* 1284, 1296, 1312, 1327). The CLB has applied the expected lenition when, in fact, it is featured in none of the historic forms. Until this is better understood, it is advisable not to apply lenition where it does not occur historically.

Trematon (KK: Treveu): early records give <u> for <n>, as borne out by such forms as *Trementon* 1187, 1188, 1282, 1346. The original is, therefore, *tre* + *men*, "stone" (+ OE *tun*) and, as with **Tremail** above, lenition is absent throughout its history and should not be theoretically applied.

Trenewan (KK: Trenowyen): once again, the CLB applies <ow> when all historic examples of the name give <ew>, <yw>. As it also applies <ow> to replace historical <aw>, <au>, one wonders how many phonic values apply to <ow> in what is claimed to be a phonemic orthography.

Trethurgy (KK: Tredhowrgi): C13 and C14 records consistently give *dever-* rather than the alternative *dowr-* in the personal name and, as the CLB does not object to this in names such as **Devoran** (KK: Devryon), the decision to alter it here is baffling.

Trevalga (KK: Trevelgi): the <-el-> of the CLB's version of this name is entirely unjustified as the historic forms all contain <-al->: *Trevalga* 1238, 1262, 1284, 1296; *Trevalge* 1333, 1420; *Trevalgye, Trevalga* 1584. It will be noted from these that the CLB's final <-i> stems from the one late exception penned by an English observer (Norden), the traditional final being <-a>. If the CLB was uncertain about this name, it could have used the site's alternative name: *Menaliden* (*c.* 1150) < *menedh + ledan*.

Trevellas (KK: Trevelys): the CLB's choice of <-lys> is at fault. Historic forms give *-lles,* 1302, 1306, 1327, 1337, 1376, *c.* 1720) and *-llas* 1341. Although Padel postulates a personal name **Melyt*, he stresses that there is only slight evidence for such a name. Nonetheless, the CLB opts for this rather than the historical evidence.

Treverva (KK: Trevurvo): this name invites further study and discussion. Padel's suggestion is that a personal name **Urvo* , of uncertain existence, might be involved if the earliest historic form *Trewruvo* (1327) is a mistake for **Trewurvo*. However, *Trevruvo* (the first <v> representing <u>) is also attested from 1327 and , therefore, an entirely different word or name may be involved. The safest option here would be to select a known historic form, perhaps *Trewruvo.*

Trewellard (KK: Trewylardh): again the CLB has included an unjustified feature based upon assumption rather than fact. The personal name consistently ends with <-d> in all historic references, covering a period from 1307 to present, without the slightest hint of assibilation, even though it might have been expected this far west. The <y> vowel is attested from four C14 examples.

Trewidland (KK: Trewydhlann): the second element of this name is of obscure derivation. Padel rejects a Cornish version of the Welsh personal name *Gwyddelan* on the grounds of misplaced stress. His second suggestion, a possible but unattested Cornish cognate of Welsh *gwyddlan*, "cemetery" has been seized upon by the CLB and presented by it as fact. However, as Padel stresses, there is no record of any such feature at the site. A further point is that the historic record consistently gives apparent four-syllable versions: *Trewithelon* 1297; *Trewythelan* 1298; *Trewethelan* c. 1320; *Trewhythelan* 1394; *Trewhythelen* 1417. The variations in the final vowel of these examples makes it unlikely that the second element is a compound containing *lan*.

Trewint (KK: Trewyns): An Old Cornish name which did not evolve to a assibilated form. Its preserved ancient form is an important survival and should be retained rather than misrepresented.

Treyarnon (KK: Treyarnenn): from 8 historic references available, 3 give <ar-> for the first syllable of the second element; 3 give <yar->; with one <har-> and one <gar->. The <yar-> forms most likely result from pronunciation, and <ar-> is likely to be the original, perhaps a lenited personal name *Garnon. The final vowel varies between <e>, <a> and <o>. Again, a choice from the historical list is the best option and I would suggest *Trearnon* c. 1210.

Truro (KK: Truru): this form (first attested in 1278) has been popular for much of the period of the Cornish revival but it is a contracted form of the original, recorded as *Triueru* c. 1193, 1195, 1196, 1198, 1214, 1278; *Tryuereu* C12, C13; *Triveru* 1201, 1214, 1227, 1278; *Tryveru* 1264, 1284, 1297, etc. Perhaps *Truru* has become too established to change but I would prefer the more complete form *Tryveru*.

Twelveheads (KK: Deudhek Stamp): the CLB's translated name is a nonsense, meaning "twelve stamping mills" when there was only one, equipped with twelve heads, or hammers; or, at most, two stamps of six heads each. The name is late (C17), and there is no historic Cornish equivalent or alternative.

Tywardreath (KK: Chi war Dreth): the CLB has failed to notice the peculiar convention of manorial names containing Old Cornish *ty* to retain the old form throughout the Middle and Late Cornish periods (see my notes under **Perranporth** above). This is an important historical feature that should be protected.

Upton Cross (KK: Krows Trewartha): this is pure invention. As detailed earlier, *crows* was never historically used to denote a crossroads and the English name Upton (at this location) did not have a Cornish alternative.

Victoria (KK: Trevudhek): another example of mishandled invention. Victoria is a settlement founded in the 1880s and named after a public house which was, in turn, named after Queen Victoria. There is neither precedent nor reason for the CLB's application of <tre-> which it then follows with the **masculine** Cornish form of Victoria!

The feminine is British *Boudicca*, which would lead to a hypothetical revived Cornish **Büdheca* (by analogy with historic forms of the male saint *Budoc*, e.g. the toponymic surname *Trevithick* and place-names *Pluvuthek c.* 1400 [Budock] and *Eglosbuthekbyan* 1469 [Budock Vean])

Wadebridge (KK: Ponsrys): if it is necessary in the first place to Cornicize this Eng. name, it is worth considering that the original was simply OE *waed*, "ford" (*Wade* 1312-1484), Middle Eng. *brigge* only being added in the late C15 after the bridge was built.

Wainhouse Corner (KK: Stumm an Gwinji): another Eng. name with no known Cornish alternative. It contains no definite article and, therefore, the CLB's inclusion of one is unnecessary. **Gwinji* is a modern invention and "Corner" was only added to the name in 1660. However, the CLB is correct in identifying that "Wainhouse" is actually "winehouse" (*Winhouse* 1417; *Wynhous* 1430; *Wynehous* 1440).

Warbstow (KK: Lannwarburgh): again, a *lan* is, both physically and archaeologically, a distinct and very different site from an Eng. *stow* and should not be used to translate it unless a genuine Celtic *lan* exists or is known to have existed. The Eng. (female) saint (known at various English sites) is *Waerberge* (*Werburge c.* 1180, 1305) and, therefore, the use of <-gh> is incorrect.

Week St Mary (KK: Gwigvaria): the original place-name was simply *Wike* (1277, rendered as *Wich, Wihc* 1086), St Mary not being prefixed until 1291 (note that, this time, the CLB has not prefixed <Sen> to the saint's name). This is not Cornish *gwyk*, "forest settlement" but OE *wic*. This variously translates as: "earlier Romano-British settlement; dwelling; specialized farm or building; dairy farm; trading or industrial settlement". Unless the exact meaning of *wic*—as applicable to the individual site—can be ascertained, translating it into Cornish is impossible.

Werrington (KK: Trewolvrin): the CLB appears to have mistranslated the first element of this OE name which derives from *Wulfredinga tun*, "farm/settlement of Wulfred's people/family".

Zelah (KK: An Hel): this name is certainly Middle Eng. *sele*, "hall". However, it is questionable whether the use of a definite article that does not feature in the original is necessary or correct.

Zennor (KK: Sen Senar): as a Celtic saint is involved, the use of the prefix <Sen> is not correct and contrary to traditional Cornish practice. Indeed, only one of the 19 historic forms of the place-name (as opposed to those that merely record the church dedication) includes the use of "St". There are, in fact, records of an alternative Cornish name that give a far better option: *Egglose Zennor* 1561 and *Eglos Senor* 1781. The CLB's choice of <Senar> is the best historical form of the saint's name and, therefore, a truly historical *Eglos Senar* can be adopted.

CONCLUSION

It is unfortunate that, throughout the period of revival of the Cornish language, some linguistic enthusiasts have tended to treat place-names as their own preserve. At best, this is a mistaken attitude. It is, at least equally, the preserve of the historian and we ignore this at our peril.

Place-names and their study contain an undeniably important linguistic element but, of greater importance is their historical evolution. Unless the latter is fully researched and taken in full account, great damage can be done to them by exercises such as that by the Cornish Language Board which is the subject of this paper. The CLB's recommendations are replete with mistranslations, insufficient research and flights of fancy created by unwarranted assumptions.

Many of the Cornish names are poorly represented and the CLB has, in some cases, seen fit to manipulate history in order to make it adapt to the ideology of a modern orthographical system. This can never be acceptable practice. If historical integrity has to be laid aside in order to satisfy the requirements and rigidity of any modern linguistic system, then it is surely the responsibility of that system to be able to adapt and be flexible enough to ensure that the historic evidence is both observed and protected. Indeed, place-names are historical monuments and merit the same degree of protection as one would expect to be applied to historical and archaeological structural remains.

The exercise also demonstrates the difficulties and, arguably, the unwise practice of translating non-Cornish place-names into Cornish where no recorded Cornish alternative historically existed. For example, the above entries contain several instances where an Old English element simply cannot be translated for lack of evidence of its exact meaning, and several more where the Old English element has simply not been translated correctly. Names such as these have a history of their own and it cannot be right to concoct a false one. This also applies to those names that can be shown not to have evolved from their Old Cornish forms.

There are many questions to be applied to the whole practice of representing Cornish place-names in a purer Cornish form than that which appears on the modern map or signpost: in West Cornwall, for instance, are several names displaying written representations of Late Cornish pre-occlusion. This is a real and valuable historical development and should not be discarded simply because it does not accord with the requirements of a modern orthographical system. As stated above, it is for the modern system to adapt to the history and not the other way round. Whatever the current system of revived Cornish, can it harm that system to write *Trewynt* (for *Trewint*), or *Pedn an Wlas* (for Land's End)? If it is seen to do so, the only conclusion to reach is that the fault must lie within that modern system and that the system itself must change.

REFERENCES

Gover, J. E. B. 1948. *The Place Names of Cornwall*. Unpublished MS at R.I.C. Truro.

Hodge, Pol. 2005. "Spelling" in *Agan Yeth* 4. Cornish Language Board.

Mills, A. D. 1993. *A Dictionary of English Place Names*. Oxford.

Padel, Oliver J. 1985. *Cornish Place Name Elements*. Nottingham.

Padel, Oliver J. 1988. *A Popular Dictionary of Cornish Place Names*, Penzance.

Pool, P. A. S. 1985. *The Place Names of West Penwith* (*2nd edition*). Heamoor.

Pool, P. A. S. 1990. *The Field Names of West Penwith*. Hayle.

Pool, P. A. S. 1994. "The Field Names of the Manor of Mulfra", in *Journal of the Royal Institution of Cornwall*, New Series II, Vol. II, Part 1. Truro.

Svensson, O. 1987. *Saxon Place Names in East Cornwall*. Lund: Lund University Press.

Thomas, C. 1993. *Tintagel: Arthur and Archaeology*. London.

Weatherhill, Craig. 2005. *Place Names in Cornwall and Scilly*. Salisbury and Launceston.

Weatherhill, Craig. *Cornish Place Name Index*. Unpublished archive at Newbridge, Penzance.

Weatherhill, Craig. Forthcoming. *Cornish Place Names and Language*. Second, revised edition. Wilmslow.

Williams, Nicholas. 2006. "Saint in Cornish", in *Writings on Revived Cornish*. Westport: Evertype.

"STUDYING CORNISH PLACE NAMES": REVIEW OF THE CORNISH LANGUAGE BOARD'S *THE FORMATION OF CORNISH PLACE NAMES*

Craig Weatherhill

Graham Sandercock, Wella Brown, 1996, *The Formation of Cornish Place Names* (A background to Cornish, an occasional series, number two), 12pp.: Kesva an Taves Kernewek, The Cornish Language Board. ISBN 0 907064 63 9. £1.75.

INTRODUCTION
The second of the Cornish Language Board booklets in the series: "A background to Cornish, an occasional series", published in 1996, was *The Formation of Cornish Place Names.*

As a general introduction, this booklet is helpful but, nonetheless, its twelve pages contain unacceptable errors, particularly with regard to several of its cited place-names. In their own introduction, the authors open with the sentence: "Many students first take an interest in the Cornish language through studying place names", but the errors and leaps of faith contained in this little booklet speak against such study having taken place in its preparation. As a result, the Cornish Language Board has produced a second booklet that both misinforms and misleads its readers.

ANALYSIS
Page 2 contains a list of international city and town names shown in their native language forms alongside their English language equivalents. The last of these names is: ***Bosvenegh*/Bodmin**. The preceding review article mentionss that evidence suggests it likely that the qualifying element in the Cornish form of this name is (both lenited and unlenited) *mene(g)hy*, 'churchland', rather than *menegh*, 'monks'. This view is shared by Oliver Padel (Padel 1985) and it does seem curious that the Cornish Language Board has chosen not to heed its own advice given in the very first paragraph of the same page: *"However, for the serious student, attention should be drawn to more authoritative works, particularly the recent work of Oliver Padel".*

Page 4: Under Section 1c, headed: "**A name can be a noun with an adjective**", it is mentioned that: "*The adjectives hen ('old') and *kamm ('crooked') are unusual in that they come before the noun*". This is rather a misconception. In place-names, hen is only found as part of a compound, in which usual word order is reversed; the adjective coming first and often causing lenition to the following element, for example **Hendra** (< *hen* + *tre*). Numerous adjectives are found in these compounds, e.g. *hyr*, 'long' takes part in *hyr-yarth*, 'long-ridge' and *hyr-nans*, 'long-valley'. *Cam* (KK **kamm*) does appear after the noun as expected in such place-names as **Gilly Gabben** (< *kelly* + *cam*), thus exposing the error of the booklet's statement.

The introduction to Section 1*d*. unnecessarily complicates the process in which: "**A name can consist of two nouns**". The authors advise that: "*we have to interpret it as 'the **something** (of) or (by) or (on) or (with) **something**"*, giving examples such as **Cargreen**, 'rock of a seal'; **Millendreath**, 'mill on beach'. Bearing in mind that this booklet is designed to be a simple introduction, a far easier alternative would be to translate these names as: 'seal rock', 'beach mill'.

Page 5: It is unfortunate that, in the first list of 8 toponyms under Section 1d, the authors cite **Kelly Bray** as 'copse on a hill' when, as mentioned in the previous review article, simple research shows that this is not the derivation. In addition, this place-name does not consist of two nouns, but a noun followed by an adjective. It is *kelly*, 'copse, grove' + *bregh*, 'dappled', as shown by the historically recorded form *Kellibregh c.* 1286.

In the same list, **Egloshayle** is translated as 'church by estuary'. Whether this is the site on the Camel Estuary or the alternative Cornish name for Phillack, the translation must surely be 'church by the Heyl', this having been the Cornish name for both estuaries.

The second list of seven names under the same Section looks at toponyms containing personal names and translates **Liskeard** as 'Kerrys' court'. There is some uncertainty attached to the second element of this name. If a personal name, the *c.* 1010 record *Lys Cerruyt* rather suggests a personal name similar to **Kerwyd*, **Kerwyt*, rather than **Kerrys* which has been gleaned from later versions of the place-name.

The third list of names under this Section illustrates how two nouns might be joined by *an*, 'the'. It cites **Castle an Dinas**, translating it as 'castle of the fort'. The two examples of this name in Cornwall are both tautologies and likely to have been coined in error. The St Columb Major site is recorded simply as *Dynas* 1345, 1427; then *Castle of Dynas* 1478 before becoming *Castel an dynas c.* 1504. The current name is not Cornish but Cornucized English and how it came into being is clarified by this sequence.

The next name, **Crows-an-wra**, is given by the authors as 'cross of the witch'. This translation may be correct but *gwragh* more often means 'old woman, hag, crone'. In Late Cornish, its meaning expanded to include 'giant', as shown by place-names such as **Towanroath** (< *toll an wragh*) and **Loban Rath** (<*la[b]m an wragh*).

Ponsanooth, in the same list, is confidently translated as 'bridge of the goose' by the authors, perhaps by analogy with **Ponsongath**, 'bridge of the cat' (St Keverne). This, again, is far from certain. Equally, the final element could be *godh*, 'stream', this being favoured by Padel (Padel 1985). The CLB's choice might have been encouraged by the 1521 form of the name as *Pons an Oeth* (three other forms, from 1555 to 1620 have -*woth*), this containing the <oe> vowel favoured by the modern Kemyn system in its spelling of **goedh*, 'goose'. One would prefer not to think that modern ideology has been permitted to take precedence over historical analysis in this case.

Page 6: Section 2 looks at common place-name elements but repeats the statement on Page 4 that: "adjectives follow the noun except *hen*, ('old') and **kamm*, ('crooked')". See above for criticism of this statement.

Page 7: Section 2*a.* is a list of nouns denoting a habitation or settlement. This list includes **kar, ker*, which is translated as 'fort, town'. It must be pointed out that this element cannot be demonstrated in Cornwall to represent 'town', but this criticism is minor compared to the treatment given to the cited place-name, **Carveth**. The authors translate this as 'fort of the grave' (rather than 'fort at a grave', as the name does not contain a definite article), *ker + vedh*. Three examples of this place-name exist in Cornwall and none of them have any such derivation:

> **Carveth** (Cuby): *Caervegh* 1334, 1335, 1339, 1355 (*ker*, 'fort' + *begh, bygh*, 'small')
>
> **Carveth** (Mabe): *Kervergh* 1327; *Carvergh* 1538 (*ker*, 'fort' + *mergh*, 'horses')
>
> **Carveth** (St Austell): *Karnarh* 1224 (probably *carn*, 'tor, cairn' + *ardh*, 'height')

It is clear that, in this case, the CLB has simply failed to carry out the necessary research but has, instead, relied upon mere speculation.

Also included in this list is **Landlooe**, this name being translated by the authors as 'enclosure by inlet'. This translation is doubly erroneous. As shown by several other examples, *land-* in East Cornish place-names is often Old Cornish *nant*, 'valley' (there is no known Early Christian *lan* site here), while the second element refers to the name, rather than the type, of the watercourse. The name is, therefore, 'valley of the Looe River' (OC. *nant* + *Logh*), this derivation being agreed by Padel (Padel 1985).

Page 8: The list of nouns (2*b*.) denoting man-made features includes **Trevorrow**, the CLB authors interpreting this as 'farm by roads' (*tre* + *fordhow*). Once again, this is horribly in error. One **Trevorrow** is listed, this being in Ludgvan parish, and the historic forms of this name are as follows:

> *Treworveu* 1299; *Trevorveu* 1309, 1345, 1346; *Treforfu* 1327; *Treworvou* 1345, 1346; *Trevorow* 1590; *Trevorou* 1755.

These examples show quite clearly that the qualifying element is anything but the plural of *fordh*, 'road, way' but is likely to be a personal name **Gorveu* or the like.

Creak a Vose, also included in the same list, is confidently interpreted by the authors as "barrow by a dike". This is not strictly true. Had the authors undergone the research, they would have found that early forms of the name are: *Crucgkeyrvos* 1346; *Crukarfos* 1368. The derivation is thus: *crug*, 'barrow, tumulus' + a compound *ker-fos*, 'fort-wall, fort-rampart'.

Lizard is cited, again with confidence, as Cornish *lys ardh*, 'high court'. In fact, *ardh* is not an adjective but a noun, 'height, high place'. As mentioned in the previous review article, however, the language of this place-name is in some doubt. It may be English, French or Cornish. The assumed Cornish meaning makes little sense with regard to the site: there was no major administrative center here that would have earned the title of *lys*, and there is no noticeable "high place" in this markedly flat-topped landscape. Also, the unsibillated Old Cornish final element would be unprecedented so far west. Other examples of *ardh* on the very same peninsula appear as *–arth* and *–are*. Historic spellings such as *Lisart* 1086; *Lesard c.* 1250-1348 (6 exx.); *Lesart* 1302 are suggestive of a French derivation. However, and to add to the doubt, a Cornish origin is also suggested by: *Lysarth* 1327 and *Lesarth* 1323, 1326, 1327. It is possible, of course, that a reversion to -*ard* may have resulted from the influence of a resemblance to the English word 'lizard' but the uncertainty of this name's origin is too considerable to allow the application of assumption being presented as fact.

Page 9: List 2*c*. **Nouns denoting natural features**, firmly translates **Sellan** as "dry pool' (*segh* [KK *sygh*] + *lyn*), but not one of the eleven available historic forms bears out this interpretation of the qualifying element. Nine of these consistently show –*lan*, with two examples (from a single year) of –*len*, this probably arising from the unstressed vowel becoming schwa.

Gunvena also appears in List 2*c*. This is translated by the authors as "down on mountain" (*gun* [KK *goen*] + *menedh* [KK *menydh*], although, in Cornish place-names, *menedh* usually means 'hill, hillside'). This is, presumably, **Gunvenna** in St Minver parish which is *gun* + *fynnow*, 'boundaries' (*Goenfynou* 1275; *Goenfinou* 1284, etc.), with no involvement of *menedh* whatsoever. The name is included, with this derivation, in Padel's *Cornish Place Name Elements* (1985) and, as his work is recommended on Page 2 of the booklet, one wonders why the authors did not consult it. The authors of the booklet might, however, be referring to **Gonvena**, Egloshayle and, if so, would still be in error. This site was *Gwynveneth* 1286; *Gwenvene* 1315 (a compound *gwyn-veneth*, "white / fair hill[side]").

A further name in the Section 2*c*. list continued on Page 10 (**Rostowrack**) has been "corrected" by the CLB authors to **Rosdowrek*. This treatment is disturbing. It is a known feature of Cornish place-names that a final –*s* of a generic will often cause provection to the initial of a qualifier (found, for example, in **Rospannel, Rospeath, Nan[s]pean**). The decision to "correct" such a feature is baffling and fails to pay necessary heed to the historic development of place-names.

Page 11: List 2*d*. gives adjectives commonly found in place-names. In this list, the CLB authors render **Redruth** as **Rysrudh*, thereby ignoring another feature of place-name history. This feature is the common retention of an Old Cornish form before the initial R of a qualifier. In West Cornwall, this feature is not only found in the name **Redruth** but also in names such as **Bodrifty** and **Bodriggy**. Again, this should not be subjected to "correction" in order to satisfy the requirements of a modern ideology.

The Section 2*d.* list further contains what is arguably the most glaring error of the entire booklet: the interpretation of **Lanyon** as 'cold valley' (*nans* + *yeyn*). Cornwall contains three sites with this name. The first, in Wendron parish, has thus far, revealed only two historic forms: *Lanyne, Lanyon* 1566, insufficient evidence to form definite judgements on the interpretation of either of its elements, although they certainly do not suggest that **nans** is involved. **Lanyon** in Gwinear, formerly *Coswin Wolward*, was renamed when the impressive seventeenth-century house was built by members of the Lanyon family who had originally hailed from the **Lanyon** in Madron parish. The best known by far of the three sites and undoubtedly the one borne in mind by the booklet's authors, the Madron site has the following historic forms:

> *Liniein, Leniein, Lenien* 1214; *Linyeine* 1244; *Lenyen* 1285; *Lenyeyn* 1314; *Lynyeyn* 1326; *Lynieyn* 1327; *Lynyen* 1333, 1344; *Laneyn* 1390; *Lanyayn* 1443; *Lennyen* 1447; *Lanine* 1794. (now generally pronounced 'lan-YON', instead of the traditional 'le-NINE')

The name is **lyn** + **yeyn**, 'cold pool', this being agreed to by all authorities, including Pool and Padel, and the pool referred to is probably the biggest of several in a marshy area close to the original medieval site of **Lanyon** (now known as Old Lanyon) 500 metres SW of the present farm. The variant vowel of the unstressed generic probably results from a tendency towards schwa. Why, then, has the CLB chosen to ignore these authorities and the historical evidence and, instead, to invent a new interpretation with *nans*, 'valley' which is clearly not involved at all? Even more regrettable is that the Cornish Language Board seems happy to present this to the public as fact.

This entry is immediately followed by **Treveddon**, translated by the authors as 'narrow farm' (*tref* [KK **trev*] + *yn* [KK **ynn*]). This site, in the parish of Grade-Ruan, has the following historic forms:

> *Trevedren* 1244; *Trevedern* 1302; *Trevedryn* 1542; *Trevedden* 1696; *Treveddorn* 1866.

It is plain from these records that the qualifier is not **ynn*, even in its preoccluded Late form **idn**. Instead it is likely to be a personal name.

Once again, the CLB has failed to carry out the necessary research and state a mere and erroneous guess to be factually correct.

CONCLUSION

Place names are historical monuments and must be treated as such. Linguistics play an important part in their study but equally important, if not more so, is the role of historical research. That a critical review of a 12 page booklet should necessitate an article of this length is damning and it is clear that, where the study of Cornish place-names is concerned, the Cornish Language Board is "unfit for purpose" in that it approaches the subject solely from the viewpoint of the linguistic enthusiast and is happy to present unresearched guesswork and erroneous assumption as "fact" to an unsuspecting public.

This is not to say that place-name research is easy. It is not and even the most authoritative scholar in the field can occasionally be in error. When such occasions arise, however, it is because the historical evidence proves to be inadequate when a previously undiscovered form of the name comes to light. This type of error is inevitable and the serious scholar will then proceed to correct it at the earliest opportunity.

What is not excusable is where that evidence exists in abundance (and authorities on the subject are in agreement), it is then ignored or neglected to be replaced by assumption and guesswork, particularly when that guesswork is masked by a method of production that appears to present it as factual and researched interpretation. That the Cornish Language Board should recommend the work of such scholars as Oliver Padel and then proceed to ignore that evidence several times in a 12 page booklet can only be deplored.

As historical features, Cornish place-names can only be realistically explained or rendered in revived Cornish by utilizing the fullest research and historical spellings of Cornish words and elements. It is simply not enough to transform them into forms based upon what is a modern and artificially created orthography that bears insufficient resemblance to historically known spellings. The result appears alien and utterly un-Cornish. For this reason, the form known as *Kernewek Kemmyn* is, in the writer's view, wholly unsuitable for this task. It is too rigid a system that does not allow for (particularly) Old and Late Cornish features and, as Padel rightly comments (Padel 1988): "in my opinion, it removes itself undesirably far from the spellings of the Middle Cornish texts (which are also, very often, those of medieval Cornish place-name spellings, and are therefore particularly apt here)".

In closing, it is noticeable that several bodies, including the Cornish Language Board and the Historic Environment Unit of Cornwall Council, appear to rely solely upon J. E. B. Gover's unpublished MS for historic forms of Cornish place-names. This was produced in 1948 and, as Padel has pointed out, has to be used with some caution (Padel, pers.comm.). Six decades of further research has uncovered many more historic spellings which can be found in other archive collections at the Institute of Cornish Studies and, indeed, the reviewer's own archive collection, currently undergoing conversion into a computer database. Information from both is available on request.

REFERENCES

Gover, J. E. B. 1948. *The Place Names of Cornwall*. Unpublished MS at R.I.C., Truro.

Padel, Oliver J. 1985. *Cornish Place Name Elements*. Nottingham.

Padel, Oliver J. 1988. *A Popular Dictionary of Cornish Place Names*. Penzance.

Pool, P.A.S. 1985. *The Place Names of West Penwith*. Second edition. Heamoor

Weatherhill, Craig. 2005. *Place Names in Cornwall and Scilly*. Salisbury and Launceston.

Weatherhill, Craig. *Cornish Place Name Index*. Unpublished archive at Newbridge, Penzance.

Weatherhill, Craig. Forthcoming March 2007. *Cornish Place Names and Language* (Second revised edition). Wilmslow.

RECOGNIZABILITY OF TRADITIONAL CORNISH PLACE-NAMES AND SURNAMES IN THE VARIETIES OF REVIVED CORNISH

Ray Chubb and Craig Weatherhill

INTRODUCTION

One of the aims of the Single Written Form, for use in Statutory Education and Public Life, should be to impart to school children a sense of the Cornish language heritage around them in place-names in Cornwall and the surnames of people of Cornish descent. Children should be able to make the link in as direct a way as possible between what they have learned in school the surnames of some of their friends in the playground and the names that they will see on sign boards when returning home from school.

It therefore seems imperative that the four existing forms of revived Cornish recognized in the MacKinnon Report i.e. Common Cornish (KK), Late or Modern Cornish (Late), Unified Cornish (U) and Unified Cornish Revised (UCR) should be examined with a view to determining their suitability for enabling children to connect with the Cornish language heritage around them.

METHOD

Set out below are two tables. The first lists elements found in Cornish placenames in their most common form, the second lists some elements of Cornish surnames and in some instances the complete surname. English translations have not been given, these can be referred to in dictionaries if necessary. Each of the four forms of revived Cornish have been compared to the element. The form of Cornish that appears to provide the quickest recognition from Cornish learnt in the classroom is given 4 points, the next quickest 3 points and so on. If, for example, three forms of revived Cornish have the same spelling and they all provide the quickest recognition they are given 4 points each and the remaining form is allocated 1 point.

The method of assessing how close a particular form of Cornish is to a place or surname element does, of course, involve a certain amount of subjectivity. Our own preference in revived Cornish is Unified Revised, however we think it would be possible for a person with any other spelling preference to carry out the same exercise and, if they approached it honestly as we hope we have done, come up with similar results.

Placename	KK	kk	UC	uc	UCR	ucr	RLC	rlc
Arth	Ardh	1	Arth	4	Arth	4	Arth	4
Bean	Byghan	2	Byghan	2	Byan	3	Bean	4
Brea	Bre	3	Bre	3	Bre	3	Brea	4
Carn	Karn	1	Carn	4	Carn	4	Carn	4
Cadgwith	Kaswydh	1	Cajwyth	3	Cajwyth	3	Cadgwith	4
Cos/Coose/Cuit	Koes	1	Cos	3	Cos	3	Cooz	4
Creeg	Krug	1	Cruk	2	Crug	3	Creeg	4
Dower/Dever	Dowr	4	Dowr	4	Dowr	4	Dowr	4
Dren/Dreyn	Dren	4	Dren	4	Dren	4	Drean	1
Eglos	Eglos	4	Eglos	4	Eglos	4	Eglos	4
Enys/Ennis/Ninnis	Ynys	1	Enys	4	Enys	4	Ennis	4
Eythen/Ithon	Eythin	1	Eythyn	3	Eythyn	3	Eithen	4
Fenten/Venton	Fenten	3	Fenten	3	Fenten	3	Ventan	4
Glas/Glaze	Glas	3	Glas	3	Glas	3	Glaze	4
Goon/Gun	Goen	1	Gun	3	Gun	3	Goon	4
Marhas/Maraz	Marghas	2	Marghas	2	Marhas	4	Marhas	4
Pen/Pedn	Penn	1	Pen	4	Pen	4	Pedn	4
Pol	Poll	2	Pol	4	Pol	4	Poll	2
Pras/Praze	Pras	3	Pras	3	Pras	3	Praze	4
Res/Red	Rys	1	Res	4	Res	4	Res	4
Ros/Rose	Ros	4	Ros	4	Ros	4	Ros	4
Ryp/Reb	Ryb	3	Ryp	1	Ryb	3	Reb	4
Scawen	Skawenn	1	Scawen	4	Scawen	4	Scawan	2
Skyber/Skibber	Skiber	2	Skyber	4	Skyber	4	Skiber	2
Stras/Straze	Stras	3	Stras	3	Stras	3	Straze	4
Towan	Tewynn	1	Towan	4	Towan	4	Towan	4
Tre	Tre	4	Tre	4	Tre	4	Trea	1
Tyr/Tire/Teer	Tir	4	Tyr	2	Tyr	2	Teer	3
Wartha	Wartha	4	Wartha	4	Wartha	4	Wartha	4
Wollas	Woeles	1	Woles	3	Woles	3	Wolas	4
Subtotal P	*KK*	*67*	*UC*	*99*	*UCR*	*105*	*RLC*	*107*

Surname	KK	kk	UC	uc	UCR	ucr	RLC	rlc
An+gove	gov	3	gof	2	gof	2	gove	4
Bray	bre	4	bre	4	bre	4	brea	4
Che+gwidden	chi+gwynn	3	chy+gwyn	3	chy+gwyn	3	chy+gwidn	4
Che+noweth	chi+nowydh	1	chy+noweth	4	chy+noweth	4	chy+noweth	4
Coad	koes	1	cos	3	cos	3	cooz	4
Craze	kres	1	cres	3	cres	3	creaz	4
Innes/Ennis	An+ynys	1	An+enys	4	An+enys	4	An+ennis	4
Hen+dy	hen+ji	1	hen+jy	4	hen+jy	4	hen+jy	4
Laity	le'ti	1	lety	3	lety	3	laity	4
Magor/Meagor	magor	4	magor	4	magor	4	magor	4
Mundy	moenjy	1	munjy	4	munjy	4	moounjy	2
Nancarrow	nans+karow	1	nans+carow	4	nans+carow	4	nans+carow	4
Pol+mear	meur	2	mur	1	muer	3	mear	4
Pen+gelly/gilly	gelli	1	gelly	4	gelly	4	gilly	2
Res or Ros+corla	Korlann	1	corlan	4	corlan	4	corlan	4
Tre+gear	ger	3	ger	3	ger	3	gare	4
Tre+loar	lowarth	3	lowarth	3	lowarth	3	looar	4
Tre+menheere	menhir	3	menhyr	3	menhyr	3	menheer	4
Subtotal S	*KK*	35	*UC*	60	*UCR*	62	*RLC*	68
Subtotal P	*KK*	67	*UC*	99	*UCR*	105	*RLC*	107
Total P & S	**Kemyn**	102	**Unified**	159	**UCR**	167	**Late**	175

CONCLUSIONS

It can be seen from this exercise that the Common form of revived Cornish is the least suitable for enabling children to recognize the Cornish around them and the the Late or Modern form is the most suitable. The maximum possible score is 192, therefore it could be said that a child learning through Late Cornish would have a significantly better chance of recognizing Cornish in the environment than a child who is learning through Common Cornish. Even through Unified Cornish, the next to the lowest score, a child would have a much better chance. This exercise does not provide a totally conclusive answer but it is a great improvement on unsubstantiated statement. What it does clearly show is that further research using students in the early stages of learning Cornish through the various forms would have to be carried out before the Common form could safely be adopted as a Single Written Form. We would suggest that the results indicate that no such research would be necessary if any of the other forms are choosen as a Single Written Form.

It is very important that children learning Cornish should be able to make a link easily to the Cornish that they see around them in order that the language's improved recognition under the European Charter for Regional and Minority Languages helps to instill in them a pride in the place in which they live. This in turn helps them to respect what they see around them and encourages them to stay in Cornwall to follow a career.

For these reasons alone it is our view that Common Cornish is unsuitable as the Single Written Form and the results of this exercise tend to confirm this view.

DECONSTRUCTING KERNOWEK KEMYN: A CRITICAL REVIEW OF *AGAN YETH* 4

Bernard Deacon

In 2003 the UK government belatedly and somewhat reluctantly included Cornish among the languages it was statutorily bound to protect under the terms of the Council of Europe's Charter for Regional or Minority Languages. As a result the Cornish language entered a new world. Throughout the twentieth century it had been the jealously guarded preserve of the tiny group of amateurs and enthusiasts attracted to the Cornish Revivalist movement. But now its status has become that of a public language, the heritage of the Cornish people and the birthright of all those who live and will live in Cornwall. This is a momentous step. But the potential benefits are threatened by the failure of the twentieth century Cornish Revival to produce an agreed system for spelling Cornish. Instead, a deep and apparently irreconcilable divide exists between proponents of different spelling systems for the revived language. As a result, many observers sympathetic to the language have called for the involvement of outside experts to establish a standard written form of Cornish for use in schooling and in signage.

The demand for outside involvement stems from a major frustration confronting anyone attempting to evaluate and assess the current debate on the way Cornish should be spelt, for all contributors to the debate share the same shortcoming. They are all pleading a special case for one or other of the existing spelling systems. The three papers in *Agan Yeth: Cornish Language Studies* 4, by Pol Hodge, Ken George and Julyan Holmes, are no exception. They set out a vigorously argued case why Kernowek Kemyn "should now be used officially in public documentation and in education". But in doing so they also turn a blind eye to the widely-expressed demand for a compromise standardized Cornish spelling system that might be more inclusive and acceptable to *all* users of Cornish. This article contains a preliminary assessment of some of the arguments in *Agan Yeth* 4.

Of course I am not immune to this criticism; I cannot escape the fundamental problems bedevilling this long overdue "debate" about Cornish spelling. This contribution too is an example of special pleading. Ultimately, I believe that the base of Cornish should be shifted to the later early modern period, or somewhere around 1700, in order to get as close as possible to the eminently sensible proposal put forward by John Humphreys on Radio 4 (17 September 2005) that revived Cornish should pick up at the point when its native speakers ceased to use the vernacular language. After all, had Cornish survived into the age of the tape recorder, as did Manx, we would not be having this debate. The vast majority of languages trace a continuity of development to the versions spoken in the present day. Only in the most unusual circumstances does a society decide to break that chain and consciously revert to an archaic form of the language spoken half a millennium earlier. Yet this is exactly what those who have chosen late medieval Cornish have done, in my view mistakenly, when sufficient knowledge now exists of the early modern language for the latter to be the preferred form. This "common-sense" default position for any revived language—pick up where the last speakers left off—should only be rejected in exceptional circumstances. The case of those who wish to use a medieval base for Cornish has to be equally exceptional in order to convince the 99.95% of people in Cornwall who cannot speak Cornish to follow them.

However, I do not intend to spend the rest of this paper building a case for Revived Late Cornish. Instead, I want to deconstruct the arguments put forward by our Kernowek Kemyn colleagues. First, the publication of these articles is to be welcomed. The authors of *Agan Yeth* 4 have taken a major step forward by admitting that a debate about the spelling of Cornish actually exists, and they should be congratulated on this belated recognition. Their willingness to discuss this must now be embraced openly and transparently by their detractors. Nevertheless, the three articles in *Agan Yeth* 4 contain the usual strange combination that we have come to expect from those who defend Kernowek Kemyn, namely a mix of "scientific" truth statements asserted with excessive bravado combined with highly questionable assumptions, the whole shot through with glaring contradictions. I do not intend to confront directly here the linguistic content of the arguments put forward in *Agan Yeth* 4, leaving that to others who are far better qualified to do so. Instead I want to use this as an occasion to foreground some less familiar aspects of the language debate, ones that are usually ignored by defenders and critics of Kernowek Kemyn alike. These lie outside the preferred linguistic paradigm within which the "debate" is artificially restricted, at least on the surface. I intend to discuss the

70

language which is used in *Agan Yeth* 4 rather than discuss its content. I want to use this opportunity to examine the rhetorical strategy employed by Kernowek Kemyn supporters and the values explicitly or implicitly underlying their arguments. The debate about which Cornish spelling system to use is at heart not a question of simply identifying and adopting the "correct" linguistic solution but one about competing assumptions about what the Cornish language actually is and what its purpose should be in the twenty-first century.

The three articles in *Agan Yeth* 4 aim to construct a particular mental model of Cornish. In doing this they provide a fascinating insight into the mind-set of the Kernowek Kemyn evangelist. Their arguments might be viewed as comprising a discourse, a set of related concepts, statements and suppositions that convey their macroproposition—that the late medieval period is the best basis for the revived language and that Kernowek Kemyn is the preferable way to spell it. A series of local meanings are then created through the implications, presuppositions, allusions, etc., adopted and through the lexical and syntactical choices the authors make.

THE ASSUMPTIONS OF KERNOWEK KEMYN

Wht are the taken-for-granted assumptions about the Kernowek Kemyn project? Ultimately, its discourse of Cornish revolves around its value system rather than technical arguments over quantity rules, minimal pairs and phonemes. Core defenders of Kernowek Kemyn adopt a narrow and restrictive genre for discussion—that of linguistics. In doing so they echo the tendency of the historic Revival and collude with some of their detractors, who also contain debate within this genre. The net result of such a genre selection is conveniently to restrict the debate to those schooled in the terminology of linguistics, excluding all other factors as being irrelevant. This allows the gatekeepers of the language to confine discussion to a tiny proportion of, in the main self-appointed, "experts" who have the right to speak, while prohibiting all others who may have a stake in the language and who feel equally deeply about it. As the Cornish language is the birthright of all those who consider themselves Cornish and of generations yet unborn who might wish to learn about their heritage, to restrict debate in this way only to "experts" in linguistics or "fluent" Cornish speakers is to adopt a mind-bogglingly exclusive franchise. On the contrary, given that the twentieth century Revival only created a relatively tiny pool of such "fluent" speakers, we have a unique historic opportunity to involve as

71

many people as possible in the consultation over a standardized spelling, as Cornish tentatively moves from the private to the public sphere and into the light of public scrutiny. Indeed, I would go further. We have a positive duty to widen out the debate if public money is now going to be used to support the language.

With half an eye on that impending public scrutiny much is made in this issue of *Agan Yeth* of "choice": "most Cornish speakers have already chosen KK as their standard written form" (p. 27) and "the majority of speakers have already chosen this as their standard" (p. 34). Putting aside the pathetically small number of "speakers" for a moment, what "choice" has in reality been exercised by consumers of Cornish? As Kernowek Kemyn inherited the institutional resources of the language movement and the Cornish Language Board in the 1980s it also benefited from the legitimacy of apparent continuity, not to mention the publishing resources of the Board, which enthusiastically set about re-publishing Cornish texts in this newer version of medieval Cornish. Thus, when the curious seeker after knowledge met Cornish texts in bookshops and libraries, the chances were that they were Kernowek Kemyn texts. And when enquiring after local Cornish classes the likelihood was that these would be using Kernowek Kemyn. However, in how many of these texts or classes was the putative learner actually offered a choice? In how many texts and classes is the background to the current pluralist spellings of Cornish set out and the criteria for making a sensible choice explained, coolly and logically?

In reality, very little if no information has been provided by Kernowek Kemyn or by organizations such as the Language Board and magazines such as *An Gannas* that have adopted it (or by other Cornish language organizations come to that) that might come anywhere near providing our Cornish punters with useful information on which meaningful choices can be based. Quite the opposite, as we have all met Kernowek Kemyn learners who, at an advanced stage, still seem oblivious to the fact that there is more than one form of "Cornish". "Choice" is precisely what is not on offer. This can be further illustrated by looking at the organization Kowethas an Yeth Kernewek. This body noisily re-launched itself in 2005 as an umbrella for all forms of Cornish. Yet the more prosaic reality is readily visible on its website, where the only Cornish on offer is Kernowek Kemyn. Furthermore, there are no links to the websites of organizations using other spellings and an entire absence of information on the background to the spelling debate. For 'Cornish" read "Kernowek Kemyn". Real "choice" requires real, and as far as possible, objective, information and that information is seriously lacking at present.

Choice implies pluralism and diversity and it is gratifying to see that the authors of *Agan Yeth* 4 at last admit that pluralism is a feature of the current Cornish language movement. Yet the Kernowek Kemyn learner remains locked in an imagined world of uniformity and homogeneity. This is a world of Cornish rather than Cornishes, where there is just one pronunciation of Cornish, where one spelling provides signs faithfully recording clear sounds which never change. But in reality, as George states, "like any language, the number of phonemes in traditional Cornish changed over time, and we cannot be sure of how many there were at a given epoch" (p. 21). However, this careful recognition of complexity is replaced by a confident, arrogant certainty on the part of George's disciples who, running amok on internet discussion lists, apparently sincerely believe that they are dealing with a transparently simple language where each sound can be represented by one symbol. The less comfortable truth is that the phonemes of Cornish have changed radically over the course of its history.

The historical language was anything but homogenous (like all living languages). Indeed, we are told there was a major change in pronunciation somewhere in the fifteenth or early sixteenth centuries (p. 31). Because of this we face an unavoidable choice: on which era do we base our pronunciation of Cornish. Kernowek Kemyn has chosen 1500 (p. 31). But why this date? As George admits, if he was "starting from scratch with reviving Cornish ... there would be an argument for going the other way, i.e. earlier" (p. 33), presumably basing the pronunciation on the Cornish of, say, 1400. However, such proper uncertainty over a chosen date then dissolves as the *Agan Yeth* 4 authors unite in demanding that "the spoken system must be accurate" (p. 41). But, as their own discussion makes crystal clear, there are a number of different historic pronunciations and therefore a number of potentially "accurate" possible spelling systems. A choice must be made. George has gone for 1500 although now he might prefer an earlier date; I prefer a date around 1700; others want to go for 1550 or 1600. Unfortunately, the discussion about which epoch to base Cornish on now appears to take second place. It needs to be reopened and resolved first before we can begin to talk about "accurate" spelling systems.

Furthermore, an aim of achieving "accuracy", a "logical system-atized" spelling based on Cornish as it was at one fixed point in time may well be incompatible with another stated aim that a standard should be "compatible with all styles of Cornish ... of every period" (p. 41). George argues that "it would be possible to read a passage written in KK using the pronunciation of LateC. But it would need some practice" (p. 32). But why on earth would we want to read Modern Cornish in Kernowek Kemyn when a perfectly valid and easier alternative exists—a logically systemized spelling system based on the pronunciation of Late Cornish? This possibility would be aesthetically more pleasing, simpler to learn, more fluent when heard spoken and possess clear and transparent links to the traces of the language that exist around us in the twenty-first century Cornish environment. That possibility already existed even in 1986 as George shows in his thesis and in *The Pronunciation and Spelling of Revived Cornish* (pp. 110ff), where the phonemes of "Late" Cornish are set out in some detail. Now that we know much more about the pronunciation of Modern Cornish it is surely time to revisit its hasty and premature rejection in the mid-1980s, based on an over-simplistic discussion (George, 1986, pp. 33-34).

In seeking "accuracy", Kernowek Kemyn's greatest strength, its single-minded systematization, becomes also its greatest weakness. In emphasizing systematization and phonemic, morphemic and etymo-logical fitness its defenders sight of the historical language as it really was. Fundamentally, they are not discussing the really existing language at all, with all its quirks, ambiguities and inconsistencies, but a Cornish language as they wish it had been. Moreover, the disturbing implications of a language that did not live up to their expectations are air-brushed out of the picture through constructing a conceptual binary polarization between Cornish and English and, by implication, between "good" and "bad".

CONSTRUCTING THE KERNOWEK KEMYN "OTHER"

All three authors are at great pains to differentiate between Cornish and English; the two languages, we are reminded incessantly, are "distinct" (e.g. pp. 11, 14). This desire to keep them hermeneutically separate reaches the height of absurdity with the claim that "Kernesh (Cornish dialect) is not a bridge between the two [English and Cornish]. It is also a separate language in its own right" (p. 11). If Anglo-Cornish dialect is a separate language then clearly a rather loose definition of language is being adopted. But even this flimsy argument must be pursued in order to ram home the message that Cornish is different from English. In the Kernowek Kemyn world English borrowings are not just "borrowings"; they become "flagrant borrowings" (p. 29), corrupting the pure unsullied language of their imagination. Changes in pronunciation as the language developed are not just linguistic developments. They have to be sorted between "those features which were a natural development in Cornish and those which could be interpreted as corruptions from English" (p. 33). The key word here is "interpreted" for there is little if no *scientific* justification for such a distinction. Pursuing the chimera of linguistic purity in this way leads to the view that what Cornish people were actually saying—in Cornish—by the seventeenth and eighteenth centuries was a "breakdown" and should be rejected as it destroys the "unity" of the language (p. 37). This is a romanticized idea of "unity" which, together with notions of purity and Celticity, has for too long been imposed on the Cornish language by the Revival. The genre of scientific linguistics slips here, to reveal the language of nineteenth-century romantic nationalism. Within this, every nation had to have its distinct language and each language had to seek uncontaminated purity.

It is a short step for the Kernowek Kemyn enthusiast to define their opponents as those "people" who are "so attached to … English graphemes" (p. 23). If Cornish is distinct from English any opposition to Kernowek Kemyn can be conveniently re-defined as "English influence" (p. 23) and those who demur from the project to differentiate Cornish as far as possible from English stand accused by implication of un-Cornish activities. "Is Cornish in an English style really what we want?" (p. 17) then becomes a rhetorical question with which no right-minded Cornish patriot would dare to disagree.

This disturbingly totalitarian argument serves to distract attention from the fundamental problem at the core of the Kernowek Kemyn case. We read that Old Cornish, Middle Cornish and Late Cornish were not "distinctive Cornish orthographies", but were "English" (p. 20). All historical Cornish literature was therefore actually "English" in its spelling. Even Middle Cornish, the chosen basis for Kernowek Kemyn, was, in its written form, "over-rated" and was merely "based on English" (p. 30). This notion, that all the written Cornish handed down to us by our ancestors was affected by English, should tell us something. It surely tells us that Cornish, in all its historical phases, did in fact borrow freely from English vocabulary and was influenced by English grammar—something hardly unexpected given the relative power of the two languages. It also chimes with a broader historical reality. However much we might regret it, Cornish culture and society has been bound up with and affected by its neighbour to the east of the

Tamar for at least a millennium. Nineteenth century romantic nationalist dreams are just that—romantic dreams—and bear little relation to the unsettling truth which is that Cornish is not totally distinct from English. Granted, Cornish is a different language, but it is not and has not been, since the first miracle play was written, uninfluenced by English.

But Kernowek Kemyn logic denies this unpalatable truth, preferring to take refuge in its own fantasy world where Cornish is sealed from the "corrupting" influence of English. Determined to avoid English at all costs it does not stop with the unjustifiable rejection of widely used English vocabulary in Middle Cornish (see Williams 1997, 174–79). Its logic leads it to reject historic Cornish spellings entirely. Kernowek Kemyn is proud to have moved furthest from Middle Cornish spelling and revels in being "less close to the MidC textual spellings than either Unified or UCR" (p. 31). At the same time, ironically, Modern Cornish is criticized in *Agan Yeth* 4 as creating "a complete barrier between the new Cornish user and the bulk of traditional Cornish literature" (p. 41). Yet Kernowek Kemyn itself creates a barrier between the Cornish user and all Cornish literature of whatever period. At least the Modern Cornish learner is able to read the Cornish of the Bosons, Rowe, Tonkin, Gwavas and company. But Kernowek Kemyn learners are airily told that "if anyone seriously wishes to study the texts, then they must use the original spelling in the manuscripts" (p. 31). In its written form Kernowek Kemyn has ceased to be "Cornish" in any recognizably historic sense even while claiming to base its pronunciation on the Cornish of the late medieval period. Links with history are broken in the name of a linguistic purity that denies what really happened in the past. It is this denial of our past that others cannot accept. And, inevitably, Kernowek Kemyn is unable in practice to deny that past. Its whole case is premised on the basis of re-interpreting spellings which were "English". But when necessary Kernowek Kemyn spellings are justified because "they are historic" (p. 23) even as the historic spelling is rubbished as "English". Contradictions abound!

The excessive distance travelled by the *Agan Yeth* 4 authors to distance Cornish from English is best explained by resort to issues of identity and not linguistics. The vast majority of Cornish learners— irrespective of spelling system—come to Cornish for reasons of identity, as an expression of being Cornish or from a desire to commit themselves to Cornwall. Yet ever since the 1920s when Morton Nance based revived Cornish on the late medieval period, those choosing to adopt Cornish as a symbol of their identity have also had to jettison half a millennium of Cornish history. Interestingly, most of the leading lights of the Revival movement have been marginal to popular working class Cornishness, themselves influenced deeply by a middle class "English" culture. This has had two consequences. First, it strengthened the appeal of a medieval, apparently purer, more unambiguously non-English "Cornish". Second, it convinced the revivalists that the Cornishness of the people was a corrupt anglicized cultural wrong turn and one that could be either safely ignored or condescendingly patronized. This attitude cut the Cornish Revival off from the majority of Cornish people, whose distinctiveness was a product not of medieval Cornwall but of the industrialization of the eighteenth and nineteenth centuries, an industrialization that, ironically, produced the confidence that underpinned the Cornish revival of the late 1800s. While the majority of Cornish speakers have adopted a medieval language and rejected the ambiguities of the Cornish identity since the Reformation, inhabiting a dream world where they possess the more "Cornish" credentials, the majority of Cornish people were and are a product of exactly those post-Reformation ambiguities.

The Kernowek Kemyn project goes even further. Arguing that Middle Cornish was no more "Cornish" in its spelling than was Late Cornish and aware (though sometimes reticent about it) of the uncomfortable truth that medieval Cornish was also deeply affected by English, Kernowek Kemyn rejects historic spelling entirely, preferring a simpler form that inscribes Cornish's non-Englishness visibly in texts and on signs. But the net result is that Cornish becomes an alien and foreign product for most actual Cornish people. While Kernowek Kemyn may well have produced a more logical system it has also stripped out the links between language, history and identity. If Kernowek Kemyn became the standard form the Cornish language would be left becalmed on a timeless and lifeless beach safely remote from the tides of history. It would certainly not be English but it would also not be recognizably "Cornish" either. Such a Cornish resembles nothing more than the "Christmas game" that our forebears complained of when rising against the imposition of religious change in 1549. Then they rejected the breaking of the links with their traditions and customs. Similarly, Kernowek Kemyn has to be rejected because it also breaks too abruptly with tradition.

Cornish is not Latin nor Esperanto—a diverting intellectual problem to be solved like a crossword puzzle. It is a living language with a history and a tradition. Moreover, it is a critically important bearer of the Cornish identity. But in being so, and this is the bit that revivalists have found difficult to swallow, it also bears the contradictions of our past. The answer is not, however, to ignore those contradictions by taking refuge in a Cornish language that rejects all historic forms. Instead, it is healthier psychologically to embrace the ambiguities. By doing so we can come to terms with the reality of our identity and align the language revival more closely with the popular consciousness of being Cornish. Doing this inevitably involves adopting a later and more sensible base for the revived language, thus finally healing the rift between revivalism and the Cornish people.

However, I am now in danger of leaving the Kernowek Kemyn discourse far behind. So far I have identified an over-simplistic approach resting on outdated notions of "purity" and "corruption", a failure to engage with the real complexities of the historic language and a greatly overdrawn binary opposition between Cornish and English as some of the elements of the Kernowek Kemyn discourse. Yet perhaps the most striking and regrettable aspect of this discourse is not so much its assumptions and content but its tone.

THE RHETORIC OF KERNOWEK KEMYN

As in former interventions (Dunbar and George 1997) the overall style of the discourse is stridently and overtly confrontational, infused with a sense of righteousness. It is assumed that those who do not wish to adopt Kernowek Kemyn are misguided unfortunates who will gratefully see the light once the phonological and orthographical holy grail of Kernowek Kemyn is laid out before them. The result is a patronizing and condescending attitude towards those who cannot or do not wish to debate merely on the narrow grounds of graphemes, phonemes, quantity rules, minimal pairs and the like. Thus we are bluntly advised on page 6 that "unless you intend to take your fourth grade, write a novel in the language or do something useful [?], stop reading this now". All genres of argument act to exclude those who do not or cannot share the language of that genre. The language of linguistics and its specialist terminology does not normally need to exclude people explicitly. But, just in case they aren't already excluded the above quote implies very firmly that the real debate should only be carried on by those cognoscenti initiated into the mysteries of linguistics. The role of the rest of us is to stand around and wait for the tablets to be brought down from the mountain after the restricted selectorate who might qualify (how?) to discuss such things make their decisions.

Perhaps dazzled by their own faith in Kernowek Kemyn, the loyalists remain blind to the wider perspective, impervious to the way the twentieth century history of the Revival could be read as a story of the hi-jacking of the Cornish language by a tiny group who have used it as a vehicle to pursue their own visions. After a century of revivalism the result—around 100 fluent speakers if that—a proportion equal to 0.02% of the Cornish population, is hardly an earth shattering endorsement of the methodologies adopted by the Cornish revival. Yet such inconvenient evidence is either denied, or refuge is sought in comforting conspiracy theories; the Cornish language has failed to grow exponentially, we are told, because "the authorities have refused to fund it properly" (p. 17). Really? Nothing at all to do with the twee amateurism of the early language revivalists or the shambolic impression given by the Cornish language movement over the past 20 years then.

Arrogance is moreover coupled with a second rhetorical strategy of the Kernowek Kemyn discourse—vituperative name-calling. Those who prefer to use other, more historical, forms of spelling or who base their Cornish on its pronunciation at a more modern period are described as "splinters" (during discussion at Tremough conference on language planning, September 2005). Or they are dismissed as "anarchists, kilt-wearers and flag wavers" and "conservatives" (pp. 16–17). Once demonized as part of this unusual collection of fellow-travellers they can be safely classed with "those who don't have the capacity to debate" (p. 17). This style of argument—first stereotype and caricature your opponents and then, second, define them as unfit to debate and therefore to be actively excluded from that debate—when linked to an unswerving faith in Kernowek Kemyn, is much more reminiscent of seventeenth than twenty-first century, more relativist, discourses. Kemyn spokespersons seem locked in a strangely old-fashioned world, where computer based methodologies rub shoulders with pre-modern discourses and nineteenth century taken-for-granted assumptions.

A third aspect of Kernowek Kemyn discourse is a a deep lack of interest in or knowledge of the work of the other groups active in disseminating the Cornish language since the 1980s. This is best illustrated in their approach to Modern Cornish, of which they apparently know little and care less. The Cornish of the seventeenth and eighteenth centuries is routinely dismissed as having a "reduced competence" (p. 26, though here George is gracious enough to admit that this is "arguable"). The later manuscripts are described as "reduced and sometimes faulty" and contrasted with the "subtle, sophisticated, literary language" of the late medieval plays (pp. 35–36). While Kernowek Kemyn was "devised" in the 1980s, Modern Cornish was being simultaneously "concocted" (p. 19), a revealing choice of words that is fundamentally at odds with the trope of "objective" scientific rationality that Kernowek Kemyn defenders like to think they adopt in discussing the mechanics of the language. Moreover, this drip feed of disparagement is sometimes coupled with complete misrepresentation. We are informed that "proponents of a Late [Cornish] base ... use no source texts earlier than CW [Creation of the World]" (p. 26). This came as news to me. Those of us who wish to base Cornish on its later period, that of the bulk of the prose works in the language and on the register actually used by Cornish people living around 1700, of course have to resort to source texts earlier than CW if words or grammatical forms are unavailable in the later texts. We too adopt a policy of *tota Cornicitas*; it is just that the base is shifted towards a more modern period when, arguably, we have a lot more first hand knowledge of the pronunciation of Cornish—both from the rich variety of spellings used by native writers and the revealing work of Edward Lhuyd. So let's not exaggerate the difference in approach between those who favour Modern and those who prefer late medieval Cornish.

Occasionally the discourse in *Agan Yeth* 4 about Modern Cornish moves into a pure cloud cuckoo land of incomprehension. Thus we are informed that "a supporter of late Cornish once admitted that 'we will' and 'we will not' are written in exactly the same way and that this caused so much confusion he had to ring up his mates to see if they were coming or not" (p. 15). This is sheer, unadulterated nonsense. In no version of Modern Cornish spelling could this pair be possibly given the same spelling, as 'we will' is *ny vedn* and 'we will not' would be *na vedn ny* or *na veddony*. But, as the ordinary Kemynite foot soldier appears to be told little if anything about historical forms of Cornish, he or she will presumably swallow anything, however bizarre or outrageous, with few questions asked. Or at least that's what the inner core of the Kernowek Kemyn project seems to assume.

A fourth and final rhetorical strategy used by Kernowek Kemyn writers is more recent. It involves deliberately emphasizing the plurality of Cornish spelling systems. Thus we are told that "there are at least eight different orthographies of Revived Cornish (not three as is sometimes heard)" (p. 27), This echoes discussions I have had with supporters of Kernowek Kemyn where it was noticeable how eager they have become to differentiate between Unified and UCR, despite the former being dismissed by George as now a "historic" spelling system (p. 24). On the surface this strategy may seem strange as for two decades Kernowek Kemyn supporters went out of their way to deny the existence of any form of Cornish other than Kernowek Kemyn, the "official" choice of the Language Board back in the chaotic days of the mid-1980s. But this *volte-face* can be understood as part of a strategy of muddying the waters for the non-Cornish user (and for many Cornish users). By exaggerating the choice of spelling systems the aim is to elevate the role of Kernowek Kemyn as a giant among these competing pigmies, the only spelling system fit to receive the government endorsed mantle of "official" status. But, as George almost admits, in reality only Kernowek Kemyn, UCR and Modern Cornish have any "significant" following (p. 27).

A blustering, hubristic tone, name-calling, selective misrepresentation and exaggeration are therefore some of the rhetorical strategies adopted in *Agan Yeth* 4 and are part of the Kernowek Kemyn discourse. Unfortunately, the authors of *Agan Yeth* 4 appear to be naively unaware and unconcerned how many people are alienated by this rhetoric. Furthermore, it appears to give the green light to the vicious personal attacks indulged in by the more vigorous supporters of Kernowek Kemyn, attacks that can in turn trigger off equally rabid responses from some who align themselves with other spelling systems. The net result has been a downward slide in the tone of debate and the stoking up of bad feeling within what is already a very small group of Cornish users. Kernowek Kemyn, as the largest group, has a particular responsibility here. The failure of leading Kernowek Kemyn proponents to present a more tolerant and less aggressive face to their detractors and their persistent use of a confrontational style that leaves little or no space for compromise has deepened and entrenched differences within the Cornish language movement. Had they developed a less dismissive and more open discourse back in the late 1980s, it is quite possible that we would not be in the sad situation we are today.

CONCLUSION

What I have done here is reconstruct the discourse of Kernowek Kemyn, a discourse that creates an over-polarized "us and them" attitude to the language, that over-simplifies the real complexities of the historical language, that trades excessively—to the point of totalitarianism—on concepts of homogeneity and certainty and that at bottom rests on outdated values of romantic nationalism that are inappropriate to the needs of Cornish as it becomes a public language. I have also tried to suggest that the debate about a standard orthography is as much, if not more, about values and assumptions as it is about linguistics. (Although even within the restricted genre of the latter the over-confident claim that "the principal written objections to Kernowek Kemyn ... made by Nicholas Williams ... have been dealt with in *Cornish for the 21st century*" (p. 23) has been exploded by Williams' comprehensive critique of Kernowek Kemyn, *Towards Authentic Cornish* (2006).)

Moreover, underlying the aggressive certainties of the Kernowek Kemyn discourse, and the disturbingly intolerant, hectoring and bullying attitude it encourages amongst a minority of its supporters, there is a detectably growing desperation. In *Agan Yeth* 4 George states that the users of other Cornish spellings "feel themselves to be increasingly marginalised" (p. 33). Here again, George shows his lack of awareness of what is actually happening in the non-Kernowek Kemyn universe. The evidence of *Agan Yeth* 4 suggests the precise opposite: that, while UCR and Modern spelling users are becoming more confident, it is the users of Kernowek Kemyn who are beginning to experience the chill winds of marginalization. The plaintive question on page 17—"so who is hosting this conference [the Language Planning Conference at Tremough in September 2006]? And why?" betrays a fear that other agendas have imposed themselves and that Kernowek Kemyn speakers are being ignored. (In fact, the conference was organized by a group that included activists from all spelling factions.)

Of course, such paranoid suspicion goes far wider than Kernowek Kemyn and is a major factor preventing a healthy debate about the future of Cornish and its spelling. But the Kernowek Kemyn publicists must take the lion's share of blame for this situation. Having wrested the institutions of the language revival away from Unified Cornish in the 1980s Kernowek Kemyn was determined to present itself as a de-facto "standard" Cornish, trusting that in a Darwinian environment of the survival of the fittest and the absence of public funding, other forms of Cornish would wither away. That strategy has backfired badly. Living in their sealed world and refusing to engage in a real debate about Cornish, Kernowek Kemyn enthusiasts palpably failed to notice that other Cornishes not only survived; they thrived. Now belatedly aware of this, they resort to the argument "that the majority of Cornish speakers had their debate about it 20 years ago, and chose KK.... The few that do not like KK want to re-open the debate" (translated from p. 2). But what proportion of current speakers and users of Cornish were active 20 years ago? And, as I've argued above, what real "choice" has been given to that new generation (probably a majority) who have come to Cornish since the 1980s? In reality this is not a re-opening of the debate. The debate never went away; it was just that Kernowek Kemyn backers refused to engage in it unless it was on their own terms. (Note the complete lack of response to my call in Deacon, 1996 for a new umbrella group to reflect the pluralism of Cornishes). There were always some who rejected the Kernowek Kemyn adopted in the 1980s and who questioned the legitimacy of the decision taken at that time.

At least *Agan Yeth* 4 shows that the inner core of Kernowek Kemyn now accepts that the debate is continuing and they have to re-engage with it. And behind this there is also a dawning realization that, in the twenty-first century unlike the twentieth, the Cornish language may well cease to be the plaything of a few and become the property of the many. If we seriously wish to move towards that re-positioning of Cornish then one thing that has to happen is a flowering of debate about the language and the purposes of the Revival. And this has to be within the language schools as much as between them. There is now growing evidence that the guru-fetishization that has held back the Cornish language revival since the days of Henry Jenner is finally being overcome. Users of both UCR and Modern Cornish are no longer accepting the claims of their gurus at face value but are actively discussing, accepting or rejecting them. It is time for Kernowek Kemyn users to follow suit and engender a debate within Kernowek Kemyn, about how to live with a situation of pluralism, about how to build bridges to other medievalists, about how to achieve a workable solution that can accommodate the presence of Modern Cornish, about what compromises can and should be made, about the role of Cornish in the twenty-first century and about how to build a genuine rather than imposed unity within the Cornish language movement so that we can face the many enemies of Cornish with more confidence—together.

Perhaps when that discussion starts taking place we can then begin to think outside the box. For example, why do we need one standard spelling for signage purposes; what is wrong with two standards as happens in Norway; why not different standards for different purposes? Whatever solutions we arrive at will have to be innovative, flexible and inclusive and will have to be unique, like the Cornish language itself.

REFERENCES

Agan Yeth: Cornish Language Studies 4 (2005), Cornish Language Board.

Deacon, Bernard. 1996. "Language revival and language debate: modernity and postmodernity" in Philip Payton (ed). *Cornish Studies Four,* University of Exeter Press, 88-106.

Dunbar, Paul, and Ken George. 1998. *Kernewek Kemmyn: Cornish for the Twenty-First Century.* Cornish Language Board.

George, Ken. 1986. *The Pronunciation and Spelling of Revived Cornish.* Cornish Language Board.

Williams, Nicholas. 1997. *Clappya Kernowek: an introduction to Unified Cornish Revised.* Agan Tavas.

Williams, Nicholas. 2006. "'A modern and scholarly Cornish-English dictionary': Ken George's *Gerlyver Kernewek Kemmyn*" in *Writings on Revived Cornish.* Westport: Evertype.

THE CORNISH LANGUAGE BOARD AGAINST THE WORLD: THE BOARD'S *POLICY STATEMENT* OF NOVEMBER 2006

Bernard Deacon

When the process of establishing a suitable Single Written Form for the Cornish language reaches fruition, one of the first tasks will be the establishment of a properly constituted and financed language board. This will seek to command respect and further the interests of the language in the same way as the Welsh Language Board. It will also take over the functions of the present Cornish Language Board.

The Cornish Language Board was originally founded in 1967 at a time when Unified Cornish was a proto-standard spelling for Cornish. At that time the Cornish Language Board enjoyed a high degree of legitimacy among users of Cornish. However, after the divergence of opinion over the spelling and temporal base of Cornish in the early and mid-1980s the Cornish Language Board saw its legitimacy disappear. Since then it has faced a fundamental problem in that it is engaged in two incompatible projects. The first is the entirely laudable aim of increasing access to and knowledge of the Cornish language and promoting its adoption. But the Cornish language has undergone considerable change since the mid-1980s. It has left homogeneity behind and entered a new, more pluralist and diverse phase. The Cornish Language Board has signally failed to recognize this changed context and, furthermore, compounds this conservatism by equating "the language" with just one of its current variants, thus excluding the energies and expertise of many language activists. This is because it was captured by a small group in the 1980s who since that time have used it as a vehicle for their second aim: to promote only one form of the language, that spelling of late medieval Cornish known as Kernowek Kemyn.

In the 1980s, the Cornish Language Board over-hastily and eagerly rushed to embrace Ken George's Kernowek Kemyn, replacing Unified Cornish on the grounds that Kernowek Kemyn was more "authentic". It took no soundings amongst external experts in the Celtic languages and no advice more generally from other academics. This was unfortunate, as the much-vaunted "authenticity" of Kernowek Kemyn could not even survive the millennium. Academic opinion has been unenthusiastic to say the least, and it was not long before Kernowek Kemyn was subjected to a withering barrage of objections raised by professional linguists (these include Everson 1999; Mills 1999 and 2002; Penglase 1994; Price 1998 and Williams 1990, 1995, 1996, 1998, 2001, 2006a and 2006b). The phonological base that Kernowek Kemyn purported to "reveal" turned out to be at best highly debatable and at worst a chimera. At the point when it became crystal clear in the 1990s that Kernowek Kemyn was not meeting with universal acclaim those who controlled the Cornish Language Board might have admitted their error, pending a full and properly conducted re-assessment of the basis for the revived language. However, they spurned this chance and instead set out to exacerbate the ill-feeling that had emerged within the language movement after 1986 by vigorously promoting Kernowek Kemyn with renewed missionary zeal and a blind arrogance. This has inevitably led to a total loss of credibility amongst those who prefer to use dialects of Cornish based on more modern periods. As a result the useful work done by the Cornish Language Board over the years, for example in publishing manuscript texts of the Cornish corpus, has been fatally compromised by the embarrassing sectarian zeal with which it pursues its preferred re-spelling of medieval Cornish.

Over the past five years we have seen the recognition of Cornish in the European Charter for Regional and Minority Languages, the appearance of a Cornish Language Strategy, the beginnings of public funding for the language and the formation of the Cornish Language Partnership, the body that now oversees the spending of this money. In the light of these developments, it might be expected that the Cornish Language Board would finally begin to recognize the changing environment in which it operates. Sadly this is patently not so. Its latest November 2006 *Policy Statement* betrays no hint of a willingness to alter course. On the contrary this document reveals the Board's utter inability to move from a heads in the sand attitude and react to the moves to inject greater dynamism and restore confidence in the Cornish language that are now happening around it. Instead of welcoming those changes and engaging with the opportunities presented by the formation of the Cornish Language Partnership and the onset of limited public funding the Cornish Language Board prefers to ignore them. Faced with the challenge of working with other groups to establish a

Single Written Form for the language for signage and schooling, the Cornish Language Board merely retreats even further into what it fondly regards as the safety of its bunker. And as it does so it resorts to its tired tirade of increasingly threadbare textual defiance.

This *Policy Statement* is replete with the usual disingenuous assertions and highly contentious claims that have become typical of those who advocate Kernowek Kemyn (for another example see *Agan Yeth* 4). To take just one, it states that the Cornish Language Board is "completely democratic and representative" (pp. 8–9). It is in fact completely unrepresentative as the major body represented—*Cowethas an Yeth Kernewek*—is another organization committed to Kernowek Kemyn. Indeed, the same names crop up on the committees of both the Cowethas and the Language Board. Those organizations that use other forms of Cornish are not represented and have never been invited to send representatives. It also repeats several unsubstantiated claims, for example that Kernowek Kemyn "accurately represent[s] the historic pronunciation" of Cornish. This is questionable on two counts. First, Kernowek Kemyn only represents one historical pronunciation and second, as we have seen above, its claim to represent late medieval pronunciation has been challenged regularly over the years by several scholars of Middle Cornish. This continuing stubborn refusal to admit that Kernowek Kemyn is not an "accurate representation" of any historical pronunciation has now reached absurd levels. Because Kernowek Kemyn prefers to adopt words and grammar from Breton and Welsh rather than use attested Middle Cornish forms, rejects other vocabulary and grammar on the grounds that they are influenced by English, and moreover spells its ideological construct in a manner that moves the revived language further from the historical corpus of Cornish, it would be better described as a most "inaccurate representation" of the historic language.

Not content with parading the unproven fictions of the Kernowek Kemyn bunker as palpable fact the authors of the Cornish Language Board *Policy Statement* couple this with other statements that possess no evidential base at all—for example that Kernowek Kemyn is "important for both the practical and academic soundness of the language" (pp. 16–17) and that it is "academically superior" (pp. 18–19). In view of the weight of academic work that casts doubt on Kernowek Kemyn these statements beggar belief and might cause us to enquire where the authors of this *Policy Statement* have been living for the past twenty years. The same authors do not hesitate to grasp the opportunity for another gratuitous attack on the form of Cornish it calls Late Cornish and which is known to its users as Modern Cornish. Modern Cornish speakers attempt to use the Cornish spoken by those last generations of Cornish speakers in the seventeenth and eighteenth centuries. But, selectively misrepresenting the work of Edward Lhuyd, the Welsh linguist who conducted a survey of spoken Cornish around 1700, the Cornish Language Board sneeringly disparages a dialect that was actually spoken by Cornish people.

These examples from the Cornish Language Board's pamphlet reveal what is basically a polemic transparently designed to further one particular spelling system and obfuscate the situation for those with little knowledge of Cornish or of recent debates within the language movement. Clearly, they are incompatible with a serious organization that claims to speak for "the Cornish language". Furthermore, such polemical arrogance works to undermine the trust and confidence across differing viewpoints which is gradually and painstakingly being constructed under the auspices of the Cornish Language Partnership. On the contrary, in its document the Board takes a positive delight in refusing to help in the struggle to overcome two decades and more of mutual distrust and miscomprehension. By subverting moves to reach a considered solution to the problems posed by pluralism, the Cornish Language Board has chosen, sadly, to place itself outside the mainstream debate. But in doing so it becomes a major part of the problem facing the language movement.

The users of Kernowek Kemyn for whom the Cornish Language Board claims to speak now need urgently to reconsider the role of this organization. The best thing they could do for the future of the language would be to press their supposed representatives to dissolve the Cornish Language Board and hand over its functions to a reformed body that recognizes and represents the whole language movement in all its diversity. That moment has now arrived, for now we have the Cornish Language Partnership which brings together all those engaged in promoting and using the Cornish language (including the Cornish Language Board) alongside public sector bodies. Therefore, much of the original rationale for the Cornish Language Board no longer applies. For example, the Partnership has had a translation policy and advisory service in place for several months. It is therefore unfortunate to note in its *Policy Statement* (pp. 10–11) that the Cornish Language Board are continuing to offer an alternative advisory service for those wishing to use "Cornish" in their businesses or for signage. While claiming to use the "correct historical forms", this service no doubt advises use of Kernowek Kemyn. Maintaining this would seem to be a deliberate and brazen attempt to undermine the work of the Cornish Language Partnership.

As a first step, functions of translation, education and research need to be immediately transferred to a new body answerable to the Cornish Language Partnership. This can ensure that we have a language board that for the first time in 20 years will act on behalf of all language users, present a united public face and be properly accountable. As soon as the Single Written Form is agreed, responsibility for publishing and exams should also be divested to a properly accountable body. The Cornish Language Board has one final chance to move with the times, show its willingness to join with the rest of the language movement and use its resources for the benefit of the whole movement. If it refuses to take this opportunity it will consign itself, and rightly so, to the dustbin of history.

REFERENCES

Everson, Michael (1999) 'An event of great signicance [sic]: a review of George's *Gerlyver Kres'* in Philip Payton (ed.), *Cornish Studies Seven,* University of Exeter Press, Exeter, 242-53.

Mills, Jon (1999) 'Reconstructive phonology and contrastive lexicology: problems with the *Gerlyver Kernewek Kemmyn'* in Philip Payton (ed.), *Cornish Studies Seven,* University of Exeter Press, Exeter, 193-218.

Mills, Jon (2002) 'Computer assisted lemmatisation of a Cornish text corpus for lexicographical purposes', PhD dissertation, University of Exeter.

Penglase, Charles (1994) 'Authenticity in the revival of Cornish' in Philip Payton (ed.), *Cornish Studies Two,* University of Exeter Press, Exeter, 96-107.

Price, Glanville (1998) 'Modern Cornish in context' in Philip Payton (ed.), *Cornish Studies Six,* University of Exeter Press, Exeter, 187-93.

Williams, Nicholas (1990) 'A problem in Cornish phonology' in Martin Ball et al (eds), *Celtic Linguistics: Readings in the Brythonic Languages,* John Benjamins, Amsterdam.

Williams, Nicholas (1995) *Cornish Today: an examination of the revived language,* Sutton Coldfield.

Williams, Nicholas (1996) '"Linguistically sound principles": the case against Kernewek Kemmyn' in Philip Payton (ed.), *Cornish Studies Four,* University of Exeter Press, Exeter, 64-87.

Williams, Nicholas (1998) 'Pre-occlusion in Cornish', *Studia Celtica* 32, 129-54.

Williams, Nicholas (2001) 'A modern and scholarly Cornish-English dictionary: Ken George's *Gerlyver Kernewek Kemmyn'* in Philip Payton (ed.), *Cornish Studies Nine,* University of Exeter Press, Exeter, 247-311.

Williams, Nicholas (2006a) 'Bewnans Ke: implications for Kernowek Kemyn' in Nicholas Williams (ed.) *Writings in Revived Cornish,* Evertype, Westport, 187-95.

Williams, Nicholas (2006b) *Towards Authentic Cornish,* Evertype, Westport.

A REVIEW OF *THE NEW TESTAMENT* IN KERNOWEK KEMYN

Nicholas Williams

An Testament Nowydh. Translated by W. Brown, J. H. Chesterfield, J. M. Davey, R. J. Edwards, G. Sandercock and R. K. R. Syed (general editor). 2004. Kesva an Taves Kernewek—The Cornish Language Board. [Redruth, Cornwall]. ISBN 1 902917 33 2.

INTRODUCTION

0.00 This is the second version of the New Testament in Cornish to have been published in recent years. My translation, *Testament Noweth agan Arluth ha Savyour Jesu Cryst* (Spyrys a Gernow, Redruth, 2002) was based on the original Greek and written in Unified Cornish Revised. The readers of this review will understand, therefore, that I am by no means an unbiased commentator. My judgement of *An Testament Nowydh*, however, goes beyond any antipathy to a rival publication. In the following pages I have done my best to be as fair as I can to the translation by the Cornish Language Board, but my judgement remains largely negative.

My own version of the New Testament in Cornish was welcomed. See, for example, the review by Alan M. Kent in *An Baner Kernewek/The Cornish Banner* 109, August 2002 (available at **www.evertype.com/gram/tn-review-amk.html**). I am now unhappy about certain portions of my translation. I have, moreover, noticed a number of misprints and inaccuracies. An on-line errata page will now be found at **www.evertype.com/gram/tn-errata.html**.

0.01 The Bible in traditional Cornish. Middle Cornish literature deals almost exclusively with religious themes and there are many allusions to the Bible in the texts. The writers were presumably educated clerics, who would have been familiar with the scriptures in the Latin of the Vulgate. Quotations from the Vulgate are not uncommon in the mystery plays:

deus mei miserere 'God have mercy upon me' Psalm 50:3 (OM 2251)

literas nobis in via '[opened] the scriptures to us on the way' Luke 24:32
(RD 1326)

in manus tuas domine spiritum meum commendo 'into thy hands, Lord, I
commend my spirit' Luke 23:46 (BM 4329-30).

Some passages in Cornish in the texts are themselves based almost
verbatim upon the scriptures. It was probably not until the period of
the Reformation, however, that there was any serious thought of
translating the bible into Cornish. Penglase believes that a Cornish
version of the scriptures existed, was in circulation in medieval
Cornwall and that evidence for it can be seen in the portions of
scripture quoted in Cornish in Tregear's homilies (*Études Celtiques* 33
(1997), 233–243). This view has been disputed, and I myself remain
wholly sceptical that such a translation ever existed.

We have a few portions of scripture in Cornish from the Late
Cornish period, in particular by William Rowe of Sancreed, by John
Boson and John Keigwin. It was not, however, until the beginning of
the Cornish revival that the work of translating the scriptures began in
earnest. Jenner and Nance both translated portions of the New
Testament and A. S. D. Smith published a translation of St Mark's
gospel in 1936. A second, emended edition appeared in 1960. By 1989
the four gospels, Revelation and some of the Pauline epistles had been
published—all in Unified Cornish.

The present translation is in Kernowek Kemyn, a variety of Cornish
adopted by the Cornish Language Board in 1986. I have explained the
reasons for my unhappiness with Kernowek Kemyn in many places
and on many occasions. I regret therefore the appearance of any of
sacred scripture in this questionable form of Cornish.

0.02 The editor's address of September 2006. In September 2006 the
editor gave an address on the Cornish Bible Project, in which he
suggested that any Biblical translation must be made from the original
language (in the case of the New Testament from Greek). He also
observed that it must be rigorously checked for accuracy and
translators into Cornish in particular must have an excellent knowledge
of Cornish. We will see in the following pages that *An Testament Nowydh*
falls far short of fulfilling any of these criteria. The editor also calls
those involved with the translation of *An Testament Nowydh*
"experienced Cornish linguists", a description which can perhaps be
questioned.

The editor in his address stresses how important it is that the translation should be faithful to the original and indeed he puts this criterion above all others. But it is only realistic to remind ourselves that a Cornish version of the New Testament will not be the reader's primary source for the New Testament itself. The reader will inevitably know Cornish as a second language, and his first language is likely in the majority of cases to be English. If the reader really wishes to study in detail the exact meaning of this or that passage in the New Testament, he will not primarily be relying on any Cornish translation.

The Cornish New Testament is going to be used in the first instance as an adjunct to the Cornish revival. Of course the text must be treated with the greatest respect, but the primary function of the New Testament is to provide good, fluent and idiomatic Cornish. If the translation of the New Testament by the Cornish Language Board is in the first place written in an unhistorical orthography and if, in the second place, the language in it is neither accurate nor idiomatic, how faithful the translation remains to the original Greek is a much less important question.

GENERAL COMMENTS

1.00 The list of translators. In the Introduction in Kernowek Kemyn the names of the translators and the books which they translated are set out (page ix). Here we read that R. J. Edwards, among other things, translated '1 ha 2 Kolosse' i.e. the first and second epistles to the Colossians. There is only one epistle to the Colossians. The statement is a typographical error and only one epistle to the Colossians is ascribed to Edwards in the corresponding English list on page xi.

1.01 The sources of the translation. The editor says

> Some twenty commentaries have been used to assist us with problems of interpretation, and some fifty Bible translations have been consulted, both ancient (Latin, Syriac) and modern (from Tyndale, Luther and the Geneva Bible onwards) in various languages—among them Welsh, Breton and Irish, mainly to suggest phraseology in difficult passages (page xii).

Was this to be absolutely sure of the meaning and to decide between this or that nuance of interpretation, or, more likely, to find the simplest way of translating the text? The translators would have done better to read continuously the whole corpus of traditional Cornish, and the prose writer John Tregear in particular, to see how native speakers used the language.

The editor writes:

> This New Testament is not a translation of another translation—it is based strictly on the Greek text (page xii).

As we shall see below, this statement is not entirely true. The translation of the text itself was quite clearly based in many places on the Revised Standard Version (RSV) and in some others on the Authorized Version of 1611.

The editor explains something of the translators' working methods and tells us that the dictionaries of Nance and George have been used as well as W. Brown's *Grammar of Modern Cornish*—a work which I have have criticized elsewhere as giving a misleading and indeed mistaken view of traditional Cornish (see TAC: 235-81).

1.02 The Influence of *Testament Noweth*. My own *Testament Noweth* is nowhere mentioned in the Introduction, but has clearly had some influence on the present work. In the *Raglavar* or Introduction to my Cornish version of the New Testament I pointed out that 'according to' in the traditional language is *war lergh*; indeed I indicate that the words *warlergh Sen Luk* 'according to St Luke' actually occur at line 391 of *Beunans Meriasek*. Until the publication of my *Testament Noweth* in 2002 it had been customary to use the less authentic *herwyth* for 'according to' in the titles of the Gospels and indeed the two works *An Aweyl herwyth Synt Mark* and *An Awayl herwyth Sen Mathew* are cited in the footnotes on page xiv of this translation. In the present work, however, the four gospels are described as *war-lergh Matthew, war-lergh Mark, war-lergh Luk* and *war-lergh Yowann* respectively. I do not understand why the hyphen is necessary in *war-lergh*, nor can I approve of the form *Yowann* 'John', which is questionable in both spelling and phonology (see below), but I should like to take some of the credit for having replaced the less authentic *herwyth* with the more natural *war lergh*.

It should be noted also that the titles of the individual Gospels in Unified Cornish that were published over the years called their authors *Sen Mathew, Synt/Sen Mark, Sen Luk* and *Sen Jowan* respectively. There is no hint anywhere in this Kernowek Kemyn translation of *Sen/Synt* in the titles of the gospels. I should like to think that, perhaps, the complete absence of *Sen/Synt* anywhere owes a little to my article "'Saint' in Cornish" (*Cornish Studies Seven* (1999) 219–41, reprinted in

Writings on Revived Cornish (Evertype 2006) 120–37), where I discuss the medieval usage in Cornish.

Noteworthy also is the similarity between 1 Timothy 1:17 in my *Testament Noweth* and the same verse in the present work:

> *Dhe Vytern an osow, dyvarow, dywel, an Dew unyk, re bo onour ha glory bys vyken ha benary! Amen* (Testament Noweth)

> *Dhe Vyghtern an oesow, divarow, diwel, an Dyw unnik, re bo enor ha gordhyans trank heb worfenn. Amen* (Testament Nowydh).

1 Timothy was translated by R. Edwards, and as I say in my *Raglavar*, I used his Unified Cornish version of *Revelation* and 11 epistles while preparing my own translation.

THE TRANSLATION ITSELF

2.00 Questionable personal names and place-names. The treatment of personal names and place-names in *An Testament Nowydh* is unsatisfactory, largely because Kernowek Kemyn is both highly schematized and at the same time very inconsistent.

In *Cornish Today* (CT3: 67-8; 196-98) I explain in detail with evidence why biblical names like *Jesu, Jonas, Jowan, Judas, Judi* and *Jerusalem* must have been pronounced in Middle and Late Cornish alike with an initial *J* rather than a *Y*. The translators of *An Testament Nowydh* have chosen to ignore my evidence and thus use a whole series of names that are without warrant in the traditional language, e.g. **Yesu, *Yakob, *Yason, *Yesse, *Yoanna, *Yosafat, *Yosep, *Yowann, *Yudas, *Yunias, *Yustus, *Yeriko, *Yerusalem, *Yoppa* and **Yudi*. At the same time they spell the equivalent of 'James' as *Jamys*—presumably because the name was so obviously borrowed from English. They do not accept that all the other names were borrowed from English or Middle French as well and, like *Jamys*, were all pronounced with an initial *J*. This decision by the translators leads to some bizarre results. The two disciples of Jesus are referred to throughout as *Jamys ha Yowan* 'James and John', when it is quite clear that the two names alliterated in Hebrew and Greek and should alliterate in Cornish as well. Similarly one finds *mab Maria, broder Jamys ha Yoses ha Yudas ha Simon* (Mark 6:3). Curiously, one name from the Old Testament has escaped attention, for we read of *perthyans Job* 'the patience of Job' at James 5:11, rather than the expected *perthyans *Yob*.

2.01 Variant forms of the same personal name. This translation writes *Yosep* 'Joseph' with a final <p> rather than <f> throughout, e.g. at Matt. 1:16, 1:18, 1:19, 1:20, 1:24, 2:13, 2:19, 13:55, 27:57, Mark 15:43, 15:45, Luke 1:27, 2:4, 2:16, 3:23, 3:24, 3:30, 4:22, 23:50, John 1:45, 4:5, 6:42, 19:38, Acts 1:23, 4:36, 7:9, 7:13, 7:14, 7:18, Heb. 11:21, 11:22 and Rev. 7:8. The form in final <p> is presumably based on the spellings *Iosep* PA 215a & c, *iosep* RD 3155, etc. It should be pointed out, however, that final [f] also occurs in the texts, e.g. *ioseph* RD 3, 22, 31; and Rowe writes *Joseph* twice. The editors of *An Testament Nowyth* are inconsistent with the spelling, however, since in a footnote on the name *Yoses* at Matt. 27:56 we read: *War-lergh re a'n dornskrifow* **Yosef**.

This translation is inconsistent as far as the Cornish for 'Abraham' is concerned. In 2 Corinthians and Galatians St Paul refers to the great patriarch of the Jews as *Abraham*:

has **Abraham** *yns i* 2 Cor. 11:22
Kepar dell grysis **Abraham** *yn Dyw* Gal. 3:6
dhe vos mebyon **Abraham** Gal. 3:7
a dharganas an aweyl dhe **Abraham** Gal. 3:8
rag skrifys yw bos dew vab dhe **Abraham** Gal. 4:22.

In his epistle to the Romans, however, he calls him *Abram*:

Pandr'a levery ytho y hwrug **Abram** *y gavoes* Rom. 4:1
y synsys fydh dhe **Abram** *avel gwiryonedh* Rom. 4:9
an ambos dhe **Abram** *h'ay henedh* Rom. 4:13
oll mebyon **Abram** Rom. 9:7
dhiworth has **Abram** Rom. 11:1.

Names with stressed *i* in the root syllable also appear in more than one guise. The name 'Simeon' is rendered **Symeon**, for example, at Luke 2:25 and 3:30. We read **Simeon** *henwys Niger*, however, at Acts 13:1. The same difficulty is to be seen with the name 'Silvanus': we find **Silvanus** *ha Timothi* 2 Cor. 1:19 and *dre* **Silvanus** 1 Peter 5:12, but *Powl,* **Sylvanus** *ha Timothi* at 1 Thess. 1:1 and at 2 Thess. 1:2. Notice also a different kind of hesitation in **Barsabas** Acts 1:23 but **Barsabbas** Acts 15:22. Most remarkable of all, perhaps, is the hesitation between <ks> and <x> is the single sentence:

Re'n routh a ros gorhemmynow dhe **Aleksander**, *neb re bia herdhys yn-rag gans an Yedhowon, hag* **Alexander**, *ow kwevya y leuv, a vynnas styrya an dra dhe'n kuntelles* Acts 19:33.

2.02 Variant forms of the same place-name. We read of *Tyr ha Sidon* at Matt. 11:21, Mark 7:24 and Luke 10:13, but at Mark 3:8 the names appear as *Tyr ha Sydon*. We also find *Sesarea* at Matt. 16:13, Mark 8:27, Acts 8:40, 9:30, 10:1, 10:24, 11:11 and 12:19; on the other hand, the name is spelt *Sesaria* at Acts 18:22, 21:8, 21:16, 23:23, 23:33, 25:1, 25:4. 25:6 and 25:13. Compare also *ha dos dhe Bethphage* Matt. 21:1, but *pan dheuth nes dhe Bethfage ha Bethani* Luke 19:29 and *Aleksandria* Acts 27:6, 28:11 but *Alexandria* Acts 6:9.

The translation contains two different ways of spelling the place of origin of Joseph of Arimathea. Usually it is called *Arimathea*:

> *den rych a **Arimathea**, henwys Yosep* Matt. 27:57
> *Hag ott, yth esa den henwys Yosep, esel an konsel, ha den da ha gwiryon, (ny wrussa assentya dh'aga thowl na dh'aga gweythres)—yth esa a **Arimathea*** Luke 23:50-1
> *Yosep a **Arimathea**, onan a dhyskyblon Yesu* John 19:38.

But it may also be called *Aramat*:

> *y teuth Yosep a **Aramat*** Mark 15:43.

There is now justification for *Aramat.The town is called **Baramat** at PA 214a, **Baramathia** at PC 3099, RD 22 and **Baramathya** at RD 627. Notice also *ynys **Malta*** 'the island of Malta' Acts 28 (heading) and *Malta* 'Malta' Acts 28:1 but *MELITA* on the map on page 425.

At Luke 21:37 we read *ha godriga y'n vre henwys an **Menydh Oliv*** whereas at Acts 1:12 we find *dhiworth an **menedh** henwys **Olivet**. Both *meneth olyff* and *meneth olyved* are attested in Middle Cornish, but it is curious that two different forms should be used in Luke and Acts, since both books were written by the same author and the Greek name is the same: εἰς τὸ ὄρος τὸ καλούμενον Ἐλαιών Luke 21:37 and ἀπὸ ὄρους τοῦ καλουμένου Ἐλαιῶνος Acts 1:12. Since the heading at Luke 21:34 is *Ynnians dhe Woelyas* in the Kernowek Kemyn and 'The Need to Watch' in the TEV, one suspects that the Lucan passage is based on the TEV and the passage in Acts on another English translation. This suspicion appears to be correct. The English of Luke 21:37 in the TEV reads: 'and spend the night on the Mount of Olives' (cf. *Menydh Oliv*), whereas the RSV at Acts 1:12 reads 'from the mount called Olivet' (cf. *an menedh henwys Olivet*). This all seems to suggest that these two passages of *An Testament Nowydh* were not translated from the Greek.

2.03 Inconsistencies in the use of <k> and <s>. It would seem that this translation has no consistent method for converting biblical names into Kernowek Kemyn. This is particularly true with names containing Greek κ before a front vowel. Some times it is allowed to remain and appears as Kernowek Kemyn <k>; at other times it is rendered in Kernowek Kemyn <s>, as though from an intermediate Latin <c>. We thus find the following inconsistencies:

GREEK <κ> = KERNOWEK KEMYN <k>

Narkissus 'Narcissus' Rom. 16:11
Priskilla 'Priscilla' Acts 18:2, 18:26
Skeva 'Sceva' Acts 19:14
Syrofenikek 'Syrophoenician' Mark 7:26
Syrofenikia 'Syrophoenicia' (heading at) Mark 7:24.

GREEK <κ> = KERNOWEK KEMYN <s>

Fenisia 'Phoenicia' Acts 11:19, 15:3, 21:2
Kappadosia 'Cappadocia' Acts 2:9
Lysia 'Lycia' Acts 27:5
Syprus 'Cyprus' Acts 4:36, 11:19, 27:4.

The hesitation between *Syrofenikia* 'Syrophoenicia' and *Fenisia* 'Phoenicia' is striking.

Sometimes no final decision is made as to which form is the "correct" one. We thus find, for example *Kenkrea* 'Cenchrea' Rom. 16:1 but *Senkrea* Acts 18:18; *Kyrene* 'Cyrene' Matt. 27:32, Mark 15:21 and Luke 23:26 but *Syrene* Acts 2:10, 6:9, 11:20 and 13:1; *Lukius* 'Lucius' Rom. 16:21 but *Lusius* Acts 13:1; *Makedoni* 'Macedonia' Rom. 15:26 but *Masedonia* Acts 16:9, 16:10.

2.04 English forms of personal names used in preference to Cornish ones. Various forms of the Cornish name for 'Herod' are found in the Middle Cornish texts: *Erod, Herodes* and *Erodes*:

me a wra sur y thanfon the'n turont **erod** *yn scon* PC 1602-03
gorreugh ef the **erod** *scon* PC 1614
myghtern **erod** *gans onour re thanfonas ihesu thy's* PC 1842-43
nag **erod** *an arluth cref* PC 1858.

bos **herodes** *war an wlas* PA 108b
I eth bys yn **herodes** PA 109a
The **herodes** *y thesa pur wyr worth pylat sor bras* PA 110a
Herodes *a wovynnys orth Ihesus crist leas tra* PA 111a
Herodes *a leuerys ʒen eʒewon* PA 113a
herodes *reth tenyrghys* PA 115b.

hag a gallos **erodes** PC 1601.

The present work calls 'Herod' throughout by the English form of the name *Herod*, e.g. at Matt. 2:1, 2:3, 2:7, 2:12, Mark 6:14, 6:16, 6:17, 6:20, 6:22, Luke 1:5, 3:1, Acts 4:27, 12:6 and 13:1. This name is found in the traditonal language only in Late Cornish:

Nena **Herod**, *pereeg e prevath crya an Deez feere* Rowe
Rag **Herod** *vedn whelaz an Flô rag E latha* Rowe
Ha E ve enna terebah Mernaz **Herod** Rowe
Nena **Herod** *perêg E gwellaz fatal o geaze gwreaze anotha gen an Teze feere*
   Rowe
Potho **Herod** *maraw, mero Elez Neue theath tha Joseph* Rowe.

When the Middle Cornish variants *Erod*, *Herodes* and *Erodes* were available, it seems curious that the form *Herod* should have been chosen, since *Herod* is either Late Cornish or English.

In the present translation Solomon is always called **Solomon**, e.g. at Matt. 1:6, 1:7, 6:29, 12:42, Luke 11:32, 12:27, John 10:23, Acts 3:11, 5:12, 7:47. In traditional Cornish, however, Solomon is known as *Salamon*:

Salamon *the vap kerra a'n coul threha eredy* 'Solomon, your dearest son, will complete the building of it' OM 2341-42
dun the gyrhas **salamon** *ha goryn ef yn y dron* 'let us go to fetch Solomon and let us set him on his throne' OM 2371-72
lowene thy's **salamon** 'Hail to thee, Solomon' OM 2377
ov arluth ker **salamon** *awos lavur na dewon nefre ny fallaf theughwhy* 'my dear lord Solomon, never will I fail you because of labour or affliction' OM 2404-06
dun the leuerel yn scon d'agan arluth **salamon** 'let us go to tell our lord Solomon quickly' OM 2579-80
Yma **Salamon** *ow leverall in y proverbis* 'Solomon says in his Proverbs' TH 8
Raghenna yma **Salamon** *ow declaria openly in Ecclesiasticus* 'Therefore Solomon declares openly in Ecclesiasticus' TH 8
In weth mytern **Salamon**, *a ve diskys dre an spuris sans* 'Also king Solomon was taught by the Holy Spirit' TH 31

Ken rug oll an x tryb a Israell departia a theworth Roboam mab **Salamon**
'Although all the ten tribes of Israel separated from Rehoboam the
son of Solomon' TH 50a.

It is difficult to understand why this translation does not use the
traditional Cornish form of the name.

The present work spells the Kernowek Kemyn equivalent of
'Matthew' as **Matthew**, e.g. as the title of the first gospel, at Matt. 9:9,
10:3, Mark 3:18 and Luke 6:15. It is a feature of Kernowek Kemyn that
it is based on the erroneous view that Middle Cornish maintained half-
length in vowels. The spelling <Matthew> with internal <tth> is to
show that the consonant is long and that the stressed vowel is
correspondingly short. In which case Kernowek Kemyn differs from
both Welsh and Breton, which write the name *Mathew* and *Mazhev* or
Maze respectively, i.e. with a single medial consonant. More importantly Kernowek Kemyn differs from traditional Cornish, which also
spells the name with a single medial consonant:

h'essoge goky **mathew** RD 983
a synte mari **mathew** RD 1387
ow leverall in ix **mathew** TH 8a
scriffis in xxviii chapter a **mathew** TH 17
scriffys in v. chapter a **mathew** TH 17a
in vii chapter a **mathew** TH 19a
in v-as chapter a **mathew** TH 26a
therag declaris in v. **mathew** TH 26a
in v-as a **mathew** TH 27
gyrryow crist in xi. **mathew** TH 27a
ow screffa war an pempas chapter a **mathew** TH 27a
han kythsame gere na in pempas a **mathew** TH 28
in v-as chapter a S **mathew** TH 29
in iii-a chapter a mathew TH 29a
Ha in aweyll S **mathew** *inweth* TH 31a
dell vsy S **Mathew** *ow recordya* TH 35a
peswar aweylar only, luk, mark, **mathew***, ha Jowan* TH 37a
in xvi-as chapter a S **Mathew** *in vaner ma* TH 43a
Ha in xviii-as chaptu [sic] *a* **mathew** TH 44a
an iii aweylar, mark, **mathew** *ha luke ow hagrya* TH 52a
In xvii a **mathew***, ny a rede* TH 56a
in 26. chapter a **mathew** SA 59a
mathew *res in ker vaggya* CW 1335
mathew *dew an tas serrys* CW 2148

in xxii a S Mathe TH 20a
in delma. mathe v TH 21a
blonogath y das. mathe .xxvi TH 22a.

The only example of a spelling with <tth> is *An Duah a an bozvevah Chaptra a* **Matthew** from William Rowe, which is based on the English from which he is translating.

The name **Belsebul** 'Beelzebub, Beelzebul' occurs at Matt. 10:25, 12:24, 12:27, Mark 3:22, Luke 11:15, 11:18 and 11:19. It should be noted, however, that *Belsebul* is nowhere attested in traditional Cornish, where the name is **Belsebuk** or **Belsebuc**:

> **Belsebuk** *ha satanas eugh alemma pur thoth bras* 'Beelzebub and Satan, go hence with greatest speed' OM 541-42
>
> *aha* **belsebuc** *aha ovotte vn purvers da lemyn wharfethys* 'Aha, Beelzebub, aha, here is a fine upset that has happened' OM 881-83
>
> **belsebuc** *del y'm kyrry fystyn duwhans gueres vy* 'Beelzebub, as you love me, hurry quickly, help me' OM 890-91
>
> *ov benneth thy's* **belsebuk** *del ose pryns ha chyf duk* 'my blessing to you, Beelzebub, as your are prince and foremost duke' PC 1925-26
>
> *ha rag henna satenas ha* **belsabuk** *dun toth bras* 'and therefore, Satan and Beelzebub, let us go with all speed PC 3037-38
>
> **belsebuc** *whek wheyth the corn* 'dear Beelzebub, blow thy horn' PC 3055
>
> **belsebuc** *ha lawethan dylleugh luhes ha taran* 'Beelzebub and Leviathan, let forth lightning and thunder' RD 128-29
>
> **belsebuk** *ha sattanas kenough why faborden bras* 'Beelzebub and Satan, sing you a loud bass' RD 2358-59
>
> **belsebuc** *ny a vyn moys thege gore in lel forth* 'Beelzebub, we will go to set them on the right way' BM 2320-21.

Since *Belsebuk* is so well attested in the traditional language, it should have been used in preference to a non-Cornish form *Belsebul*.

2.05 Inconsistencies in the use of Cornish forms of toponyms. The Cornish for 'Rome' is attested in the texts:

> *an epscop a* **rom** *the vos pen* TH 50
> *ny alsa an epscop a* **Rom** TH 50
> *In* **Rom** *me ew senator* BK 2493
> *bys in* **Rom** *gans pen Lucy* BK 2839.

The Cornish for 'Spain' is attested:

arluth ow tevos a **spayn** RD 2147
Me, Alphatyn myghtern **Spain** BK 2608-09
Welcum, Mightern **Spain** *deffry!* BK 2643.

The Cornish for 'Egypt' is attested:

Yn **egip** *whyrfys yv cas* OM 1415
bys yn **egip** *the pharo* OM 1422
myghtern **Egip** *mylprevys* BK 2629
ha Myghtern **Egyp** *kefrys!* BK 2641.

The Cornish for 'Bethlehem' is attested, either as **Bethlem** or **Bethalem**:

rag y feth map yn **bethlem** OM 1934
pur evn y **bethlem** *iudi* PC 1607
a fue genys yn **bethlem** PC 1652.

poue Jesus gennez en **Bethalem** *a Judeah* Rowe
Ha an gye lavarraz tho tha, en **Bethalem** *a Judeah* Rowe
Ha Che **Bethalem** *en Pow Judah* Rowe
oll an Flehaz a era en **Bethalem** Rowe.

In the present work 'Rome' is **Rom** (e.g. Acts 2:10, 18:2, 19:21, 23:11, 28:14, 28:16, Rom. 1:7, 1:15, 2 Tim. 1:17); 'Spain' is **Spayn** (e.g. Rom. 15:24, 15:28) and 'Egypt' is **Ejyp** (e.g. Matt. 2:13, 2:14, 2:15, 2:19, Acts 2:10, 7:9, 7:10). Inconsistently, on the other hand, 'Bethlehem' is referred to by the English form of the name: **Bethlehem** Matt. 2:1, 2:5, 2:6, 2:16, Luke 2:4, *dhe* **Vethlehem** Matt. 2:8, Luke 2:15.

2.06 Invented forms of names. At Luke 16 (heading), 16:20, 16:23, 16:24, 16:25, John 11 (heading), 11:1, 11:2, 11:11, 11:14, 11:38 (heading), 11:43, 12:2, 12:9 (& heading) this translation calls 'Lazarus' by the name **Lasarus*. The Greek says Λάζαρος while English says *Lazarus*. The Cornish form of 'Lazarus' is attested in Cornish, however:

Lasser *o den bohosek a thuk lavyr pur anwhek abraham an reseves pan o marov dotho eff hag in y hascra heb greff in golovder an gvythes* 'Lazarus was a poor man who endured severe hardship; Abraham received him to himself when he died and in his bosom without pain kept him in glory' BM 450-55.

This passage from *Beunans Meriasek* refers to the Lucan parable. It is therefore difficult to understand why this translation does not call Lazarus by his Cornish name, *Lasser*, rather than by an invented form **Lasarus*.

Throughout *An Testament Nowydh* the translators refer to the town where Jesus dwelt as **Nasara*, e.g. at Matt. 2:23, 4:13, 21:11, Mark 1:9, 1:24, 10:47, Luke 1:26, 2:4, 4:16, John 1:45, 18:5 and 19:19. Whenever it occurs in traditional Cornish, Middle or Late, the place-name always contains a medial <z> rather than <s>:

> *ihesus crist an* **nazare** PA 69c
> *Ihesus crist a* **nazary** PA 255b
> *divithys a* **nazare** PC 328
> *ihesu parde a* **nazare** *an fals crystyon* PC 1111-12
> *me yw ihesu an* **nazare** PC 1114
> *gans ihesu a* **nazare** PC 1278
> *worth ihesu a* **nazare** PC 1717
> *er byn ihesu* **nazare** PC 1971
> *an profus a* **nazare** PC 2197
> *ihesu Cryst a* **nazare** PC 2361
> *a gous ihesu* **nazare** PC 2498
> *ef yv ihesu* **nazare** PC 2795
> *pous ihesu an* **nazare** PC 2854
> *ihesu ru'm feyth a* **nazareth** PC 1117
> *Ha garah* **Nazareth** Rowe.

The spelling **Nasara* is inauthentic and unwarranted.

The name *Cedron* is attested in the Middle Cornish texts:

> *nynsus pons war thour* **cedron** 'there is no bridge over the river Cedron' OM 2804
> *war thour* **cedron** *may fo pons* 'that there may be a bridge over the river Cedron' OM 2811
> *mars ty a theg a neyl pen the dour* **cedron** 'unless you carry the one end over the river Cedron' OM 2814-15
> *war* **cedron** *ov crowethe yma pren da ren ow thas* 'a beam lies upon the Cedron, by my father' OM 2544-45.

There can be no doubt that in Middle Cornish the name was pronounced with an initial [s]. At John 18:1, however, we read *Yesu eth dhe-ves gans y dhyskyblon dres dowr *Kedron* 'Jesus went away with his disciples across the river Kedron'. It is difficult to see why *Kedron* has been used in Kernowek Kemyn rather than a form with initial <S>.

2.07 Inconsistencies in capitalization of names and adjectives. There is hesitation in the present translation with respect to the capitalization of proper names. We thus find *an bobel* **Yedhowek** 'the Jewish people' Acts 12:11, *hudoryon* **Yedhowek** 'Jewish magicians' Acts 19:13, *an gemmynieth* **Yedhowek** 'the Jewish community' Acts 25:24 but *an genedhel yedhowek* 'the Jewish nation' Acts 10:22, *fals profoes yedhowek* 'a false Jewish prophet' Acts 13:6, *y'n kryjyans yedhowek* 'in the Jewish faith' Gal. 1:14, *hwedhlow yedhowek* 'Jewish myths' Titus 1:14; *burjesi* **Romanek** 'Roman citizens' Acts 16:37, 16:28 but *trevesigeth romanek* 'a Roman colony' Acts 16:12; and **Menydh** *Sinay* 'Mount Sinai' Acts 7:30, 7:38, Gal. 4:24, 4:25, **Venydh** *Sion* 'Mount Zion' Heb. 12:22, but *menydh Sion* 'Mount Zion' Rev. 14:1.

2.08 Inconsistencies in initial mutation of names. The conventions adopted for the present translation appear inconsistent with respect to the lenition of the initial consonant of proper names. We thus find *dhe* **Barnabas** 'to Barnabas' Acts 15:36 but *dhe* **Varnabas** Gal. 2:9; *dhe Kefas* 'to Cephas' 1 Cor. 1:12 but *dhe Gefas* 1 Cor. 15:5; *dre Belsebul* 'by Beelzebul' Matt. 12:24, Luke 11:15, 11:18, 11:19, but but *dre Velsebul* Matt. 12:27; *a Vethani* 'from Bethany' John 11:1 but *a Bethani* 'from Bethany' Mark 11:12; *dhe Peder* 'to Peter' Matt. 16: 23, 17:24, 26:40, Mark 14:37 but *dhe Beder* Mark 16:8 fn. (page 97). Remarkable also are *dhe Maria Magdalena* 'to Mary Magdalen' in the heading at Mark 16:9 but *dhe Varia Magdalena* at Mark 16:9 itself. Finally notice *dhe Bethphage* Matt. 21:1, *dhe Bethfage* Luke 19:29, *dhe Bethsaida* Mark 8:22 but *dhe Vethlehem* Matt. 2:8 and Luke 2:15.

2.09 Inconsistencies in population names. The New Testament contains many population names, some of which are used in the titles of the epistles. *An Testament Nowydh* is remarkably inconsistent with these names also. Here is a list of population names and collective names taken from *An Testament Nowydh*. In all cases the English equivalent ends in either *-ans* or *-ians*:

Herodianys 'Herodians' Matt. 22:16, Mark 3:6
Nikolaitanys 'Nicolaitans' Rev. 2:6
Samaritanys 'Samaritans' Matt. 10:5, Luke 9:52, John 4:9, 4:39, 4:40, Acts 8:25

Efesyon 'Ephesians' Acts 19:28, 19:34, 19:35
Romanyon 'Romans' John 11:48, Acts 16:21

tus Filippi 'Philippians' Phil. 4:15 and title
tus Galatia 'Galatians' Gal. 3:1 and title
tus Galila 'Galileans' Luke 13:1, 13:2, John 4:45, Acts 2:7
tus Kolosse 'Colossians' title
tus Korinth 'Corinthians' Acts 18:8, 2 Cor. 6:11 and title
tus Thessalonika 'Thessalonians' title.

The word **Samaritanys** 'Samaritans' looks like a plural and one would therefore expect the singular to be **Samaritan**. This occurs at John 8:48. On the other hand **Samaritanek** is used at Luke 10:25 (heading). On the Bible corrections website (**www.bibelkernewek.com/amendyansow**) *den a Samaria* in the original text at Luke 17:16 has been corrected to **Samaritan**. This means that now 'Samaritan' is **Samaritanek** at Luke 10:25 but **Samaritan** at Luke 17:16 and John 8:48.

The title of the Epistle to the Ephesians is *Dhe Dus Efesus*. Oddly enough, when the men of Ephesus shout 'Great is Artemis of the Ephesians!' (Acts 19:28, 19:34, 19:35) this is translated into Kernowek Kemyn as *Meur yw Artemis an **Efesyon***. There would appear, therefore, to be two different expressions for 'Ephesians' in Kernowek Kemyn, although the distinction between them is not clear. Moreover the expression ***Efesyon** itself seems to be badly formed, for it looks like a plural in *-yon* of ***Efes**, which, however, if it is anything, is a suffixless form of the name of the city Ephesus; it does not suggest an Ephesian (see further § 7.18 below).

'Israelite' is translated **Ysraelit** at John 1:47 and Rom. 11:1. The plural 'Israelites', however, is not the expected ***Ysraelitys** (cf. *Elamitys* 'Elamiites' Acts 2:9), but **Ysraelyon** at Rom. 9:4, 2 Cor. 11:22. Like *Efesyon*, **Ysraelyon** seems curiously badly formed, since it looks as though it is the plural of *Ysrael* 'Israel'.

Populations terms beginning with *tus* 'people' are presumably based on forms like Lhuyd's *Tîz Kimbra* (AB: 222), *Tîz Lezou* (AB: 223). The plural form *Romanyon* is curious, however. In traditional Cornish the Romans are known as *an **Romans***:

*y epistyll then **romans*** TH 4a
*S Pawle thyn **romans** an iii-a chapter* TH 7a
*S pawle in kynsa chapter thyn **romans*** TH 14
*dell vgy S paul thyn **romans** ow kull mencion* TH 14a

Yma S poule in delma ow declaria thyn **romans** TH 25
An **Romans** *a vyth wystyys* BK 2136
Merough ple ma an **Romans** BK 2808
durt an **Romans** *meskez gen a Brittez* NBoson.

The ending -*yon* added to *Roman* is particularly perplexing in the light of Lhuyd's singular *Norman* and plural *Normanno* (AB: 224). If a native plural suffix was desirable, surely **Romanow* would have been the form of choice.

The adjective 'Roman' in Kernowek Kemyn apparently is *Romanek*:

heb agan bos dampnys, ha ni burjesi **Romanek** Acts 16:37
pan glywsons aga bos burjesi **Romanek** Acts 16:38
Yw lafyl ragos dhe skorjya burjes **Romanek** Acts 23:25
Lavar dhymm, osta burjes **Romanek?** Acts 23:27

The singular of the plural noun **Romanyon** 'Romans' is **Roman** 'Roman' at Acts 22:29 and 23:27. We thus have the noun **Roman** 'Roman', plural **Romanyon* 'Romans' but the adjective **Romanek** 'Roman, belonging to Rome'. In the light of **Samaritanek** 'Samaritan' and **Samaritanys** one might rather expect **Romanek** 'a Roman' and **Romanys* 'Romans'. Or one might expect **Samaritan**, **Samaritanyon* by analogy with **Roman**, plural **Romanyon*.

We find *Herodianys, Samaritanys* and *Nicolaitanys* in *An Testament Nowydh*. It might therefore have been most logical for this translation to have adapted traditional *Romans* to make it **Romanys**.

Although the term 'Pharisees' is not strictly a population name, it is used in the New Testament, as are the terms 'Herodians' and 'Nicolaitans', to refer to a distinct group. The Cornish for 'Pharisees' is well attested in Tregear's Homilies, though not elsewhere. I have collected the following 13 examples:

an dus perfect han **pharyses** TH 9
Onyn an **pharasys** *o docture an law* TH 20a
dell rug an **phariseys** *gans aga pestilens tradicions* TH 22
ny gesan ow kull bithwell agys an **pharises** TH 22a
vght lelldury an scribis han **pharysys** TH 26a
Ha dre an scribis han **pharises** TH 26a
passia an scribes han **pharises** TH 26a
dell rug an scribis han **pharises** TH 26a
an scribis han **pharases** *ha dre reson na ges fawt vith* TH 26a-27
kepar dell rug an scribis han **pharases** TH 27

*gyllwall an scribis han **pharases** TH 29a*
*fatell ra Scribes ha **pharises** setha in chare moyses TH 34*
*stall po cheare an scribys han **phariseis** TH 48a.*

The present work translates 'Pharisees' as **Fariseow*, for exampe, at Matt. 3:7, 5:20, 9:11, Mark 2:16, 2:18, 3:6, Luke 5:17, 5:21, 6:2, John 1:24, 3:1 and 7:32. Yet we regularly find *skribys* 'scribes' with an -*ys* plural, e.g. at Matt. 2:4, 5:20, 7:29, 9:3, Mark 1:22, 2:6, 2:16, 3:22, Luke 5:21, 5:30, 6:7, 9:22, John 8:3, Acts 4:5. The plural *skribys* is derived from Tregear, who, as we have seen, also writes *pharyses, pharasys*. Indeed, as can be seen form the above citations, the phrase **scribys ha pharysys** is well attested in TH. This translation thus arbitrarily nativizes the plural *Farysys* to **Fariseow* but leaves the ending of *scribys* as it was. In the Kernowek Kemyn New Testament 'scribes and Pharisees' appear regularly as **skribys ha **Fariseow***, one nativized and the other not. There is no warrant at all for the plural **Fariseow*, rather than the more authentic *Farysys* or *Faryses*. But to leave *skribys* with a plural in -*ys* seems curiously inconsistent.

2.10 Inconsistency in the word for 'Greek'. In *An Testament Nowydh* there is hesitation in the way 'Greek (person)' is translated into Kernowek Kemyn. On occasion one finds *Grek: an venyn o* **Grek** 'the woman was a Greek' Mark 7:26; *dhe'n Yedhow yn kynsa keffrys ha dhe'n* **Grek** 'to the Jew first and also to the Greek' Rom. 1:16, *an Yedhow yn kynsa ha'n* **Grek** *ynwedh* 'the Jew first and also the Greek' Rom. 2:9, 2:10, *ynter an Yedhow ha'n* **Grek** 'between the Jew and the Greek' Rom. 10:12, *hag ev* **Grek** 'although he was a Greek' Gal. 2:3, *Yedhow na* **Grek** 'neither Jew nor Greek' Gal. 2:28. On other occasions, however, one reads *Greka: mes y das o* **Greka** 'but his father was a Greek' Acts 16:2, *bos y das* **Greka** 'that his father was a Greek' Acts 16:4; *omma nyns eus* **Greka** *na Yedhow* 'here there is neither Greek nor Jew' Col. 3:10.

2.11 Further inconsistencies in spelling. We have seen above that several proper names are spelt in different ways at different places in the text. The same is true of common nouns as well. Notice, example, the following: **Diswryans** 'Destruction' at Mark 13:1 (heading) Luke 21:5 (heading) and 21:20 (heading), but **Diswrians** at Matt. 24:1 (heading) and *diswrians* Matt. 7:13, Phil. 1:28, 3:19, etc.

The two items *yagh(h)e* and *yagh(h)eans* vary in spelling, as though correct orthography had not yet been finally determined. I have noticed the following: **yaghe** 'heal' Matt. 9:32, but **yaghhe** Luke 13:10, 14:1,

18:35, John 4:43, 9:1; and *yagheans* 'healing' Matt. 9:1, but *yaghheans* Matt. 8:5, 8:14, 8:28, 9:27, 14:34, 15:29, 17:14, 20:29, Mark 1:29, 2:1, 5:1, 6:53, 7:31, 8:22, 9:14, 11:11, Luke 4:38, 5:17, 7:1, 8:26, 9:37, John 5:1, Acts 9:32.

There are a number of borrowings in the text whose English equivalents end in *-ity* (Frech *-ité* < Latin *-itat(em)*). In the present work the suffix in some of these is *-ita*, in others it is *-yta*:

abstract nouns ending in -ITA
awtorita 'authority' Matt. 8:9, 21:23, 21:24, 21:27, Mark 1:22, 1:27, 11:28,
    11:29, 11:33, Luke 4:32, 4:36, 7:8, 9:1.

abstract nouns ending in -YTA
dijastyta 'unchastity' Matt. 5:32, 19:9
restoryta 'restoration' Luke 4:18, Gal. 6:1.

It is difficult to see why the suffix has different spellings, when from the point of view of etymology and pronunciation it is the same element in all cases.

Also remarkable is the inconsistency in spelling between *pynakyl* 'pinnacle' Matt. 4:5, Luke 4:9 and *tabernakel* 'tabernacle' Heb. 8:2, 13:10. Perplexing also are two neologisms we encounter in *An Testament Nowydh*: *oferyasel* 'priestly' Heb.7:1 (heading) but *arghoferyasek* 'high-priestly' Acts 4:6.

Kernowek Kemyn is often canvassed as an easy system to master. I find, however, that it contains distinctions that are simply baffling.

LEXICAL PURISM
3.00 One of the most notable features of Kernowek Kemyn is its dislike of words that appear similar to English. In order to avoid such items, Kernowek Kemyn favours either words that are attested only in Old Cornish, but which disappear from Cornish thereafter, or to borrow words *holus bolus* from Welsh and Breton. This use of obsolete or borrowed words in order to avoid English borrowings renders much Kernowek Kemyn even less authentic than it is already. Regrettably *An Testament Nowydh* has provided great scope for lexical purism. Although this purism, as we shall see, is not infrequently itself inconsistent.

3.01 *Urdh* 'order'. In the Epistle to the Hebrews there are five examples of the expression 'the order of Melchizedek' (Heb. 5:6, 5:10, 6:20, 7:11,

7:17) translating the Greek κατὰ τὴν τάξιν Μελχισεδεκ. Melchizedek, referred to in Hebrews was a priest of the Lord, mentioned in the book of Genesis. His importance to the author of Hebrews was that he did not belong to the Aaronic order of priests. In all cases in the present work 'according to the order of Melchizedek' is rendered into Kernowek Kemyn as *herwydh *urdh Melkisedek*. ***Urdh** (UC *urth*) is an invention of Nance's being attested nowhere in traditional Cornish. Indeed Nance himself admits in his 1938 dictionary that the word is borrowed from Welsh and Breton, being replaced in traditional Cornish by *ordys* (< **ordrys*) 'orders'. Since Nance's dictionary appeared, however, Tregear's homilies have come to light and it is quite apparent from them that the correct term in Cornish for 'order' in the religious or ecclesiastical sense is *ordyr*:

> *ow leverall thynny an* **ordyr** *a rug Du appoyntya the vos gwethis in y egglos* 'telling us of the order which God appointed to be maintained in his church' TH 33a
>
> *An power han auctorite na, kepar dell veva fuguris in la goyth thyn* **ordyr** *a prontereth* 'That power and authority, as it was granted in the Old Law to the order of priests' TH 38a
>
> *[An] rena ew oll an* **ordyr** *a prontereth thea tyrmyn an appostlis* '[Those] are all the order of priests since the time of the apostles' TH 38a
>
> *ow tochya an primacie, bo an vhell* **ordyr** *a sans egglos* 'concerning the primacy or the supreme order of Holy Church' TH 46
>
> *war an succession an epscobow a rome, neb a rug dos ha folya pedyr in* **ordyr** *Evyn thea y dyrmyn* 'upon the succession of the bishops of Rome who happened to follow St Peter even from his own day' TH 48a-49.

When the author of the Epistle to the Hebrews uses the term κατὰ τὴν τάξιν Μελχισεδεκ he is speaking about an order of priests. This in traditional Cornish is rendered as **ordyr** *prontereth*. The term **urdh* used in the present work is unnecessary and inauthentic.

3.02 *Loeth* **'tribe'.** Although the expression *eghenn Benyamin* 'the tribe of Benjamin' is used at Rom. 11:1, the phrase *a* **loeth** *Benyamin* 'of the tribe of Benjamin' occurs at Phil. 3:5. *Loeth* is also used everywhere else for 'tribe', e.g., Luke 2:36, Acts 13:21, Heb. 7:13 and most notably in the list of the twelve tribes of Israel at Rev. 7:5-8. The word *loeth* is the respelling in Kernowek Kemyn of the word which is attested as *luid* 'procinctus [battle array]' and as *luit* in the phrase *hebrenciat luit* 'dux [miliary leader]' (literally 'leader of a battle array') in the *Old Cornish*

Vocabulary. Since *luid, luit* means 'battle array', it is difficult to see why in the present work it has been pressed into service as 'tribe'. The answer must lie in Nance's English-Cornish dictionary of 1952 which gives *lyth* s.v. 'tribe'. The word *luid* or *lyth* does not appear to have survived into Middle Cornish, and in Old Cornish it meant 'battle array, host, army'. In traditional Cornish the word used is *tryb*:

*Ken rug oll an x **tryb** a Israell departia a theworth Roboam mab Salamon* 'Although all the ten tribes of Israel departed from Rehoboam the son of Solomon' TH 50a.

There is no reason for using *loeth* to refer to the tribes of Israel.

3.03 **Trodreghi* **'circumcise'**, **trodreghyans* **'circumcision'**. In the present work the word **trodreghi* has been used for 'to circumcise', e.g. at Luke 1:59, John 7:22, Acts 7:8, 15:5, 21:21, 1 Cor. 7:18, Gal. 5:2, 6:12, 6:13 and **trodreghyans* for 'circumcision', e.g. at John 7:22, 7:23, Acts 11:2, Rom. 2:25, 2:26, 2:27, 2:28, 2:29, 3:1, 4:10, 4:11, 4:12, 1 Cor. 7:18, 7:19, Gal. 2:7, 2:8, 2:12, 5:3, 5:6, 5:11, 6:15. These words appear to be a recent invention. The Breton for 'circumcise' is *amdroc'han* and the Welsh is *enwaedu*. It was on the basis of the Welsh form that Nance suggested **enwosa* 'circumcise' in his 1952 English-Cornish dictionary.

The verb 'circumcise' is attested once in traditional Cornish:

*Rag ny gone ny kylmys the vos **circumcisis**, na the offra in ban the ley, oghan, devas, ha gyffras* 'For we are not compelled to be circumcised, nor to offer up to God calves, oxen, sheep and goats' TH 27a.

It would seem, at first glance, that the *circumcisia* was such an obvious borrowing from English, that it was rejected for the present work, and the recent coinage **trodreghi* was used in its place. Yet from the Epistle to the Ephesians onwards, the present translation seems to reverse that policy, since both *circumcisia* and a noun derived from it, **circumcisians* 'circumcision' are used:

*perthewgh kov agas bos Jentily kyns y'n kig, 'an re heb **sirkumsisyans'** Eph. 2:11*

*Rag yth on ni an **sirkumsisyans** gwir* Phil. 3:3

*Ynno ev ynwedh y fewgh **sirkumsisys** gans **sirkumsisyans** na veu gwrys dre dhorn, ow ti'ska korf an kig yn **sirkumsisyans** Krist* Col. 2:11

*Ha hwi neb a veu marow yn kammweythresow ha heb **sirkumsisyans** agas kig* Col. 2:13

ha Yesus, henwys Yustus, tus an **sirkumsisyans** Col. 4:11

Rag yma lies den heb rewl a gews yn euver hag in hwowek, dres oll an re a'n **sirkumsisyans** Titus 1:10.

There is no reason for the different translations in the two parts of *An Testament Nowydh*. The Greek verb and noun are the same throughout, περιτέμνω 'circumcise' and περιτομή 'circumcision'. The half-hearted reluctance to used *circumcisia* in this translation is quite baffling. Invented words for 'circumcise' and 'circumcision' are used—even though *circumcisia* exists in traditional Cornish and is itself employed in part at least of this translation. In which case the use of the invented forms **trodreghi*, **trodreghyans* are both inauthentic and unnecessary.

3.04 *Froeth* **'fruit'.** The Greek for 'fruit' is the masculine noun καρπός, which is translated throughout the Gospels in the present work as *frut*, plural *frutys*. In the Epistles, however, the matter is not so simple, since καρπός is translated by two differing words: A) *frut* and B) *froeth*:

A **frut**

Piw a blans gwinlann heb dybri rann a'y **frut** 1 Cor. 9:7

rag yma **frut** *an golow yn oll dader* Eph. 5:9

Mes bywa y'n kig, hemm yw **frutys** *a'm ober* Phil. 1:22

mes my a hwila an **frut** *owth ynkressya dh'agas reken* Phil. 4:17

hag yn oll an bys hi a dheg **frut** *ha tevi* Col. 1:6

ow toen **frut** *yn pub ober da* Col. 1:10.

B **froeth**

Mes pana **froeth** *a'gas bo* Rom. 6:21

rag may tykkyn **froeth** *rag Dyw* Rom. 7:4

mes ni agan honan, a'gan beus kynsa **froeth** *an Sprys* Rom 8:23

Mes **froeth** *a'n Spyrys yw kerensa* Gal. 5:22

wo'tiwedh y teg **froeth** *kres a wiryonedh* Heb. 12:11

henn yw **froeth** *diwweus a wormel y hanow* 13:15.

The word *froeth* is the respelling in Kernowek Kemyn of *fruit* 'fructus [fruit]' in the Old Cornish Vocabulary. It is nowhere attested in Middle Cornish, which always uses *frut*. Here are a very few examples:

ha war an pren **frut** *degis* PA 153c

may teth **frut** *may fen kellys* PA 153d

War bup **frut** *losow ha has* OM 77

saw a'n **frut** *ny fyth kymmyas* OM 79

frut a'n wethen a skyans OM 167
a bup kynde a frutys, beautyfull tege ha wheg TH 2
an frutys an spuris sans TH 9.

The last example translates 'fruits of the Spirit' Gal. 5:22, rendered *froeth a'n Spyrys* in Kernowek Kemyn. In the present work *frut* is much commoner than *froeth* and it would seem that there was no real objection to *frut*, for all that it was obviously borrowed from English. One can legitimately ask, then, why was *froeth* used at all?

3.05 *Henavogyon* 'elders'. The term **henavogyon* 'elders' is used at Acts 4:5, 4:8, 4:23 and 6:12. **Henavak* 'senior, ancient', plural **henavogyon* is a ghost-word, invented by Nance on the basis of Nicholas Boson's *empack* and by comparison with Welsh *hynafol* 'ancient'. I have suggested elsewhere that the phrase *an empack Angwin* in *Nebbaz Gerriau* is a misreading for *an empirick Angwin* 'Angwin the Empirick', and that Dick Angwin was probably, *inter alia*, a herbalist and healer (an 'empirick' in the language of the time). The attested terms in Cornish for 'elders, seniors' are *tus hen* BM 2929 and *eleders* TH 32. There is no justification for the use of **henavogyon*.

3.06 Further purisms. Among further purisms might cite **oferyas* 'priest' (e.g. Heb. 7:5, 7:11, 7:14, 7:16, 7:17, 7:20, 8:3, 8:4) and its derivatives **arghoferyas* 'high priest' (e.g. Matt. 6:3, 26:51, 26:57, 26:58, 26:65, Luke 3:2, Heb. 5:1, 7:26, 7:27, 7:28, 8:1) and **pennoferyas* 'chief priest' (e.g. Matt. 6:3, 26:59). Elsewhere, however, the word used for 'priest' is *pronter* (e.g. Matt 8:4, Luke 1:5, 2:8, 5:14, Mark 1:44). There are also two words used for 'priesthood' in the work A. *prontereth* (e.g Luke 1:9, 1 Pet. 2:5, 2:9) and B. **oferyaseth* (e.g. Heb. 7:11, 7:12, 7:23). **Oferyas* is a Middle Cornish respelling of *oferiat* 'presbiter [priest]' in the *Old Cornish Vocabulary*. It may be that those behind the present work believed that the Middle Cornish word *pronter* was insufficiently Celtic in appearance. In fact *pronter* is the Cornish development of Latin *presbyter*, via an insular Celtic stage **premiter* (cf. Old Irish *cruimther* 'priest'), and is thus etymologically identical with the Latin gloss given for the OC word *oferiat*. *Oferiat* occurs once only in Old Cornish and nowhere else, whereas *pronter* is common in Middle and Late Cornish:

pronter boys me a garse 'I should like to be a priest' BM 524
vn pronter ov cuthel guyth 'a priest doing works' BM 785
pronter ef a hevel suyr 'he certainly seems to be a priest' BM 1903

henwys oys **pronter** *grassijs* 'you are called a gracious priest' BM 2550

han **prounter** *heb deweth a rug offra* 'and the eternal priest who offered' TH 11

thyn minister neb ew an **pronter** *a thu* 'to the minister who is the priest of God' TH 42a

rag y bos an **prounter** *a thu* 'because he is the priest of God' TH 48a

nena ne ra an **pronter** *vsya girreow e honyn* 'then the priest does not use his own words' SA 62

inter dowla an **pronter** 'into the hands of the priest' SA 66

An **prounter** *ez en plew East* 'the parson who is in the parish of St Just' JTonkin

Drake **Proanter** *East the Toby Trethell* 'Drake parson of St Just to Toby Trethell' Pryce

E a roz towl dho **proanter** *Powle* 'he gave a fall to the parson of Paul' WGwavas.

Notice also that Tregear uses the expression *vhell pronter, uhell prownter* to mean 'high priest' TH 11, 48a and the author of *Sacrament an Alter* uses the phrase *pensevik pronter* with the same sense at SA 66. *Prontereth* 'priesthood' is attested twice at TH 38a. There is no need to use the poorly attested Old Cornish word *oferyas* instead of the more frequently occurring *pronter*—and indeed, some parts of *An Testament Nowydh* use *pronter* rather than *oferyas*. There seems to have been no consistent policy on this matter in the translation.

At Rom. 1:25 we read *ha servya an* **kroadur** *yn le an Kreador* 'and served the creature rather than the Creator'. *Kroadur* is the Kernowek Kemyn respelling of *croadur* 'creatura [creature]' in the *Old Cornish Vocabulary*. In Revelation, however, the word for creature is **kreatur**, e.g at Rev. 4:7, 4:8, 4:9, 5:8, 5:11, 5:13, 5:14. 6:1, 6:3, 6:5, 6:6. 6:7, 7:11 and 15:7. The Middle Cornish equivalent of *kreatur* 'creature' is well attested:

> *haccra mernans byth ordnys 3e* **creatur** *ny vye* PA 151b
> *a ugh oll* **creaturs** *erell* TH 2
> *fatell ve oll an* **creaturs** *gwrys da ha perfect* TH 2a
> *generall in oll* **creaturs** *consernya agan creacion* TH 3
> *te* **creature** *unkinda* CW 155.

It is difficult to see why *kroadur* was used at all.

The word *golusek* is used for 'rich', e.g. at Matt 19:16 (heading), 19:23, 19:24, Mark 10:17 (heading), Luke 18:18 (heading), 18:25, 1 Cor. 4:8, 2 Cor. 8:9, Ephes. 2:4, Rev. 13:16 and 18:19. *Golusek* is a Kernowek Kemyn respelling of Nance's *golusak*, itself based on *wuludoc* 'diues

[rich]' in the *Old Cornish Vocabulary*. It did not survive into Middle Cornish, probably because it would have been acoustically so close to *gallosek* 'powerful'. Elsewhere in the present translation the word used for 'rich' is *rych*, e.g. at 1 Tim. 6:9, 6:17, James 1:10, 1:11, 5:1, Rev. 2:9, 3:18, 6:15, 18:14, 18:15. *Rych* is the only word for 'rich' in Middle Cornish and here is a selection of examples:

> *y box **ryche** leun a yly* PA 35a
> *han purpur **ryche** a vsye* PA 161a
> *sendall **rych** yn luas pleg* PA 232c
> *yn erna **rych** ef a vyth* PA 259c
> *gans dylles **rych** del deguth* OM 1925
> *cytes **rych** trevow a brys* PC 132
> *yn purpyr **rych** ru'm laute* PC 2123
> *nyn guel an **rych** galosek* BM 441
> ***rych** lour o in pup termen* BM 447
> *selwel **rych** ha bohosek* BM 876
> *kefrys **rych** ha bohosek* BM 2183
> *the **ryche** ha bohosogyon* BM 2552
> *yma **rych** ha bohosek* BM 2695
> *tus ientyll, **rych** ha behosek* TH 6a
> *Impossybyll the then **rych** entra in gwlascur neff* TH 53
> *Arthor **rych** a ryowta* BK 1555
> ***rych** os ha fuer* BK 1697.

The use of the two words here leads on occasion to curious results. At James 5:1 the writer addresses the rich with the words *a dus **rych*** 'O you rich', but the heading before the verse is *Gwarnyans dhe'n **Wolusogyon*** 'Warning to the Rich'. Given that *golusek* is so poorly attested and *rych* so well, it is difficult to see why this translation did not dispense with *golusek* entirely.

3.07 Invented words in *An Testament Nowydh*. Among words not attested in traditional Cornish, but which occur in the present work we might include ***denel*** 'human', ***eskarogeth*** 'hostility', ***hevelder*** 'likeness', ***kigek*** 'fleshy', ***mebyoneth*** 'sonship', ***negedhses*** 'apostasy', ***pervedhel*** 'internal'. Let us look at these in turn.

> ***denel*** 'human' occurs in the expression *agan gnas **dhenel** aves* 'outer human nature' (RSV), 'physical being' (TEV) 2 Cor. 4:16. There is no adjective in the Greek which says ὁ ἔξω ἡμῶν ἄνθρωπος 'the

outside man of us'. I preferred to use *mortal*; cf. *mortall bewnans* TH 26. ***Denel*** is unnecessary.

eskarogeth 'hostility' in the expression *Yndella an an brys [neb] a wra fors a'n kig, yw *eskarogeth erbynn Dyw* 'Thus the mind which concerned with the flesh is hostility to God' Rom. 8:7. The Greek says: διότι τὸ φρόνημα τῆς σαρκὸς ἔχθρα εἰς Θεόν 'for the thinking of the flesh is hostility towards God'. I translated: *Rag henna escar dhe Dhew yw an brys yw rewlys der an kyg.* ***Eskarogeth*** is unnecessary.

hevelder 'likeness' Rom. 8:3. The word ***hevelder*** is unattested, although *havalder* 'likeness' occurs twice in the versions of the Ten Commandments printed by Pryce. The usual words for 'likeness' in traditional Cornish are *ymach, semlant* and *hevelep*. Here *hevelep* is quite clearly the right word; cf. the following examples from the texts:

ty *re thyswrug eredy* **hevelep** *tho'm face vy vrry nep o marrek len* 'thou hast destroyed indeed the likeness of my face Uriah who was a loyal knight' OM 2336-38

in **hevelep** *leskis glan ny a vethe pur dyson* 'in likeness we would have been burnt very quickly' BM 2150-51

Gesow ny the wull den the gan similitud ha **hevelep** *ny* 'Let us make man in our our similitude and likeness' TH 1a

Eff agan grege ny in dede in **hevelep** *thy ymag eff y honyn* 'He indeed made us in the likeness of his own image' TH 1a

apperia the Abraham in **hevelep** *the dus* 'appear to Abraham in the likeness of people' TH 55

fatell ylly du po ell apperia in **hevelep** *a den* 'how could God or angel appear in the likeness of a man?' TH 55

rag hem(ma) ew in **hevelep** *a bara* 'for this is in the likeness of bread' SA 66a.

Hevelder is unnecessary.

kigek 'bodily, physical' Rom. 15:27. This word is not the translator's own invention, for it is already in Nance's 1938 dictionary. But it is being given a new sense here, where it translates Greek σαρκικός 'fleshly, bodily'. The related Breton word *kigek* means 'fleshy, fat' as does the Welsh *cigaidd*. Similarly Nance in his 1938 dictionary gives ***kigek*** the sense 'fleshy'. ***Kigek*** naturally, therefore, suggests 'meaty, fleshy, fat'. It does not mean what the translator wants it to mean, i.e. 'of the flesh, of the body, physical'. In my own translation I said *yn* *taclow ow tuchya an kyg* 'in matters concerning the flesh'. **Kigek* is the wrong word.

*mebyoneth 'sonship', which occurs in *mes y kemmersowgh spryrys *mebyoneth dredho may kriyn 'Abba! Tas!'* 'but you received a spirit of sonship, by which we cry "Abba! Father!"' Rom. 8:15. The Greek says: ἀλλὰ ἐλάβετε πνεῦμα υἱοθεσίας ἐν ᾧ κράζομεν, Αββα ὁ Πατήρ 'but you received the spirit of adoption as sons, in which we cry "Abba, the Father"'. I preferred to translate *sperys kepar ha mebyon*. **Mebyoneth* is unnecessary.

*negedhses 'apostasy' is used in the heading *Gwarnyans rag Negedhses* at Heb. 5:11. The heading is clearly based on 'Warning against Abandoning the Faith' at this place in TEV. **Negedhses* is based on Nance's *negeth* 'refuser, denier' in his 1938 dictionary. The word *denaha* is attested in the traditional language (e.g. *denagh the fay* 'deny your faith' BM 3511). In the form *denagha* it occurs in dictionaries of Kernowek Kemyn. It is difficult to see, therefore, why and expression like *Gwarnyans adro dhe Dhenagha an Fydh* was not used for the heading at Heb. 5:11. Or possibly the heading might have read: *Gwarnyans adro dhe Forsakya an Fydh*. **Negedhses* is unnecessary.

*pervedhel 'internal' in the expression *agan gnas dhenel *pervedhel* 'our inner human nature' 2 Cor. 4:16. There is no such adjective in the Greek which says simply ὁ ἔξω ἡμῶν ἄνθρωπος 'the inside human being of us'. I translated *agan natur war jy*. **Pervedhel* is unnecessary.

*reydhel 'loose, debauched' in the expression *heb bos yn drogfara *reydhel na drokhwansow dyrewel* 'not being in debauchery and licentiousness' Rom. 13:13. The Greek says μὴ κοίταις καὶ ἀσελγείαις 'not in sleeping around and licentiousness'. There are several ways in traditional Cornish for saying 'immoral' and 'impure', e.g. *plos* 'dirty', *lewd* 'wicked', and for 'debauchery' one can say *fowt chastyta* 'lack of chastity', *fowt honester* 'lack of modesty', etc. **Reydhel* is unnecessary.

UNGRAMMATICAL LANGUAGE IN *AN TESTAMENT NOWYDH*

4.00 There are very many features of *An Testament Nowydh* that are mistaken from the point of view of grammar. I have space here to deal only with a handful.

*Yn hwir **'truly'.** The adverbial phrase **yn hwir* 'truly, indeed' is very common throughout the present work. It occurs, for example, at Matt. 5:18, 5:26, 6:2, 6:5, 6:16, 8:10, *etc.*, Mark 3:28, 8:12, 9:1, 9:41, 10:15, 10:29, *etc.*, Luke 4:24, 9:27, 12:37, 18:17, 18:29, *etc.*, John 1:51, 3:3, 3:5, 3:11, 5:19, *etc.*, Acts 4:27, 10:34, Rom. 2:2, 1 Cor. 11:31.

The form *yn hwir (UC *yn whyr) is unattested anywhere in Cornish. The common phrase is always yn gwyr and is not an adverb made with the particle yn (cf. yn ta 'well'), but a prepositional phrase 'in truth'. Here are some examples from the texts:

> Onan ha try on **yn gvyr** OM 3
> daggrow gois **in gvyr** hep mar OM 631
> mar kefyth **yn gvyr** hep gow OM 1138
> lauar **en guyr** thy'm certan OM 2234
> dew vody tha ough **yn guyr** OM 2461
> a gevelyn da **yn guyr** OM 2540
> tres aral re got **in guyr** OM 2549
> **yn guyr** sawys PC 296
> ty a fyth **yn guyr** hep gow PC 600
> ov hanov **in guir** heb mar BM 1155
> me a wor **in guir** heb mar BM 4266
> **In gweyr** heb mar BK 757
> gans Arthor **in gwyr** heb mar BK 1456
> es adam **in gwyre** ynta CW 473.

It can be seen that there is no hint of mutation of gwyr in any of them. Kernowek Kemyn *yn hwir is without justification.

4.01 *Traow 'things'. Not infrequently in An Testament Nowydh we find that the plural of tra 'thing' is *traow 'things', e.g. at Rom. 1:20, 2:1, 2:2, 2:3, 4:17, 8:5, 14:19. This plural is not found anywhere in Cornish written by native Cornishmen. It occurs twice in Lhuyd's preface:

> ny vendzha e besgueth hanual an **Trào** kreiez en Ladin, Quercus, rhamnus, melis, lepus, hœdus AB: 223
> pôrletryz ha pôrskientek en **traou** erel AB: 224.

There is no other example. In native Cornish the plural of tra 'thing' is either taclow or tacklennow and it refers both to concrete objects and to abstract ideas. Here are a few examples:

> yntrethon **taclow** pryve OM 936
> the wruthyl vn pols byhan **takclow** pryve PC 92
> gwelys gans an bobyll in tyrmyn na **tacklennow** invisibly TH 14
> certan **taclennow** the vos colynwys TH 16
> pan dra ew an keth **taclennow** na TH 16
> the wetha **taclenow** wo vsyys in la moyses TH 27a

ha **tacclennow** *erall kepar* TH (*note p.* 55)
kepar ha commondementys ha **taclenow** *forbyddys* TH 50a
certyn **tacclow** *arall* SA 60
Gear Christ ill changia **takclennow** *the nappith* SA 61a
Mar crug an geir an tas an nef gonis in **taglenno** *erall* SA 63
an keth **tacklowe** *es omma* CW 2446
rag debre an **tacklow** *ewe per trink* JTonkin
an **Tacklow** *gwayah ez toane bownnaz* JKeigwin
dry raag an **tacklow** *beawe* JKeigwin
ha a **Tacklow** *Cramyhaz* JKeigwin
taklawe *da ve grweze* TBoson
gwrenz ar dour dri meas meer an **taklou** *ez guayans gen bounas* JBoson
dri meas an **taklou** *ez dothan bonnaz* JBoson
chattoll ha **taklou** *ens kramia* JBoson
Der **taklow** *minniz ew brez teez gonvethes* Pryce
dreffen en **taklow** *broaz, ma angy mennow hetha go honnen* Pryce
bus en **taklow** *minnis* Pryce
Gwrâ, O Materne, a **taclow** *ma* Pryce
ha an **tacklow** *a vedn gwaynia klôs theez* Pryce.

Taclow is also attested in the present work. Notice, for example, *traow* Acts 17:20 but *taklow* Acts 17:23. Since *traow* is a solecism, its use cannot be defended.

4.02 Huni as a noun. The word *huny* in traditional Cornish is found in three expressions only, A) *pub huny* 'everybody'; B) *kettep huny* 'each one' and C) *lyes huny* 'many a one, many people'. Here are the instances of all three expressions:

A
ynno a gyk **pup huny** OM 946
aban vynnyth **pup huny** *lathe ol an nor vys-ma* OM 970
orth y sywe **pup huny** OM 1688
my a's gueres **pup huny** OM 2017
mar ny fystyn **pup huny** OM 2323
dev a mercy the **pup huny** PC 237
dreys **pup huny** *pur wyr os gy* PC 417
yn ayr deth brus **pup huny** PC 1669
degovgh genough **pup huny** PC 2047
ha why losels **pup huny** PC 2589
gentyl yv the **pup huny** RD 1800
ha'y vennath theugh **pup huny** RD 2638
bras ha byan **pub huny** BK 267

*Hayl, arluth heel drys **pub huny**!* BK 1700-01.
*ha'th soccors oll, **pub huny*** BK 2529
*thu'm arluth drys **pub huny**!* BK 2669
*adam sure dres **pub hwny*** BK 684
*vnna a gyke **pub huny*** CW 2247.

B

*ras warnough in **katap huny**!* BK 2571-72.

C

*yn della yw **leas huny*** PA 62d
*ha ʒe rag **leas huny*** PA 240a
*tollys yv **lues huny*** BM 444
*del glowas **lues huny*** BM 1160
*socour the **lues huny*** BM 3024
*dadder the **lues huny*** BM 4514.

The instances listed above are the only examples known to me of **huny** in traditional Cornish. Several points are to be noticed. No example of *huny* is found in any text later than CW and it is also absent from TH and SA. More importantly *huny* is always used preceded by *pup*, *kettep* and *lyes*. Unlike *hini*, the related word in Breton, *huny* may not be used as the singular of *re* 'ones, people' to mean 'one'. This fundamental rule about *huny* has been ignored in the present work, since *huny* (spelt **huni* here) has been used incorrectly throughout. Here are some examples:

> *Mes hwi a naghas an *Huni Sans* 'But you denied the Holy One' Acts 3:14
> *rag may fyn ni keskrevhes dre fydh y gila, keffrys gans agas *huni hag ow *huni* 'that we may be mutually encouraged by each other's faith, yours and mine' Rom. 1:12
> *Lemmyn dhe'n *huni a ober ny synsir y wober avel ro mes y'n telir dhodho. Ha dhe'n *huni n ober mes a grys dhe neb a gyv an ongrassyes ewn, y synsir y fydh avel gwiryonedh* 'Now to one who works, his wages are not reckoned as a gift but as his due. And to him who does not work but trusts to him who justifies the ungodly, his faith is reckoned as righteousness' Rom. 4:4-5
> *Synsys vydh dhyn hag a grys y'n *huni a dhrehevis a ankow Yesu agan Arloedh* 'It will be reckoned to us who believe in him that raised from the dead Jesus our Lord' Rom. 4:24
> *neb yw skwir an *huni ow tos* 'who is a type of the one who was to come' Rom. 5:14

*dhe'n *huni re beu dassevys a vernans rag may tykkyn froeth rag Dyw* 'to him
who has been raised from the dead in order that we may bear fruit
for God' Rom. 7:4

*Rag an re a ragaswonni, ev a ragdewli dhe vos gwrys an keth furv ha hevelepter
ha *huni y Vab* 'For those whom he foreknew he also predestined to
be conformed to the image of his Son' Rom. 8:29

*An eyl a grys bos da dybri puptra mes an *huni gwann a dheber losow hepken;
na skornyes an *huni a dheber an *huni na dheber, ha na vreuses an *huni
na dheber an *huni a dheber* 'One believes he may eat anything, while
the weak man eats only vegetables. Let not him who eats despise him
who abstains, and let not him who abstains pass judgment on him
who eats' Rom. 14:2

*mes y'n kontrari part hag i ow konvedhes bos an aweyl a antrodreghyans
kemmynnys dhymm kepar dell veu an *huni a drodreghyans dhe Peder* 'but
on the contrary, when they saw that I had been entrusted with the
gospel to the uncircumcised, just as Peter had been entrusted with
the gospel to the circumcised' Gal. 2:7,

*mes dhe by *huni a'n eledh y leveris bythkweth* 'but to which one of the
angels did he ever say' Heb. 1:13.

The only thing that one can say about the above quotations from *An
Testament Nowydh* is that—spelling apart—they are inadmissible as
Cornish.

4.03 *Avonyow a Dowr Byw.* The heading at John 7:38 reads *Avonyow a
Dowr Byw, which I take to be based on the corresponding heading in
the TEV which reads 'Streams of Life-Giving Water'. The word *Dowr*
without initial mutation is a misprint for *Dhowr.* With the omission of
mutation compare the heading *An Abesteli a Yaghha Meur a *Tus* (for
Dus) at Acts 5:12.

Interestingly, *Avonyow a Dhowr Byw* itself is open to question, since
the word **avon* 'river' is nowhere attested in Cornish. The word was
awon or *awan:* *auon* 'flumen l. fluuius [river or stream]' in the *Old
Cornish Vocabulary,* *torneuan an auan* 'A bank of a river' AB: 141a and
Awen-Tregare 'Tregear Water' (Padel). We thus have no way of knowing
the plural of the word. **Avonyow* (cf. *avonyow* Rev. 16:4), better
*Awonyow, is pure guesswork.

The expression 'rivers of water' is attested in traditional Cornish:
ryvars a thowre a ra resek in mes anetha y 'rivers of water will flow from
them' TH 53.

4.04 "Shaking the Creator". Perhaps the most startling error in *An Testament Nowydh* occurs at Acts 28:5. The chapter tells of St Paul's stay on the island of Malta. While piling firewood on a fire he disturbed a snake, which attached itself to his hand. The Greek text continues: ὁ μὲν οὖν ἀποτινάξας τὸ θηρίον εἰς τὸ πῦρ ἔπαθεν οὐδὲν κακόν 'But he having shaken the animal off into the fire suffered no harm'. The Kernowek Kemyn version has been based here on an English version, probably the RSV, which reads 'He, however, shook the creature off into the fire and suffered no harm'. This has been translated into Kernowek Kemyn as: *Ena eva a shakyas an **kreador** y'n tan heb godhav drog vydh.* The word to be used here was *kroadur* 'creature', the Kernowek Kemyn respelling of *croadur* 'creature' in the *Old Cornish Vocabulary*. Instead, presumably because the word looks similar to the English 'creature', the word *kreador* was accidentally substituted. *Kreador* is the Kernowek Kemyn respelling of another Old Cornish word, *creador* 'creator'. The verse here in Kernowek Kemyn can only mean: 'Then he shook the creator in the fire without suffering any harm.'

4.05 *Yth esons **for** *ymons.* The third persons plural of the long form of the verb *bos* 'to be' is given by Nance as either *usons* or *esons*. Kernowek Kemyn allows *esons* only (which form is attested in the Tregear manuscript in the form *esans*.) The forms *usons/esans* is used after a negative particle and in relative and other subordinate clauses. Here are the only examples of *usons/esans* that I can find in Middle Cornish:

A **negative**
whath ny gesans ow kull mas vn person 'still they make only one person' TH 15
ny gusans ow kull exposicion vith 'they do not make any exposition' TH 53.

B **relative (positive and negative)**
haga drog bewnans esans ow ledya 'and their evil lives which they lead' TH 6a
an pith vsans ow quelas gans aga lagasow kyge 'that which they see with their bodily eyes' TH 56a
an dra vsans ow kylwall ew an ober a thu 'that which they call is the work of God' TH 50a
dretha may thusans ow pewa 'through which they live' TH 24
An pith na gusans ow quelas 'that which they do not see' TH 56.

C other subordinate clauses

kynth usons ovth omwul creff 'though they pretend to be strong' BM 2366
Lemen pan vsons in crok 'Now that they are on the gallows' BM 1264
Lemmen pan vsons in beth 'Now that they are in the tomb' BM 1335
fatell ew kepar dell vsans y ow cowse 'that it is as they speak' TH 19a
ha fatell vsans pub vr ow hagrya 'and that they always agree' TH 34a.

If it introduces a main clause without a preceding negative particle, *usons* is replaced by *ymons, ymowns*. This is particularly common when the verb is a progressive one with long form of *bos* + *ow* + verbal noun.

ymons thy'mo ov crye 'they are calling to me' OM 1418
ymons y orth y sywe pup huny 'they are pursuing him, every one' OM 1687-88
ymons ov toys 'they are coming' OM 4476
ymowns ow kull inivri ha cam the crist 'they are being hostile to and are wronging Christ' TH 17a
y mowns ow try tane strayng then alter a thu 'they bring strange fire to the altar of God' TH 37
y mowns ow prevy clere 'they prove conclusively' TH 43a
y mowngy oll ow casa henna thynny kepar dell ewa cowsys 'they all leave that with us exactly as it is said' TH 53
y mowns ow desyvya aga honyn 'they deceive themselves' TH 57a
In della e mowns y [o] dishonora Christ 'Thus they dishonour Christ' SA 61
y mowns y ow murnya 'they are mourning' CW 1347
ow poyntya mowns pur efan 'very widely they point' CW 2158
than purpose na mowns ow toos 'for that purpose they are coming' CW 2161.

At Rom. 4:12 in the Kernowek Kemyn we read: *an re na na's teves trodreghyans hepken mes ynwedh *yth esons ow kerdhes yn olyow fydh agan tas ni Abram hag ev hwath heb trodreghyans* 'who are not merely circumcised but also follow the example of the faith which our father Abraham had before he was circumcised'. If the clause beginning *ynwedh *yth esons* is intended as relative, the particle *yth* is incorrect. If, as seems more likely, the clause is not thought of as relative, then it ought to begin *mes ynwedh ymons ow kerdhes*. It is remarkable that this elementary mistake of inflection was not spotted before *An Testament Nowydh* went to press.

4.06 *Pan *yw hi yn lavur* **for** *pan usi hi yn lavur.* At John 16:21 we read *Benyn pan *yw hi yn lavur a's teves tristyns* 'When a woman is in labour she is grieved'. There is a serious mistake here. When one is speaking about position (either physical or metaphorical) one uses the long form of *bos*: the short form **yw* is thus incorrect. The Kernowek Kemyn ought to have read: *Benyn, pan* **usi** *hi yn lavur a's teves tristyns.* It is remarkable that this syntactic error was not noticed.

4.07 Further inaccurate verbal syntax. At Gal. 2:2 the Kernowek Kemyn reads:

> *my a yskynnas awos diskwedhyans ha gorra a-dheragdha an aweyl a bregowthav yn mysk an Jentilys, yn priva dhe dus a vri, ma na vien ow poenya *po poenys war neb kor yn euver* 'I went up by revelation and I laid before them (but privately before those who were of repute) the gospel which I preach among the Gentiles, lest somehow I should be running or had run in vain' (RSV).

There is a serious syntactical problem in this verse. It is legitimate to say *ma na vien ow poenya yn euver* 'that I should not be running in vain'; but to add *po poenys* 'or I ran' without an introductory conjunction is inadmissible. There is no connection between the verb *poenys* 'I ran' with what has gone before and the phrase, therefore, makes little sense. The Kernowek Kemyn ought to have read: *ma na vien ow poenya yn euver po* **rag dout** *my dhe boenya yn euver kyns henna* or something similar. In my own version I wrote *may hallen bos certan nag esen ow ponya bo na wrug avy ponya yn ufer.*

4.08 Ungrammatical use of pronouns. At John 15:24 we read *i re welas ha kasa ha *my ha'm Tas* 'but now they have seen and hate both me and my Father'. The translation appears to be saying: *ha kasa... *my* 'and hate me', but *my* cannot be used as the logical object of a verbal noun. The translation should have read: *i re welas hag ymons y orth* **ow hasa vy** *hag* **ow kasa ow Thas.** The translation, as it stands, is ungrammatical.

At John 16:3 we read *ny aswonnsons naneyl an Tas na *my* 'they have recognized neither the Father nor me'. The translation seems to want to say: *ny aswonnsons... *my* 'they have not recognized me', but the personal pronoun *my* cannot be used as the object of a finite verb. The Kernowek Kemyn should have read: *naneyl ny aswonnsons an Tas na* **ny'm aswonnsons vy.** As it stands the translation is mistaken.

4.09 Further ungrammatical expressions. At Rom. 6:6 we read *Ni a woer y feu agan den koth krowsys ganso rag may fe an korf a begh distruys, ha rag ma na serffyn pegh na fella.* This has clearly been translated from the AV: 'Knowing this, that our old man is crucified with him, that the body of sin might be destroyed, that henceforth we should not serve sin.' There is a grammatical error in the last clause: *ha *rag ma na serffyn pegh na fella* 'that henceforth we should serve not sin.' When *rag na* 'in order that... not' introduces a final clause *ma* is not required, indeed it should not appear. The correct Cornish usage can be seen from the following examples:

> *tresters dretho ty a pyn adrus rag na vo degees* 'thou shalt fasten across it beams that it be not closed' OM 963-64
>
> *eff a dregh the ves esall a vo corruptys in corfe mabden rag na rella corruptia esylly glan erell a vo ow ionya nessa thotho* 'he cuts away a corrupt limb in the body of mankind so that it may not corrupt other clean limbs that may be close to it' TH 25a
>
> *Ha rag na rella den vith despisya an auctorite ay appostlis, yma crist ow leverell in xiii-as chapter a Jowan* 'And so that no one may despise the authority of his apostles, Christ says in the 18th chapter of John'. TH 41a
>
> *In vn dith, rag may hallans mos the crist warbarth. In vn tyller, rag na vo an naneil a nethy destitute* 'In one day that they might go to Christ together; in one place that neither of them might be destitute' TH 47
>
> *an bricke rag na vons leskys der dane* 'the brick so that they may not be burnt with fire' CW 2186-87
>
> *jystes dretha ty a place a leas rag na vo degys* 'thou shalt place beams across it so that it be not closed' CW 2268-69.

We meet the same mistake again at John 16:1, where the text reads: *My re leveris dhywgh an taklow ma, *rag ma na wryllowgh trebuchya* 'I have told you these things, that you may not stumble'. This ought to have read *My re leveris dhywgh an taklow ma, rag na wryllowgh trebuchya.*

At Rom. 4:15 the translation reads *Rag an lagha a wra konnar mes y'n le *ma nag eus lagha nyns eus drogobereth* 'For the law brings wrath, but where there is no law there is no transgression'. The syntax here is not correct, since *ma* 'where' is not used when *le* 'place' is present: *ef a vyth sur anclethys yn le na fue den bythqueth* 'he will surely be buried in a place where no man has ever been' PC 3134-35. The translator should have written *mes y'n le nag eus lagha.*

By incorrectly writing **y'n le ma na* the translator has created a further difficulty. By the sixteenth century the negative particle *ny(ns)* of main clauses was yielding to the particle *na(g)* of tag-answers and subordinate clauses. A native speaker of Cornish would probably understand the Kernowek Kemyn here to mean: 'For the law makes wrath, but in this place (*y'n le ma*) there is no law (*nag eus lagha*), there is no transgression (*nyns eus drogobereth*).'

THE TRANSLATION OF THE HEADINGS

5.00 Like many modern versions of the New Testament, the present translation breaks into short pericopes, each with its own heading. The division of the text and the headings seem to be based on three English versions: 1) the *New English Bible* (NEB) of 1961; 2) in the *New International Version* (NIV) of 1979; and 3) the *Today's English Version* or *Good News Bible* (TEV), first published in 1966. Although the wording of the headings in the present work derive from all three versions, most appear to have come from TEV.

Another feature of the present translation seems to have come from the TEV, where the headings in any one of the four gospels are followed by references in brackets to equivalent passages in the other gospels. Cross-references to elsewhere in the Bible are cited at the foot of the page in TEV, not only in the gospels, but throughout the whole Old and New Testaments. Only in the gospels in TEV, however, are cross-references printed after the heading of each pericope. *An Testament Nowydh* follows the TEV by giving cross-references to other gospels after headings in the four gospels. Unlike the TEV, however, it does not cite further cross-references to elsewhere in the Bible at the foot of the page. In the matter of pericopes, headings and cross-referencing the present work mostly follows TEV. Some headings, however, are from the NEB and the NIV.

Before examining in detail the work of the six translators, I should like take a little time to examine the way some of the headings taken from TEV, NIV and NEB have been translated. Since there are so many, I shall deal briefly with headings from St Matthew's Gospel and a very few from elsewhere.

5.01 *An Dewhelyans dhiworth Ejyp.* The heading at Matt. 2:19 is *An Dewhelyans dhiworth Ejyp* corresponding to 'The Return from Egypt' in the TEV. Cornish does not say **dheworth Ejyp*, but *mes a Ejyp* or *mes a bow Ejyp*, as is clear from the following:

ty a gam wruk yn tor-ma **mes a egip** *agan dry* 'thou didst wrongly by
  bringing us out of Egypt' OM 1646-47

Tho ve an Arleth da Deew reg da dry meaze **vez a pow Egypt** 'I am the Lord
  thy God who brought thee out of the land of Egypt' Rowe.

This idiom already occurs in this translation, because it has appeared in
the quotation from Hosea 11:1 at verse at Matt. 2:15 **Yn-mes a Ejyp** *my
re elwis ow mab*. It is curious, then, that the appropriate expression was
not used in this heading. A better translation would be: *Ow tewheles
tre mes a Ejyp.*

5.02 *Pregoth Yowann an Besydhyer.* The heading at Matt. 3:1 is *Pregoth
Yowann an Besydhyer* translating 'The Preaching of John the Baptist' in
the equivalent place in the TEV. This is the first time that we meet the
expression *Yowann an Besydhyer*, the universal title for the Baptist in the
present translation. It is a most unfortunate rendering for a number of
reasons. In the first place, as has already been mentioned, the Cornish
for 'John' is *Jowan*, not **Yowan*. This latter form originally existed in
Cornish but survived only in *Goluan* 'Midsummer'. Middle and Late
Cornish used *Jowan, Jooan* for 'John'; **Yowan* (Kernowek Kemyn
*Yowann) is a fiction.

The Welsh and Breton for 'John the Baptist' are *Ioan Fedyddiwr* and
Yann Vazedour respectively. In both expressions there is the lenition of
apposition, but there is no definite article. *Ioan Fedyddiwr* and *Yann
Vazedour* both literally mean 'John, Baptist'. The use of the definite
article in the Kernowek Kemyn expression is a calque on English and is
most unfortunate. The Cornish expression *Kesva an Tavas Kernowek*, for
example, means 'the Board of the Cornish Language' i.e. 'the Cornish
Language Board'. In exactly the same way **Yowann an Besydhyer* can
only mean 'Yowann of the Baptist'; it certainly does not mean 'John the
Baptist', which would naturally be rendered *Jowan Besydhyer* or
possibly *Jowan Vesydhyer* (cf. *Arthor Gornow* 'Arthur the Cornishman'
BK 1250, 1398). The term **besydhyer* is a modern coinage and is
unattested anywhere in Old, Middle or Late Cornish. The traditional
expression for 'John the Baptist' is well attested in the texts, however:

prest orth sen **iowen baptyst** BM 4450
S. **Johan baptist** *a ve benegas in breis y vam* TH 8
Rag in mar ver dell rug S **Johan baptist** *gyllwall an scribis han pharases in
  iii-a chapter a mathew* TH 29a
Ran **Jowan baptist**, *ran helyas* TH 43a.

The quotation from TH 29a above refers to this very passage. The Cornish for 'John the Baptist' is *Jowan Baptyst*. **Yowann an Besydhyer* is inauthentic and ought not to have been used.

5.03 *Temptyans Yesu.* At Matt. 4:1 (and again at Mark 1:12 and Luke 4:1) we read *Temptyans Yesu*, a translation of 'The Temptation of Jesus' in TEV. The word **temptyans* is also to be found in the body of the translation, e.g. at Matt. 6:13, 26:41, Mark 14:38, Luke 4:13, 8:13, 11:4, 22:40, 22:46 and 1 Cor. 10:13. At 1 Timothy 6:9, however, the word used is *temptashyon*, which also occurs in the heading at James 1:12, *Prevyans ha Temptashyon*. This latter term is well attested in traditional Cornish:

> *a wor the ves **temptacion** PC 25*
> *worth **temptacyon** a'n tebel PC 225*
> *yn **temptacyon** yn pup le PC 806*
> *na entreugh yn **temptacyon** PC 1059*
> *nag yllough yn **temptacion** PC 1077*
> *orth **temtacyon** dewolow BM 144*
> *omma the orth **temptasconn** BM 3858*
> *dre an provocacion han **temptacion** TH 3a*
> *avoydya y **temptacions** hay successions TH 3a*
> *der **temptacon** bras an iowle CW 1768*
> *der **temptacon** an teball CW 2133*
> *Ha na or ny in **temptation** Llyfr y Resolusion*
> *Ledia ny nara idn **tentation** Camden's Britannia (1695)*
> *Ha na lêdia nei idn **tentation** John Chamberlayne (1715).*

*Temptyans, is not attested anywhere in traditional Cornish. It ought not to have appeared in the present work.

5.04 *Dyskas a-dro dhe'n Lagha.* The heading *Dyskas a-dro dhe'n Lagha* (cf. 'Teaching about the Law' in the TEV) at Matt. 5:17. We also find the same phrase, *Dyskas a-dro dhe* 'Teaching about', followed by *Sorr* 'Anger' (Matt. 5:21), *Avoutri* 'Adultery' (Matt. 5:27), *Dhidhemmedhyans* 'Divorce' (Matt. 5:31), *Liow* 'Vows' (Matt. 5:33), *Dhial* 'Revenge' (Matt. 5:38), *Alusen* 'Alms' ['Charity' in TEV] (Matt. 6:1), *Bysadow* 'Prayer' (Matt. 6:5; Luke 11:1) and *Benys* 'Fasting' (Matt. 6:16).

I have long criticized the use of *yn kever* in revived Cornish to mean 'concerning, about'. The prepositional phrase means rather 'with respect to, in dealings with' and is only ever used in the traditional language when referring to people. When I was beginning work on my English-Cornish dictionary in a personal communication to Ray Edwards, one of the translators of the present work, I pointed out that the *yn kever* did not mean 'about' and was used only with a possessive adjective. It was also rather rare. In fact it occurs once in RD, twice in BM and once in 'Jowan Chy an Horth'—although a further example has now appeared in *Bewnans Ke*. Edwards used this information in his *Notennow Kernewek* where he gives all the attested examples and writes:

> **yn kever**: This is given in all the dictionaries and is in very common use in Revived Cornish to mean *about, concerning*. I was quite surprised therefore when Nicholas Williams pointed out to me, and I checked myself, that it occurs only four or five times in the texts, governing a personal pronoun [*leg.* a possessive adjective] (NK: 89-90).

I am pleased to see in the present work that *yn kever* is not used in the headings in the Gospels to translate English 'about, concerning', *a-dro dhe* being preferred. Regrettably, however, *yn kever* continues to appear elsewhere in *An Testament Nowydh*. The heading at 1 John 5:6 (a paraphrase of 'The Witness about Jesus Christ' in TEV) is *An Dustuni *yn kever an Mab* 'The Witness concerning the Son'. We also read **yn kever an Mab y lever* 'about the Son he says' Heb. 1:8, *wosa bos gwarnys gans Dyw *yn kever traow na veu gwelys hwath* 'being warned of God of things not seen as yet' Heb. 11:7, *Dre fydh Yakob, ow merwel, a borthas kov *yn kever dibarth fleghes Ysrael hag a ros arghadow *yn kever y eskern* 'By faith Jacob, when he died, made mention of the departing of the children of Israel and gave commandment concerning his bones' Heb. 11:21. Since *yn kever* does not mean 'about' and is never used with a noun, all these instances are inadmissible.

5.05 *Kerensa orth Eskerens*. The heading above Matt. 5:43 reads *Kerensa orth Eskerens* which is a direct translation of the equivalent heading in TEV, 'Love for Enemies'. The translation is not a good one, since traditional Cornish does not use the preposition *orth* after *kerensa* 'love', but rather *the* 'to', as can be seen from the following examples:

> *an tendyr **kerensa** a du an tas **the** vabden* 'the tender love of God the Father for mankind' TH 1
> *why a glowas kynsoll an kyrngeak **kerensa** a thu **the** mabden* 'you first of all heard of the cordial love of God for mankind' TH 4a

*eff a thesqethas cherite ha **kerensa** bras **thyn** ny* 'he showed charity and great love for us' TH 10a

*gwregh drehevall in ban agas colonow hag egerogh y a leis, the receva abervath inna **kerensa** bras **the** thu* 'lift up your hearts and open them wide, to receive into them great love for God' TH 16

*bo **kerensa thyn** re vsy in aga gouernans* 'or love for those who are under their governance' TH 25a

*mes vyn disquethas **kerense the** milliow an neb es ow cara ha es gwithe ow germynadow* 'but will show love to thousands of those who love me and keep my commandments' Pryce ACB.

Late Cornish in imitation of English appears to follow *kerensa* with the preposition *rag* 'for':

*ha 'ma them mar veer **crenga racta*** 'and I have as great a love for it' NBoson.

Nowhere in traditional Cornish is the word *kerensa* followed by *orth*.

5.06 Breusi an Re Erell. The heading at Matt. 7:1 (and at Luke 6:37) reads **Breusi an Re Erell**. This is clearly intended to be a translation into Kernowek Kemyn of 'Judging Others' in the corresponding places in TEV. Unfortunately the translation is incorrect. When we talk in English about 'judging others' or 'judging other people', the object of the verb is indefinite, i.e. 'any other people'. The phrase *an re erel* in Cornish, however, contains the definite article, and is therefore of necessity definite. Compare the following quotations from the texts:

*oll **an re erell** ew robbers ha laddron* 'all the others are robbers and thieves' TH 19

*so not the onyn vith **an re erell** an apostlys* 'but not to anyone of the others of the apostles' TH 43

*in myske **an re erell** y ma eff ow leverell in delma* 'and among the others he speaks thus' TH 49

*Lowena arag nation theso drys **an re erall*** 'Before a nation joy to thee beyond the others' BK 1989.

Brusy an re erel in Cornish, therefore, can only mean 'to judge the other ones, to judge the other people'. When one wishes to say 'others, other people' (indefinite) in Cornish, one uses the expression *tus erel*:

*ef a allas dyougel del glowys y leuerel yn lyes le savye bewnens **tus erel** '*he was able, as I have heard tell in many places to save the lives of others' PC 2873-76

*ihesu a fue anclethyys hag yn beth a ven gorrys gans ioseph ha **tus erel** '*Jesus was buried and set in a tomb of stone by Joseph and others' RD 1-3

*rag dowt why gans **tus erall** the vos tynnys dre error '*lest you be led through error by others' TH 18.

The heading in Kernowek Kemyn should have been *Breusi Tus Erell.*

5.07 *An Dhew Sel.* At Matt. 7:24 TEV has the heading 'The Two House Builders' and NIV reads 'The Wise and Foolish Builders'. The NEB reads here 'A firm foundation'. It would seem that the relative simplicity of the heading in the NEB led understandably to its being preferred of the the headings of the other two English versions. Here, however, it has been adapted, to 'The two foundations', rather than simply 'A firm foundation'. The ensuing heading in Kernowek Kemyn, however, is not without problems. *Sel* 'foundation' derives from *sel* 'fundamentum' in the *Old Cornish Vocabulary. Sel* 'foundation' is not attested in Middle Cornish and had probably disappeared from the language by the time of the Middle Cornish texts. The word *sel* in Middle Cornish (< Middle English *seel*) means 'a seal':

> *my a vyn lemyn ordne mab-lyen ov **sel** pryve the vos epscop yn temple* 'I will now ordain the cleric of my privy seal to be a bishop in the temple' OM 2599-601.

Compare also: *an kigg ew **selis** may halla an nenaf bos defendis* 'the flesh is sealed so that the soul may be defended' SA 60a. Indeed the present translation uses the word *sel* 'seal' at Rev. 6:1, 6:3, 6:5, 6:7, 6:9 and 6:12. In traditional Cornish the word for 'foundation' is *fundacyon*:

> *ha buldyys owgh war an **fondacion** an abosteleth han prophettys* 'and you are built upon the foundation of the apostles and the prophets' TH 33.

'To found' is either *fundya* or *grondya*:

> *omma lemen **fondya** plays dre voth ihesu a vercy sur me a vyn* 'here I will found a place by the wish of Jesus of mercy' BM 720-22
> *Omma me re **fundyas** plas ryb maria a cambron* 'Here I have founded a place beside St Mary of Camborne' BM 991-92

ov chy fundia sur ha grondya manneff uskyes 'I wish swiftly to found and establish my house' BM 1150-52.

Notice that *Fundyans Koen an Arloedh* 'the Establishment of the Lord's Supper' appears as a heading at 1 Cor. 11:23. There is no theoretical objection in this translation therefore, to the word *fundya* 'found, establish'. It would have been better to translate 'The Two Foundations' or 'The Wise and Foolish Builders', as something like *An Fundacyon Fol ha'n Fundacyon Fur*. As it is, *An Dhew Sel* is ambiguous and unclear.

5.08 *Glanhe Klavorek.* At Matt. 8:1 the TEV has the heading 'Jesus heals a man', the NIV has 'The Man with Leprosy' while the NEB reads 'Jesus cleanses a leper'. It is this last heading which has been translated as *Glanhe Klavorek*. The verbal noun *glanhe* 'to cleanse occurs at TH 8 and TH 10. Here it is being used as a noun to mean 'cleansing', which is admissible. The word *clavorek* is attested twice in Cornish. The first instance is in the *Old Cornish Vocabulary* where *claftorec* is glossed 'leprosus' [leprous]. The second time is in *Bewnans Ke*: *Gweth oge ys contrefetur, yfle pylys clovorok!* 'You are worse than a counterfeiter, you bald, leprous scoundrel' BK 178-79. In both cases *clavorek* is an adjective. In which case *Glanhe Klavorek* can only mean 'Leprous Cleansing'. It would have been better to write the Kernowek Kemyn equivalent of *Jesus ow sawya den clavorek* 'Jesus healing a leprous man'.

5.09 *An Re a Vynn Holya Yesu.* The heading at Matt 8:18 (and again at Luke 9:57) is *An Re a Vynn Holya Yesu*. This is clearly intended to be a translation of the equivalent heading in TEV 'The Would-be Followers of Jesus'. Unfortunately the Kernowek Kemyn version does not mean what was intended.

The English expression 'would-be followers' is difficult to render into Cornish and the whole has been paraphrased as 'those who wish to follow Jesus'. Yet there is nothing in the Cornish expression *an re a vyn holya Jesu* to suggest that the verb is relative. The clause would be taken by a native speaker of Cornish to mean 'The *re* will follow Jesus.' If, on the other hand, the heading had said *An re na a vyn holya Jesu*, the clause would certainly have made sense: 'Those people will follow Jesus', though clearly not the sense desired here.

If in Cornish one wishes to say 'those who', one uses the formula *an re na neb...* as in the following examples:

neb a rug benega, **han rena neb** *ew benegys, y thens oll onyn* 'he who blessed
and those who are blessed, they are all one' TH 13

cowsow da **an rena neb** *ara agys defamia* 'speak well of those who defame
you' TH 22

mar tewgh why ha cowse da only **an rena neb** *ew agys brederath ha cothmans*
'if you happen to speak well only of those who are your brothers and
friends' TH 22

So the cara agan yskerens ew an proper condicion **an rena neb** *ew an flehis a
thu, an disciples han folowers a crist* 'But to love our enemies is the
proper state of those who are the children of God, the disciples and
followers of Christ' TH 24

Alas, pan a cas vsy **an rena** *inna* **neb** *a rug seperatya aga honyn ha naha an
catholyk egglos* 'Alas, what a difficulty are those in who separated
themselves and denied the Catholic Church' TH 33.

I am not sure, either that *a vyn holya* implies sufficient volition. In the
texts *me a vyn mos* means quite simply 'I will go', rather than 'I want to
go'. If one wanted to translate 'those who wish to follow Jesus', one
should write *An re na neb a garsa folya Jesu* or *An re na neb yw whensys dhe
folya Jesu.*

5.10 *Spavennhe Annawel.* At Matt. 8:23 and at Luke 8:22 the headings
read *Spavennhe Annawel.* This seems to be a translation of the equivalent
headings in the TEV: 'Jesus Calms a Storm'. At Mark 4:35, however, the
heading in Kernowek Kemyn is *Spavennhe an Annawel,* which I take to
be a translation of the equivalent heading in the NIV: 'Jesus Calms the
Storm'.

*Spavennhe is in origin an invention of Nance's constructed on the
basis of 1) *spauen mor* 'equor' in the *Old Cornish Vocabulary*; 2) Breton
span 'interruption, cessation; pause'; 3) Cornish dialect word *spannel,
sponnel* 'quiet water by a rock on the opposite side from the tide'. In
view of the Breton and dialect forms one would have thought that
*spanhe would have been a more likely form. I am not sure, however,
that **spavenhe, *spanhe,* if it ever existed in Cornish, would have meant
'to calm (the sea)'. In the first place, it is not certain that OC *spauen mor*
'equor' meant a calm at sea, rather than simply the level surface of the
sea. Moreover the dialect word and the Breton cognate seem to suggest
that the element *span-* may have referred to a lull, a short period of less
powerful waves in an otherwise choppy sea; compare the Irish word
deibhil 'lull; temporary settling of the sea'.

In my own translation of the New Testament I followed D. R. Evans in the Matthaean narrative itself and used the word *spaven* for 'calm'. In the Lucan story, however, I used Lhuyd's *calmynsy* (*Kallamingi* glossing *Tranquillitas* 'tranquility; a calm' AB: 166a). Were I translating now, I should use *teg-awel* (Cf. *Auel vâz, têg-auel* glossing *Malacia* 'Calm, a calmness' AB: 84b).

There is only one verb in traditonal Cornish meaning 'to quieten', namely **coselhe**; cf. *The ihesu rebo grasseys hag inweth 3e veryasek thyn ol ythyv* **coselheys** 'Thanks be to Jesus and to Meriasek also that all has been quietened for us' (spoken by the Count of Rohan after the country has been pacified and cleared of brigands) BM 2180-82. Another verb that might serve here, however, is **dova** 'to tame' (cf. *Dho* **dova** glossing *Domo* 'To tame, to subdue' AB: 55b).

Ennawel is the Kernowek Kemyn spelling of *anauhel* 'procella [storm]' in the *Old Cornish Vocabulary*. We have no evidence that the word survived beyond the Old Cornish period. The correct term for a storm at sea in Cornish is **hager-awel** as can be seen from the following:

> Kensa, vrt an **hagar auall** iggeva gweell do derevoll warneny Keniffer termen dr'erany moas durt Pedden an Wolas do Sillan 'First, because of the storm he causes to rise up against us every time that we go from Land's End to Scilly' NBoson [< *Duchess of Cornwall's Progress*].

If I had now to translate 'Jesus calms the storm' into Cornish, I should use only those words that are actually attested in the language and write either *An hager-awel dovys gans Jesu* or *Jesu ow coselhe an hager-awel*. I should certainly avoid both the invented *spavenhe and OC *anauhel*.

5.11 *Myrgh an Rewler, ha'n Venyn a Dochyas Dillas Yesu*. At Matt. 9:18 the heading reads ***Myrgh an Rewler, ha'n Venyn a Dochyas Dillas Yesu***. This seems to be a translation of the corresponding heading in TEV, 'The Official's Daughter and the Woman Who Touched Jesus' Cloak.' Unfortunately the translation is not correct. A good speaker of Cornish would naturally take the heading to mean 'The Ruler's Daughter, and the Woman Touched Jesus' Clothes'—which does not seem to make much sense. It is also, incidentally, unclear why the heading speaks of *dillas Yesu*, since the text reads *Mara kallav unnweyth tochya y vantell*, the Kernowek Kemyn for 'If I can only touch his cloak' (Matt.19:21). I suggest translating this heading into Cornish as: *Myrgh an Rewler ha'n Venen Neb a Duchyas Pows Jesu*.

5.12 *Yaghe Den Avlavar.* At Matt. 9:32 the TEV has the heading 'Jesus Heals a Dumb Man', which has been translated into Kernowek Kemyn as *Yaghe Den Avlavar.* Here the verbal noun *yaghhe* 'to heal' is used as a noun to mean 'healing'. Although the verb *yaghhe* is common enough, it is not used nominally like this anywhere in traditional Cornish. The usage is like that of *glanhe* above, and is permissible. What is curious, however, is that in further headings in Matthew's Gospel and elsewhere we find 'healing' rendered by the equally unattested noun *yagh(h)eans.* The only word for 'healing' attested in the traditional language is *sawment*:

> *y a lefer der lyfryov marsus **savment** in bys ma orth an cleves* 'they will tell us by the books whether there is any healing in the world for the disease' BM 1372-74
>
> *Ser emperour bethens lethys rag **savment** dywhy lemen* 'Sir emperor, let them be killed now as healing for you' BM 1638-39.

The term *aflavar* 'dumb' is unattested in Middle Cornish, being derived from the *Old Cornish Vocabulary*. The Middle Cornish for 'dumb' is *omlavar*:

> *dal na boȝar ny ase nag **omlauar** nag onon* 'he did not leave blind or deaf or anyone dumb' PA 25b
>
> *han bothar a glew han **omlavar** a cowse* 'and the deaf hears and the dumb speaks' TH 57a
>
> *ow menya dre an dall, effreg, bothar ha **omlavar**, an a re a ve therag dorne in della* 'meaning by the blind, lame, deaf and dumb, those people who had previously been thus' TH 57a.

If one wants to translate 'the Healing of a Dumb Man' into Cornish one says *Sawment Den Omlavar*.

5.13 *Avowa Krist a-dherag Tus.* At Matt. 10:32 and Luke 12:8 the heading reads *Avowa Krist a-dherag Tus.* The corresponding heading in TEV is 'Confessing and Rejecting Christ', whereas the NEB has 'Acknowledging and disowning Jesus' at Matt. 10:32 and 'Acknowledging and disowning Christ' at Luke 12:8. 'Confessing and rejecting' or 'acknowledging and disowning' are difficult to render into Cornish and instead the Kernowek Kemyn heading seeks to translate 'acknowledging/confessing Christ publicly'. It is not certain, however, that *Avowa Krist a-dherag Tus* is an adequate translation.

Let us look a little more closely at this heading. The verbal noun *avowa* is here being used nominally, 'to admit; admitting'. In the first place, it is by no means certain that *avowa* is the best verb to use:

> *hag owth avowa forsoyth a'y wlascor trubut na goyth* 'and admitting indeed that no tribute is owing from his kingdom' BK
>
> *myns a wruk me a'n avow hag a gyf dustynyow ty the govs er byn laha* 'I admit all I did and shall obtain witnesses that you speak against the law' PC 1301-03
>
> *ma na veath y avowe hethough cercot a baly thotho me a vyn y ry* 'so that he does not dare admit it, fetch a surcoat of satin; I will give it to him' PC 1783-85
>
> *tues perfyt me an advow ythyns i ha polatis brase* 'they are perfect people, I admit, and great fellows' CW 2353-54.

In Cornish, then, *avowa* is used in the expression *me a'n avow* 'I admit it' and elsewhere to refer to the admission of facts or of guilt. Our sample is small, but in none of the above instances does *avowa* mean to 'acknowledge' someone. If we had more Cornish, it is likely that we would have instances of *avowa* with a personal object. The real problem here is that there is no grammatical object. The notional object 'Christ' is in genitival relation with the verbal noun *Avowa*. Given that *avowa* seems to mean 'to admit something', there is a risk that a good speaker of Cornish would take *Avowa Krist* to mean Christ's admission (of something unspecified) rather than 'to acknowledge Christ'.

The expression *therag tus* is not attested in Cornish, but note: *yn vr na sur me a weyl mar a pethyn ny abel the wul defens a rak tues* 'then I shall surely see whether we shall be able to make a public defence' PC 2304-06. There is, however, a better way of saying 'openly, publicly' in Cornish:

> *Pur apert hag yn golow y leueris ow dyskas* 'Very publicly and in broad daylight I uttered my teaching' PA 79a
>
> *worth ihesus ef a gowsas myns vs omma cuntullys pur apert y ret flamyas ha te ger vyth ny gewsys* 'to Jesus he spoke: All gathered here have quite publicly accused you and you have said not a word' PA 92a-c
>
> *apert vythqueth y tyskys ow dyskes the'n yethewon* 'I always taught my teaching to the Jews publicly' PC 1251-52
>
> *ha'y naghe byth ny wyla rak the gous a bref neffre the vos den a galile apert the pup vs omma* 'and never try to deny it because your speech will for ever prove openly to everybody here that you are a Galilean' PC 1407-10.

I suggest translating the heading 'Acknowledging Christ Publicly' as *Owth Aswon Cryst yn Apert* or *Avowa Leldury dhe Gryst yn Apert.*

5.14 *An Den gans Leuv Wedhrys*. The heading at Matt. 12:9 (and Luke 6:6) reads *An Den gan Leuv Wedhrys* which is clearly based on the two headings, 'A man with a withered arm' in the NEB and 'the Man with a Paralysed Hand' in TEV. The translation, however, is not the best Cornish, for it follows English idiom too closely. English says, for example, 'the girl with the red dress', 'the man with the big nose', 'the dog with the limp' where the feature possessed is introduced by 'with'. French on the other hand uses the preposition *à* 'to', for example, *jeune fille à la robe blanche* 'young girl with a white dress' or *la petite reine au nez rouge* 'the little queen with a red nose'. In *Nouveau Testament* (1971), the French equivalent of the TEV New Testament, the present heading is rendered *L'homme à la main deséchée* 'The man with a withered hand'. In Irish one either uses a descriptive genitive, for example, *cailín na súl glas* 'the girl with green eyes' (literally 'the girl of the green eyes') or one uses a dependent clause, *an fear a raibh casacht air* 'the man with the cough' (literally 'the man who had a cough on him'). Traditional Cornish in the present case would have used an adjective ('withered') + possessive adjective ('his') + noun ('hand'). Of course, that particular example is not attested, but comparable instances are found in the texts:

*ȝe vab du **mur y alloys*** 'to the son of God with the great power' PA 135c

*tebell lycour **mur y last*** 'a vile drink with a very nasty taste' PA 202b

*an golom **glas hy lagas** yn mes gura hy delyfre* 'let her out, the dove with the blue eyes' OM 1109-10

*a bur fals dyscryggygyon **tebel agas manerow*** 'O you truly false unbelievers with evil ways' OM 1855-56

*dev tek a bren rag styllyow ha **compos y denwennow bras ha crom y ben goles*** 'God, a beautiful log for rafters, and with smooth sides, with a large, curved base' OM 2441-43

*scherewys **drok aga gnas*** 'scoundrels with evil natures' PC 1142

*ytho thy'nny yth heuel dre honna war ow laute the vos map dev **mur y nel*** 'so it seems to us by that upon my word that you are the Son of God with great power' PC 1489-91

*a peue den **drok y gnas*** 'were he a man with an evil nature' PC 2969.

In Late Cornish it would seem that expressions of this kind were replaced by an idiom rather closer to English. Lhuyd heard *An lyzûan bîan **gen i ar nedhez**, ez a tivi en an halou nei, ez kreiz Plêth Maria* 'The small plant with the twisted stalk, which grows on our Hills, is called Plêth Maria' AB: 245a. It should be noticed, however, that even in its decline Cornish did not say *An lyzûan bîan gen gar nedhez 'The little plant with a twisted stalk' as in English, but An lyzûan bîan gen i ar nedhez 'The little plant with *its* stalk twisted'.

I think it is safe to say that the heading here should have been *An Den Gwedhrys y Leuv*; or, if the editors had wished to imitate Late Cornish, *An Den Gans y Leuv Gwedhrys*.

What is most remarkable about this unidiomatic heading is this: at Luke 6:8 in the narrative itself we read *Mes ev, owth aswonn aga frederow, a leveris dhe'n den gwedhrys y leuv* 'But he, knowing their thoughts, said to the man with the withered arm'. The translation uses the correct form in one place but not in the other.

5.15 *Hengov an Dus-Hen.* At Matt. 15:1 and Mark 7:1 the heading reads *Hengov an Dus-Hen*. This would seem to be based on the equivalent headings in the TEV and the NEB, 'About traditions' and 'The Teaching of the Ancestors' respectively. At any rate *Hengov an Dus-Hen* is clearly intended by the editor to mean 'The Tradition of the Ancestors' or 'The Tradition of the Elders'. The translation in very unsatisfactory for several reasons. The first is that *hengof is an invention of Nance's, based on Welsh and Breton. The attested word for 'tradition' in Cornish is *tradicion*:

> *ny a vea res thyn nena sewya an order in* **tradicions**, *delyuerys drethens y* 'would it not then be necessary for us to follow the order in the traditions delivered through them? TH 19
>
> *then* **tradicions** *na lyas barbarus nacion, ow crege in crist a ra ry crygyans* 'to those traditions many barbarous nations believing in Christ will give credence' TH 19
>
> *dell rug an phariseys gans aga pestilens* **tradicions**, *fals* **tradicions** *ha interpretacions ha gloses* 'as the Pharisees did with their pestilent traditions, false traditions, and interpretations and glosses' TH 22
>
> *Dar ny vea necessary thyn folya an ordyr an kythsame* **tradicion** *a russans dyluer then rena* 'Well then, would it not be necessary for us to follow the order of the selfsame tradition which they delivered to those people?' TH 37
>
> *ny a res thyn sewya, observia ha gwetha an* **tradicions** *an auncient egglos* 'we are obliged to follow, observe and keep the traditions of the primitive church' TH 37

ha nag en ny kylmys the wetha **tradicion** *vith, na cerimonye, mas an pith vs kyfys in Scriptur* 'and we are not bound to maintain any tradition or ceremony, other than that which is found in scripture' TH 37.

Tus hen literally means 'old people'. I cannot understand why Kernowek Kemyn spells it with a hyphen. The expression is attested once: **tus hen** *guelhevyn an pov* 'elders, aristocrats of the land' BM 2929. It means 'elders, those high in rank by dint of age'. It does not, as the editor would like, mean 'ancestor(s)', which in Cornish is *hendas*, *hendasow*:

> *kepar maner dell rug eff temptia agan* **hendasow** *ny Adam hag eva* 'just as he tempted our ancestors Adam and Eve' TH 3a
>
> *an pith a ruga gonys in agan* **hendasow** *adam hag eva* 'what he wrought in our ancestors Adam and Eve' TH 5a
>
> *Ny a rug peha kepar hagan* **hendasow** 'we have sinned like our ancestors' TH 9a
>
> *fetell ve agan* **hendasow** *ny, adam hag eve, dre an singular daddar han speciall favoure a thu golosek, creatis nobyll* 'that our ancestors, Adam and Eve, by the singular goodness and special favour of Almighty God created noble' TH 12
>
> *henna o dre pehosow agan* **hendasow** *ny* 'that was through the sins of our ancestors' TH 12
>
> *whath kenthew ow* **hendas** *cayne pur bad dean lower accomptys* 'still although my ancestor Cain is considered a very evil man indeed' CW 1446-47
>
> *me a ra dyllas thyma par del wrug ow* **hendasow** 'I will make clothes for myself as my ancestors did' CW 148-79
>
> *haw* **hendas** *cayme whath en bew* 'and my ancestor Cain still alive' CW 1480
>
> *me ny allaf convethas y bosta ge ow* **hendas** 'I cannot understand that you are my ancestor' CW 1610
>
> *am corf ythos devethys hag a adam tha* **hendas** 'you derive from my body and from Adam your ancestor' CW 1610-11
>
> *marsew ty cayne ow* **hendas** 'if you are Cain my ancestor' CW 1650
>
> *cayne whath kenthota ow* **hendas** *tha aswon me ny wothyan* 'Cain, still though you are my ancestor, I could not recognize you' CW 1660-61
>
> *ow* **hendas** *adam pur weare eave regollas der avall an place gloryous* 'my ancestor Adam very truly, he has lost by an apple the glorious place' CW 2134-36.

'The Traditions of the Ancestors' in UCR is *Tradycyons an Hendasow*.

5.16 *Diswrians an Tempel Ragleverys.* At Matt 24:1 the NEB has the heading 'Destruction of the temple foretold', which has been translated into Kernowek Kemyn as *Diswrians an Tempel Ragleverys*. The word *ragleverys* is attested in the texts where it means 'aforementioned, above-mentioned':

> *An seth yw **ragleueris** as gwyskis tyn gans mur angus war hy holon* 'The arrow which has been mentioned already struck her sharply with great pain upon her heart' PA 224ab
>
> *py ny kouze mèz nebaz bîan adrô'n Tavazo **raglaveryz** en an levar-ma* 'since he speaks only a very little about the above-mentioned languages in this book' AB: 222
>
> *Mr. Estwick a'n **raglavèryz** pleu Yst* 'Mr Estwick of the aforementioned parish of St Just' AB: 222
>
> *ha'n **raglaveryz** Mr. Keiguyn* 'and the aforementioned Mr Keigwin' AB: 222
>
> *Dre yuzhanz an **raglaveryz** Skrêflevrou* 'By using the aforementioned manuscripts' AB: 223
>
> *uynyn a'n skreflevro **raglaveryz*** 'one of the aforementioned manuscripts' AB: 223
>
> *a kuitha an **raglaveryz** legradzho me honen* 'maintaining the afore-mentioned corruptions myself' AB: 223
>
> *guythrez dha veve dhyn Tîz **rag-laveryz*** 'it were a good deed for the above-mentioned people' AB: 224.

Cf. *Trega suer ew an Spurys a ve **thyrag leverys*** 'Third indeed is the Spirity which was mentioned before' BK 260-70. In Cornish the adjective immediately follows the noun it qualifies. The heading *Diswrians an Tempel Ragleverys*, therefore, can only mean 'the Destruction of the Aforementioned Temple'—which is not exactly what was intended.

5.17 *Dyskans an Figbrenn.* At Mat 24:32, Mark 13:28 and Luke 21:29 the heading reads *Dyskans an Figbrenn*. This I take to be a translation of 'The Lesson of the Fig-Tree' in the corresponding places in the TEV. I am not sure, however, that *Dyskans an Figbrenn* means what was envisaged. The word *dyscans* in traditional Cornish means A. 'education, erudition' and B. 'teaching, instruction'. When it bears the second sense the following dependent noun refers to the person or institution giving the instruction. Here are a few examples of both A. and B.:

A

y vab rag cawas **dyskans** *sur danvenys ateva ȝyugh doctor wek* 'his son to be educated behold him indeed sent to you'

yma ȝym perfect **dyskans** *grac the crist pen an eleth* 'I now have completed my education, thanks to Christ, chief of the angels' BM 85-7

mar myn ov **descans** *servya* 'if my education is sufficient' BM 524

Ha neb nan Jevas **dyscans** *a ra trelya an dra* 'And he who is uneducated will subvert the matter' TH 18

S Ireneus martyr benegas in weth, very ogas eff a ve then tyrmyn an abosteleth, den a **dyscans** *bras* 'St Irenaeus, a blessed martyr also, he was very close to the time of the Apostles, a man of great erudition' TH 18a.

B

ha refusya an **dyscans** *an kythsam egglos ma* 'and refuse the teaching of this same church' TH 17a

han **discans** *vgy an egglos ow dysky* 'and the doctrine which the church teaches' TH 19

ha gans diligens gwetha an **discans** *a sans egglos* 'and with diligence follow the teaching of holy church' TH 19

ny a res thyn kemeras wyth, magata thyn **dyscans** *a crist han bewnans* 'we must pay attention to both the teaching of Christ and of his life' TH 24

a das kere mere rase thewhy agis **dyskans** *da pub preyse* 'dear father, much thanks to you for your good instuction always' CW 1953-54.

Figbrenn is based on *ficbren* 'ficus [fig-tree]' in the *Old Cornish Vocabulary* and is unobjectionable as a lexical item. The expression *dyskans an figbrenn*, however, would seem in the light of the above examples, to mean one of two things, either 'the erudition (or learning) of the fig-tree' or 'the teaching given by the fig-tree'. It cannot, I think, mean 'the lesson of/from the fig-tree.'

5.18 *An Ura dhe Bethani.* At Matt 26:6 and at Mark 14:3 the heading reads *An Untyans yn Bethani*. At John 12:1, however, the heading reads *An Ura dhe Bethani*. The heading at all three places in the TEV is 'Jesus is Anointed at Bethany'. It is difficult to see, therefore, why the three headings are translated in two quite different ways.

The preposition used in traditional Cornish to mean 'in' or 'at' a place is invariably *yn*:

my a wyth an gueel a ras **yn ierusalem** *nefre* 'I shall keep the rods of grace for ever at Jerusalem' OM 2059-60 *yma tregys* **in cambron** *den ov cul merclys dyson* 'there is dwelling at Camborne a man who is doing miracles indeed' BM 687-88

in cambron *an lagasek nyns usy eff* 'the goggle-eyed one is not at Camborne' BM 1018-19

in rome *dyn ny dale trege* 'we ought not stay in Rome' BM 1344

yv **in rome** *pur thyogel* 'which is at Rome indeed' BM 1628

in rome *chyff cyte an beys emperour curunys certyn* 'crowned emperor at Rome the chief city of the world' BM 2514-15

han martirdom, a pedyr ha poulle **in Rome** 'and the martyrdom of Peter and Paul at Rome' TH 47

poran **in Rome**, *neb ew an pen ha chife cyte an bys* 'exactly in Rome, which is the head and chief city of the world' TH 47

martirdom a veva **in Rome** 'and the martyrdom he suffered at Rome' TH 47a

En Termen ez passiez thera Trigaz **en St. Levan** 'Once upon a time there was living in St Levan' NBoson

ha Mean orrol **en Madern** 'another stone in Madron' NBoson

mose tuah e Bargen teer **en Pedden an Wollas** 'going to his farm at Land's End' NBoson

dha Kûz karn na huila **en Borrian** 'to Cotnewilly Wood in Buryan' Lhuyd

Leben poue Jesus gennez **en Bethalem** *a Judeah* 'Now when Jesus was born in Bethlehem of Judaea' Rowe

oll an Flehaz a era **en Bethalem** 'all the children that were in Bethlehem' Rowe

an Tempel K'res **en Loundres** 'the Middle Temple in London' Gwavas

rag ma dro da deux mill Hosket whath **in Falmeth** 'for there are about two thousand baskets in Falmouth' Gwavas.

The expression **dhe Bethani* to translate 'at Bethany' is, therefore, incorrect.

5.19 Yudas a Assent dhe Drayta Yesu. At Matt. 26:14 and Mark 14:10 the heading reads **Yudas a Assent dhe Drayta Yesu**. These I take to be the rendering in Kernowek Kemyn of 'Judas Agrees to Betray Jesus' at the corresponding places in the TEV. The same heading occurs at Luke 22:3 in the TEV but the Kernowek Kemyn equivalent has been omitted in the present translation.

It seems to me, that the Kernowek Kemyn heading may not mean what was intended. The verb *assentya* does not mean 'to consent to do something', but rather 'to agree with somebody or something', 'to raise no objections to something'. Here are some examples from the texts:

a vynnegh ol **assentye** *rak pask my thylyfrye ihesu myghtern yethewon* 'are you all willing that I should free Jesus the King of the Jews for Passover?' PC 2037-39

honna yv an forth wella **assentye** *ol the henna sur me a vyn* 'that is the best way; I will certainly agree to that' RD 582-84

Henna ol ny a **assent** 'We all agree to that' BM 2926

Mar ny **asentyyth** *gena' te a hebcor lowena war bur nebas lavarow* 'In a word if you don't agree with me, you will forfeit all joy' BK 3087-88

ena ty a vyth tregys ha myns **assentyas** *genas* 'there you shall and as many as agreed with you' CW 245-56

hanter an elath genaffa **assentyes** *yth yns sera thom mayntaynya in spyte thys* 'sir, half the angels are agreed that they will support me in spite of thee' CW 271-73.

The closest example in sense to the Kernowek Kemyn heading is the last one from the CW above. In it, however, the verb appears as a verbal adjective and is qualified by *genaffa*: *genaffa assentyes yth yns* 'they are agreed with me'. In the heading on the other hand the verb is simple present-future and is not qualified in any way. It seems to me that *Yudas a assent dhe drayta Yesu* would naturally mean 'Judas raises no objections to the betrayal of Jesus.' If I were asked to translate the heading 'Judas agrees to betray Jesus' I should say something like *Judas ow promysya dhe dhyskevra Jesus*.

5.20 *An Den gans an Spyrys Avlan.* At Mark 1:21 and at Luke 4:31 the heading reads *An Den gans an Spyrys Avlan.* This is clearly based on the corresponding heading in the TEV, 'A Man with an Evil Spirit'. As noted above when discussing the 'man with the withered hand' the use here of *gans* to mean 'having' is not correct in Cornish. Here the preposition is particularly unsuitable because *an den gans an spyrys avlan* might most naturally be taken to mean 'the man together with the unclean spirit.'

In traditional Cornish a spirit is said to reside in the person:

spyrys *a vewnans* **ynno** *bynytha na vo guylys* 'lest he be seen to have the spirit of life' OM 985-86

Marow yv pup tra ese **spyrys** *a vewnans* **ynno** 'Dead is everything that possessed the spirit of life' OM1089-90

marowe ew pub tra eʒa sperys a **vewnans vnna** 'dead is everything that had the spirit of life' CW 2456-57.

Moreover, in traditional Cornish 'evil spirit, unclean spirit' is rendered by *tebel-sperys* or *drog-sperys*:

> *me yv vexijs anhethek gans **tebel speris** oma* 'I am tormented continually by an evil spirit here' BM 2628
> *mars us **drok sperys** ogas* 'if an evil spirit is near' BM 2643
> *an **drok sperys** avodys yma* 'the evil spirit has departed' BM 2657-5.

If one wished to translate 'A man with an unclean spirit' into Cornish, a better translation would be *Den ha drog-sperys ynno, Den esa tebel-sperys ynno*, or the like.

5.21 *Assenshyon Yesu.* The heading at Luke 24:50 reads *Assenshyon Yesu*, but the heading at Acts 1:6 reads *Assendyans Yesu*. *Assenshyon* is to be preferred, since it is the only one of the two words which is actually attested.

> *Inweth a wosa y **assencion** thyn neff, according thy promes, Eff a thanvonas then dore an spurissans war ben y abosteleth, kepar dell ra S luk scriffa* 'Also after his ascension in accordance with his promise, he sent down the Holy Spirit upon his apostles, as St Luke writes' TH 36
> *na gesa aweyll aweyll vith scryffys rag sertan space a wosa an **assencyon** a crist* 'no gospel had been written for a certain time after the ascension of Christ' TH 37a
> *fatell rug pedyr in contynent a wosa an **ascencion** a crist Sevall in ban in cres an elect pobyll* 'that Peter… after the ascension of Christ stood up in the midst of the elect' TH 44a
> *mathew a screfas y aweil viii blethan wosa an **ascencion** a crist* 'Matthew wrote his gospel eight years after the ascension of Christ' TH 42a.

It is also a great pity that the two headings should be different. Since St Luke's gospel and the Acts had the same author, there ought to be some consonancy in the treatment of the two books.

5.22 *An Venyn Kevys yn Avoutri.* The heading at John 8:1 reads *An Venyn Kevys yn Avoutri* which is based on the corresponding heading in the TEV, 'The Woman Caught in Adultery'. The whole passage John 7:53-8:11 is of uncertain authenticity. It is omitted from here in the NEB and NIV marks it to show that it is not found in the earliest and most reliable manuscripts. The TEV includes it within square brackets, but alone of the three English versions provides the passage with a heading.

I am very unhappy, however, about the translation of the heading here. *Cafus* (**kavoes* in Kernowek Kemyn) means 'get, obtain, find'. The heading naturally means 'The woman who was obtained in adultery'— which is not an adequate translation. We need to say 'the woman who was caught in the act of adultery'. I suggest translating here as *An venen neb a vue kemerys ow cul avowtry* or possibly *An venen neb a vue kechys yn avowtry*.

THE SIX TRANSLATORS

6.00 We are told on page ix who were the translators of *An Testament Nowydh* and which books each one translated. They and the portions they translated are as follows:

1. W. Brown: *Romans*; 1, 2, 3 *John*
2. Dr J. H. Chesterfield: *Acts*, I and 2 *Corinthians*
3. The Revd J. M. Davey: *Galatians, Philemon, Jude*
4. R. J. Edwards: *Ephesians, Philippians, Colossians*, 1 and 2 *Thessalonians*, 1 and 2 *Timothy, Titus, James*, 1 and 2 *Peter, Revelation*
5. G. Sandercock: *Hebrews*
6. R. K. R. Syed: *Luke, John*. Revision of *Mark* and *Matthew*.

THE FIRST TRANSLATOR

6.01 The first translator, we are told, translated the Epistle to the Romans and the three Johannine epistles, 1, 2 and 3 John. Since *Romans* is the longest of these, I intend to examine it closely. It is in Romans that St Paul sets out most clearly his views on justification by faith through the incarnate Son of God. Romans is not an easy epistle to translate, or even to understand. It is, however, full of memorable phrases, 'a law unto themselves', 'death hath no more dominion', 'we are more than conquerors', 'the wages of sin is death', 'the powers that be', 'let us therefore cast off the works of darkness', etc. It is imperative that this epistle be well translated, otherwise the enterprise of translating the New Testament will be seriously deficient. In the following examples from the first eight chapters of Romans, it becomes clear that this translation is unsuccessful. Notice, that I have already dealt with some of the grammatical problems at §§ 4.01, 4.02, 4.05 and 4.09 above.

6.02 At Rom. 1:11 St Paul tell the Romans that he longs to visit them in order to impart some spiritual gift to them to strengthen them. The Greek text continues in verse 12: τοῦτο δέ ἐστιν συνπαρακληθῆναι ἐν ὑμῖν, διὰ τῆς ἐν ἀλλήλοις πίστεως ὑμῶν τε καὶ ἐμοῦ, literally 'but this is in order to be mutually cheered among you by the faith among one another, both of you and of me.' The RSV, however, reads: 'That is, that we may be mutually encouraged by each other's faith, yours and mine'. It is this that has been rendered into Kernowek Kemyn: *Hemm yw, rag may fyn ni keskrevhes dre fydh y gila, keffrys* **agas huni** *hag* **ow huni**. I have explained above that the use of *huni* here is incorrect, but it has clearly been used twice to translate the English expression 'yours and mine' in the RSV. In my own translation of this passage I attempted to be as idiomatic as possible and said: *boken kens may hallen ny oll warbarth bos kennerthys an eyl gans fedh y gela, ow fedh vy ha'gas fedh whywhy.*

6.03 At verse Rom. 3:25 the Greek text says ἐν τῇ ἀποχῇ τοῦ θεοῦ 'in the forbearance of God'. The AV says 'through the forbearance of God', the NEB and the NIV say 'in his forbearance' and the TEV merely says 'he was patient'. Only the RSV says 'in his divine forbearance' and the Kernowek Kemyn says *yn y wodhevyans* **dywek** 'in his divine forbearance'. It would seem, then, that the Kernowek Kemyn of this passage is based on the RSV, not on the Greek.

6.04 The verb *obery* is not common in Middle Cornish and I know of only one example of a finite form of it: *mar pue drok a* **oberys** 'if it was evil that I wrought' OM 291. There is no attested example of a third person singular present-future *ober, for that would be likely to be confused with the noun *ober* 'work'. The autonomous form of the verb is attested in PA and the Ordinalia, but is very uncommon after that. Let us also remember that *huny* is used only with *pup, lyes* and *kettep*. With those three points in mind let us look at the Kernowek Kemyn translation of Rom. 4:4-5:

> *Lemmyn dhe'n* ***huni** *a ober ny synsir y wober avel ro mes y'n telir dhodho. Ha dhe'n* ***huni** *na ober mes a grys dhe neb a gyv an ongrassyes ewn y synsir y fydh avel gwiryonedh.*

A native speaker of Cornish from *c.* 1500 would have great difficulty in understanding that passage and would probably take it to mean something like the following:

> Now to the ?*huni* of work his reward ?is not considered as a gift but it is paid to him (*y'n telir dhodho*). And to that ?*huni* (*dhe'n huni na*) work out of ?power/?a shirt (*ober mes a grys*) to him who gets (*a gyv*) the correct ungracious one, his faith ?is considered as truth.

In my own translation I attempted to write something that would be immediately intelligible to a speaker of traditional Cornish:

> *Dhe henna usy ow lafurya, nyns yw y wajys recknys avel ro, mes avel tra dhendylys. Saw rag kenyver a wrella trestya yn Dew usy ow justyfya an dus dhydhew, crejyans a'n par na yw recknys avel ewnder.*

Compare the RSV rendering:

> Now to one who works, his wages are not reckoned as a gift but as his due. And to one who does not work but trusts in him who justifies the ungodly, his faith is reckoned as righteousness.

6.05 At Rom. 5:14 the Kernowek Kemyn reads: *Byttegyns mernans a reynya a Adam *bys dhe Moyses* 'Death reigned from Adam to Moses'. This sentence is not correct. In Middle Cornish *bys the* is used exclusively with pronominal forms only:

> *nyn drossen ny **bys deso** PA 99b*
> *ha **bys thotho** whare a OM 642*
> ***bys thy's** vmma yn vn lam ef a vyth kyrhys OM 885-86*
> *ffystynnyn fast **bys thotho** OM 1041*
> *my a'd wor scon **bys thethy** OM 2072*
> *my a'd wor scon **bys thethy** PC 584*
> *dun **bys thotho** hep lettye PC 1455*
> *dres **bys thy'so** yn kelmys PC 1569*
> ***bys dys** omma hep ardak PC 1870*
> *ath dros **bys thymmo** omma PC 2004*
> ***Bys dotho** me agys led BM 2530*
> *Me agis gor **bys detha** BM 3307.*

With proper nouns and common nouns *bys yn* is used:

> ***bys yn meneth** ha me gwan PA 53b*
> ***bys yn Ihesus** caradow PA 64d*
> ***bys yn aga fryns** annas PA 76d*
> ***bys yn pylat** o Iustis PA 98a, PA 239a*
> *I eth **bys yn herodes** PA 109a*
> ***bys yn cayphas** ʒy ʒey yvggye PA 118d*
> ***bys yn galyle** zy whelas PA 257d*
> ***bys yn meneth olyuetd** PC 2398*
> *alemma **bys yn tryger** PC 2274*
> *pur uskis **bys in cambron** BM 982*
> *heno thea Adam **bys in tyrmyn moyses** TH 14*
> ***bys in Epscop** ma vs lemma in present tyrmyn ma TH 49*

Bys in Gooddron the'n myghtern BK 53
bys in Tremustel Penpol BK 1198
Bys in Arthor in tefry BK 1370
bys in Arthur BK 1738
bys in Arthur BK 1819
bys in Rom gans pen Lucy BK 2839.

The translation ought to have read *a Adam bys yn Moyses.*

6.06 At Rom. 6:17 the Kernowek Kemyn reads as follows:

> *Mes dhe Dhyw re bo grassys, awos hwi, a vedha kethyon dhe begh, dhe vos devedhys gostyth a'n golonn dhe'n savla a dhyskas dhodho mayth ewgh res.*

It is difficult to make much sense of this without looking at an English version. If one takes it at face value it seems to mean something like: 'But thanks be to God, because you, who were frequently slaves to sin, have come obedient in heart to the position that taught him so that you were necessary.' The intended sense, however, was: 'Thanks be to God that you, who were once slaves of sin have become obedient from the heart to the standard of teaching to which you were committed'. The verbal form *vedha* is a habitual past, rather than an imperfect. When still in unbelief the Romans were slaves to sin once only, although for a long time. The translator should have written, *neb o kethyon dhe begh.* For the rest, it is apparent that his rendition of this verse has not been completely successful.

6.07 At Rom. 7:18 the Kernowek Kemyn reads: *My a yll bos hwansek war-lergh an pyth yw da, mes ny allav y wul.* This is not, I think, translated from the Greek which says: τὸ γὰρ θέλειν παράκειταί μοι, τὸ δὲ κατεργάζεσθαι τὸ καλὸν οὔ 'for the wishing is present in me, but the doing of the good is not.' It seems rather to have been translated from the RSV: 'I can will what is right, but I cannot do it'. It is not certain, however, that the Kernowek Kemyn rendering is correct. In Cornish *whansek* is followed either by *the* 'to' or *a* 'of':

> *asson **whansek** ol **the pysy** lettrys ha lek war thu mercy* 'How desirous are we all, lettered and lay, of praying to God for mercy' PC 37-8
> *whansack nyngew **tha drevyth*** 'He is not desirous of anything' CW 1794
> ***Whanzack** nyng yw **a travyth*** 'Desirous he is not of anything' Pryce.

The expression here *hwansek *war-lergh an pyth yw da* is without warrant in Cornish.

146

6.08 At Rom. 8:3 the Kernowek Kemyn text reads:

Rag Dyw re wrug an pyth na ylli an lagha y wul, gwannhes dell o gans an kig,
ow tannvon y Vab y honan yn hevelder kig peghus, ha rag pegh, ev a
dhampnyas pegh y'n kig.

This has not been translated from the Greek but from the RSV:

'For God has done what the law, weakened by the flesh, could not do:
sending his own Son in the likeness of sinful flesh and for sin, he
condemned sin in the flesh.'

We have seen at § 3.07 above that *hevelder* is an invented word and
that *hevelep* would have been better. More importantly the word order
of the Kernowek Kemyn puts *gwannhes dell o gans an kig* next to *ow*
tannvon y Vab y honan, with only a comma between them. The most
natural way of reading the Kernowek Kemyn is as follows: 'For God
has done what the law was unable to do weakened as he was by the
flesh, sending his son in the ?likeness of sinful flesh,' That is to say the
word-order is such as to make the reader think, even momentarily that
God himself was weakened by sinful flesh! In my own translation I
attempted to write something that was less susceptible of being
misconstrued:

An pyth na alsa an laha gul, drefen y vos gwanhes der an kyg, henna re wrug
Dew. Rag Dew a dhanonas y Vab y honen y'n hevelep a'n kyg luen a begh hag
avel offryn rag pegh. Dew a a dhampnas pegh y'n kyg.

6.09 At Rom. 8:9 the Kernowek Kemyn reads *Mes nyns esowgh y'n kig,*
y'n Spyrys yth esowgh, **mar trig** *Spyrys Dyw ynnowgh yn hwir.* This
corresponds to the Greek: ὑμεῖς δὲ οὐκ ἐστὲ ἐν σαρκὶ ἀλλὰ ἐν
πνεύματι, εἴπερ Πνεῦμα Θεοῦ οἰκεῖ ἐν ὑμῖν 'but you are not in flesh
but in spirit, if Spirit of God dwells in you.' The verb οἰκεῖ 'dwells' is in
the present tense. Here and 7:17, 7:18, 7:20, 7:23, 8:11 x 2 we find *tryg*
used to translate 'dwells'. This is incorrect, however. The present-future
of *trega* 'to dwell' in Cornish means 'will dwell, will stay', as is clear
from the following examples:

*hag ef a **dryk** heb fynweth yn yffarn yn tewolgow* 'and he shall dwell
   without end in hell in darkness' PA 212d
*ny **dryk** gryghonen yn fok* 'not a spark will stay in the forge' PC 2717

*ytho gyneugh me a **tryk** y ges byth ioy na thyfyk* 'therefore shall I dwell with you; you shall have joy that fails not' RD 1309-10

*lemmyn omma ty a **dryk** bys pan pottro ol the gyk* 'now here you shall stay until all your flesh rots' RD 2021-22

*ef a **dryk** pennoth in hans* 'he will remain bareheaded down below' BM 440

*mar **tryg** in kernov defry ny a vet gans an belan* 'if he stays [i.e. will stay] in Cornwall indeed, we will meet the scoundrel' BM 2294-95

*ha nena ny a **dryg** in du ha gans du, ha du a **dryg** innan* 'and then we shall dwell in God and with God, and God will dwell in us' TH 30

*mas an sorre a crist a **dryg** vghta* 'but the anger of Christ shall remain over him' TH 40

*Howen, omma te a **dryg** rag dyfenn an pow orth bryg* 'Owain, here you shall stay to defend the country from brigandage' BK 3205-06

*ef a **dryg** bys venytha* 'he shall dwell forever' CW 2032

*rag henna bys venary eve a **dryg** ena deffry* 'therefore forever he shall stay there' CW 2053-54.

If in Cornish one wants to say 'he dwells, he lives (somewhere)' one says *yma tregys*. This is clear from the following examples:

*vmma nyn gew ef **tregis*** 'he is not living here' PA 255d

*byth na wrella compressa ow tus **vs trygys** ena* 'that he should never oppress my people who live there' OM 1424-25

*punscie y tus mar calas **vs trygys** agy the'th wlas* 'to punish his people so hard who dwell within your kingdom' OM 1482-83

*py tyller yma moyses ha py cost **yma trygys*** 'where Moses is and whereabouts he lives' OM 1551-52

*the'n tyreth a thythwadow yw reys gans dev caradow thyn ena rag **bos trygys*** 'to the promsed land which has been given us by God to dwell in' OM 1624-26

*en den ma war ow ene gans ihesu a nazare yn certan a **fue trygys*** 'that man upon my soul certainly dwelt with Jesus of Nazareth' PC 1277-79

*gans cryst y **fythyth trygys*** 'with Christ you shall dwell' PC 3233

***yma tregys** in cambron den ov cul merclys dyson* 'there dwells in Camborne a man doing miracles indeed' BM 687-88

*py **ma tregys** thym leferys bethyns dyson* 'let me be told where he lives immediately' BM 816-18

*omma **yth ese tregys** avel hermyt in guelfos* 'here I dwell like a hermit in the wilderness' BM 1963-64

***tregys** off lemen heb wov berth in castel an dynas* 'I dwell now indeed in Castle Dynas' BM 2209-10

*in ban then wlas **vgy** y vab Jhesus crist inhy **tregys*** 'up to the kingdom where his son Jesus Christ dwells' TH 11a

kyn fes tregys gans an Jowl 'though thou dwell with the Devil' BK 45
Yma tregys in Kembra 'He lives in Wales' BK1292
En Termen ez passiez thera Trigaz en St. Levan Dean ha Bennen 'Once upon
a time there dwelt in St Levan a man and a woman' JCH.

The use of *ef a dryg* 'he dwells' here for *yma tregys* is incorrect. The
translation therefore means: 'But you are not in the flesh, you are in the
Spirit, if the Spirit of God is going to dwell in you (?)truly'.

6.10 Rom. 8:3 in Kernowek Kemyn reads as follows:

*Ha nyns yw an gwrians hepken, mes ni agan honan, a'gan beus kynsa froeth an
Spyrys, a gyn ynnon agan honan dell waytyn may fyn degemmereys yn fleghes,
daspren agan korf.*

The word *gwryans* (*gwrians* in the above verse) is known to us from
Stokes' title of his edition of CW, *Gwreans an Bys* 'the Creation of the
World'. *Gwryans, gwreans* in traditional Cornish, however, does not
mean 'creation', but rather 'deed, work', as can be seen from the
following examples:

*tormentores deugh yn scon may huththaho ow colon agan **guryans** na'm bo
meth* 'tormentors come to me forthwith that my heart may be
gladdened, that we may not fail in our business' RD

*ow affirmya playn fatell wothya an bobyl mer an **gwrythyans** a thu*
'affirmingly plainly that the people knew much of the works of God'
TH 14

*han offendars a res bos rebukys ha correctys in dew tyrmyn, rag mar pethans
gerys the vois, martesyn y a yll skynnya in myschew an parna may teffans
ha tenna re erell dre aga teball examplis ha **gwrythyans**, kepar hag vn ladyr
eff a yll robbya lyas den, ha cawsya lyas onyn the vos laddron inweth* 'and
the offenders must be rebuked and corrected in due time, for if they
are allowed to go free, perhaps they may descend into villainy of that
kind so that they draw other people by their evil examples and
deeds; just like one thief, he can rob many people and cause many to
be thieves as well' TH 25a

*han rulle ew holma, kemerys in mes an **gwrythyans** a awncyent den dyskys in
discans an egglos crist* 'and the rule is this, taken from the works of an
ancient learned in the teaching of God's church' TH 34a

*me a wore hag a leall gryes **gwreans** dew y vos henma* 'I know and truly
believe that this is God's doing' CW 2127-28

*Lemmen me a wor in ta orth the worthyb ha **gwryans** the vos cle'gys* 'Now I
know by your answer and behaviour that you are diseased' BK 603-
05.

In Cornish the word for 'creation' is *creacyon*:

> *neb a rella predery an* **creacyon** *a vabden* 'who ever thinks about the creation of mankind' TH 1

> *Rag in* **creacion** *a bub tra arell visible ny rug du an tas a neff mas commondya* 'For in the creation of all other visible things God, the heavenly Father merely commanded' TH 1

> *sow in* **creacion** *a vabden an tas a vsias solempnyty bras* 'but in the creation of mankind the Father used great ceremony' TH 1

> *An kensa tra vgy ow tuchia an* **creacion** *a mab den* 'The first thing which concerns the creation of mankind' TH 1

> *pan dra rug du an tas ragan ny in agan* **creacion** 'what God the Father did for us in our creation' TH 1a

> *Whath rag procedia pelha rag descernya an* **creacion** *a then* 'Yet to proceed further to discern the creation of man' TH 1a

> *fatell ylly du gull moy ragan in agen* **creacion** 'how could God do more for us in our creation?' TH 2a

> *oll an creaturs gwrys da ha perfect in aga* **creasion** 'all the creatures made good and perfect in their creation' TH 2a

> *in oll creaturs consernya agan* **creacion** 'in all creatures concerning their creation' TH 3

> *I a gollas an originall innocency stat a vongy in aga* **creasion** 'They lost the original innocency, a state they had at their creation' TH 4

> *Omma yma dewethis an homely a* **creacion(s)** *a vab den* 'Here ends the homily of the creation of mankind' TH 5a

> *ha gans an royow na ena mabden o enduwyes in dalleth in y* **creacion** 'and with those gifts the soul of man was endued in his creation' TH 12

> *ha vnderstondys dre an oberow an* **creacion** *an bys* 'and understood by the works of the creation of the world' TH 14

> *why a wellas pub degre leas matters gwarryes ha* **creacon** *oll an byse* 'you saw in every degree many matters acted and the creation of all the world' CW 2533-35.

The word *hepken* at Rom. 8:3, quoted above, is used to mean 'only' in imitation of Breton *hepken* 'seulement'. *Hep ken* in Cornish, however does not mean 'only'. Sometimes, when the element *ken* means 'other', the phrase can mean 'without any other, without another':

> *y a dollas ij doll yn (an) grows* **heb ken** *may ȝello an kentrow bras dre y ȝewleff bys yn pen* 'they bored two holes in the cross without any others so that the great nails would go through his hands up to the head' PA 178bc

> *map den* **hep ken** *ys bara byth nyn jeves ol bewnes* 'mankind without other than bread never has the whole of life' PC 65-66

ef a'th saw **hep ken** *yly ol a'th cleues yn tyen* 'it will heal thee, without other salve, wholly of thy leprosy' RD 1695.

It is probably from the sense 'without any other, without a fellow' that the sense in Breton developed. It clearly has not so developed in Cornish, however. Most usually *hep ken* in Cornish means 'without cause, without justification, gratuitously' as can be seen from the following examples:

> *Onon gans an keth welen yn leyff crist a ve gorris an gwyskis lasche war an pen*
> *bum pur gewar dese3ys ha buxow leas* **hep ken** *ha tummasow kekyffris*
> 'With the same wand that was put into Christ's hand one (man) slashed him over the head a very well-aimed blow, and many strokes without cause' PA 138a-c
> *a debel venyn hep ras ty ru'm tullas sur* **hep ken** 'O evil woman without grace, thou hast deceived me surely without cause' OM 251-52
> *Eua prag y whruste sy tulle the bryes* **hep ken** 'Eve, why didst thou deceive thy spouse without a cause? OM 277-78
> *prag y[s] tolste sy* **hep ken** *worth hy thempte the dyrry an frut erbyn ov dyfen* 'why didst thou deceive her without cause by tempting her to pick the fruit against my prohibition?' OM 301-03
> *ov lathe guyryon* **hep ken** *whet vyngeans warnogh a gouth* 'slaying an innocent man without cause! Vengeance will yet fall on you' PC 2625-26
> *poys yv gena dyswuthel* **heb ken** *an keth flehys ma* 'I am reluctant to destroy these same children without cause' BM 1633-34
> *ty ram tullas ve* **heb kene** 'you have deceived me without cause' CW855
> *eva prag y wresta gye tulla tha bryas* **heb ken** 'Eve, why did you deceive your spouse without cause?' CW 885-86.

As we have already seen, the word spelt <froeth> in Kernowek Kemyn is unattested in Middle or Late Cornish. The verb used in *a gyn ynnon* is *kyny* 'lament', but finite forms are unattested. The only examples in Middle Cornish are:

> *nu'm cloweth neb ow* **kyny** 'no one will hear me lamenting' BK 623
> *elhas bos rys thym* **kyny!** 'alas that I must lament' BK 3147
> *attoma hager vyadge ma hallaf* **kyny** *ellas* 'here is a wretched business so that I must lament, alas!' CW 918-19
> *rag henna paynes pur vras yma ornes ragan ny may hellyn* **kyny** *dretha* 'therefore very great torments have been ordained for us so that we must lament because of them' CW 1014-16.

If a native speaker heard the expression *a gyn ynnon* he would probably recognize the verb, since *kyni* 'to lament' occurs in verse 22, but he would take the whole to mean 'that will lament in us'. If he saw *a gyn ynnon* written, however, he would almost certainly understand it as 'of a trick/device in us', cf. *me a vyn towlall neb **gyn** 'I will cast some trick' CW 441. The same native speaker would also be perplexed by the phrase *dell waytyn*. *Gweyt, gwayt* is most frequently used in the imperative with the sense 'be careful to, take care to'. The verbal noun means 'expect', e.g. *fatell yllans **gwetias** favowre a thewleff aga thas a neff* 'how can they expect favour at the hands of their heavenly father?' TH 55a. I know of only one example where it occurs, as here, in a subordinate clause:

> *Pan **waytyan** e vos maraw, nyng es drog na galaraw the'n fals a scornyas ow du* 'Since we expect that he is dead, there is no harm or affliction for the deceiver who scorned my god' BK 523-25.

A native speaker of Cornish would understand *dell waytyn* to mean 'as we expect' or possibly 'that we are careful to'. If a literate speaker of Cornish read Rom. 8:23 as translated here, assuming that he could make sense of the unhistoric spelling, he would take it to mean something like:

> '... and it is not the deed without any other/without cause, but we ourselves, have the first ? of the Spirit, which ?will lament/? of a gin in us, that we expect/as we are careful that we may be accepted as children, the redemption of our body.'

The RSV, from which the Kernowek Kemyn was translated, reads:

> '... and not only the creation, but we ourselves, who have the first fruits of the Spirit, groan inwardly, as we wait for adoption as sons, the redemption of our bodies.'

My own freer version reads as follows:

> *Nyns esa an creacyon yn unyk owth hanaja. Kynth usy bleynfrutys an Sperys genen, yth eson ny owth hanaja war jy ha ny ow cortos dhe vos recevys avel mebyon. Hen yw dhe styrya, an redempcyon a'gan corf.*

I believe that a native speaker of Cornish would find that immediately intelligible.

6.11 Rom. 15:1-4 in Kernowek Kemyn reads as follows:

Y tegoedh dhyn hag yw krev perthi difygyow an re wann, heb omblesya. Plegyn ni, peub ahanan, dh'y gentrevek rag da, rag y dhrehevel. Rag ny omblesya Krist; rag dell yw skrifys, Kablow an re a'th kabla a goedhas warnav. Rag py traow pynag a veu skrifys kyns a veu skrifys rag agan dyski rag ma'gan be, der agan perthyans ha dre gonfort an skryptors, govenek.

It should be noted straight away that the first sentence begins with the particle *y* in *y tegoedh* but that the next verb, *yw* 'is', is without any particle before it. In Cornish this can only mean that the verb is interrogative. Notice also that in the third sentence the word **kablow* is intended to be the plural of *cabel* 'censure' (cf. *heb* **cabel** 'without censure' OM 2674), but no such a plural is attested and indeed such an abstract plural is not expected; **kablow* might perhaps, therefore, be more naturally taken to mean 'cables' (cf. **capel** *gorhel* 'a ship's cable' BM 467, which is probably only a spelling for **cabel gorhel*). A native speaker of Cornish, if he could read the above passage in its unhistorical spelling would probably, after reading it several times, understand it more or less as follows:

'We ought and is it strong to bear the defects of the the weak, without pleasing oneself (or ?pleasuring) oneself? Let us bow down, everyone of us, to his neighbour for a good thing, to build him. Because Christ used not pleasure himself; for as is written: The ?censures (or ?cables) of the *re* of thy calumniation, fell upon me. For whatever ?*traou* were written before what was written for our learning so that we had/might have, through our patience and by the comfort of the scriptures, hope.'

I hope that my own version of this passage is more readily intelligble:

Aban on ny cref, y codh dhyn perthy dyfygyow an dus wan ha sevel orth plesya agan honen. Res yw dhe bubonen ahanan plesya y gentrevak rag y vyldya yn ban. Rag ny wrug Cryst plesya y honen, mes, kepar del laver an scryptur, "Y codhas warnaf vy oll an despyt a'n re usy ow cul bysmer dhys". Rag pub tra neb a vue screfys y'n dedhyow coth rag agan desky ny, screfys vue may fen ny stedfast ha may hallen ny perthy govenek dre gonfort an scrypturs.

6.12 At Rom. 15:14-16 the Kernowek Kemyn reads:

Ha surhes ov ow honan, ow brederedh, y'gas kever, hwi ynwedh dhe vos leun a dhader, lenwys a bub godhvos, gwiw dhe dhyski an eyl dh'y gila. Ha hartha y skrifis dhywgh yn rann, orth agas kovhe, der an ras a veu res dhymm gans Dyw, rag may fiv menyster Yesu Krist dhe'n kenedhlow, avel oferyas dhe aweyl Yesu Krist rag may fo offrynn an kenedhlow kemmeradow, sanshes dell re beu gans an Spyrys.

The expression *Ha *hartha y skrifis dhywgh* is a problem. I assume the intended sense is 'I wrote to you more boldly'. Unfortunately the comparative degree of an adjective when used adverbially in Cornish is normally preceded by *the*. Here are some examples:

> *may hallo pup ol* **the wel** *dotho ef ry strekesow* 'so that everyone may the better deal him blows' PC 2080-81
> *mas* **the wel** *y'm gorthebeugh* 'unless you answer me better' RD 47
> **the voy** *nefre me ath cays* 'I will always hate you more' BM 926
> *mur ty a far* **the lakka** 'you will fare much worse' BM 2456
> **the belha** *ha* **the weusa** *a vova ow mois in rag* 'further and more astray would he be proceeding' TH 17a
> *na* **the le** *regardya an discans han feith* 'nor to regard the teaching and faith less' TH 34.

The translation ought, therefore, to have read: *dhe hartha*. As it is, the word *hartha* looks like the verbal noun of the word 'to bark' (*Dho* **harha** 'latro, to bark' AB: 77a). The verb *cofhe* (Kernowek Kemyn *kovhe*) is attested once in traditional Cornish, where it means 'remember' not 'remind': *why a'm* **cofua** *vy hep gow pysough* [leg. *pesquyth*] *may feve evys* 'you will remember me without doubt, whenever it is drunk' PC 827-88. The word **kenedhlow* is the unattested plural of the Old Cornish word *kinethel* 'generatio [generation]'. Neither **sanshes* nor **kemmeradow* is attested in traditional Cornish. The expression *sanshes dell *re beu* is also open to question. Nowhere in traditional Cornish is the perfective particle used after *del*; the preterite of *bos* immediately follows *del*, as can be seen from the following examples:

> *golsowens ow lauarow a ihesu* **del ve** *helheys war an bys avel carow* PA 2ab
> *yn tre du ha pehadur acord* **del ve** *kemerys* PA 8b
> *ol ʒy voth may rollo bres a neʒy* **del ve** *ʒe gres* PA 32b
> *arluth du ʒe voth* **del ve** *ʒy ʒyscyplys y trylyas* PA 55bc
> *drok ʒen os kepar* **del ves** PA 192a
> *kepar* **del ve** *ʒen Iustis* PA 247b
> *kepar* **del ve** *thy'm yrghys* OM 872
> *th'y thyller arte glenes kepar* **del ve** PC 1153-54
> *In marver* **dell ve** *agan mam sans egglos a thewethas assaultys* TH 30a

*kepar **dell** veva fuguris* TH 38a
*crowsyys in kepar maner ha forme **dell** ve y mester* TH 47
*kepar **del** ve leveris kyns* SA 62a
*par **dell** vema vngrasshes* CW 1575
*ha **del** ve thym kyns ornys* CW 2086.

Bearing those points in mind, I think we can reasonably say, that the above passage would be understood by a native speaker of Cornish as follows:

'And I am insured myself, my brotherhood, with respect to you, that you also are full of goodness, filled with all knowledge, worthy to teach one to another. And ?to bark, I wrote to you in part, remembering you, through the grace which was given to me by God, so that I ?may be the minister of ?Jesus Christ to the generations, like a ?priest to the gospel of ?Jesus Christ so that the offering of the ?acceptable generations may be, ?sanctified as he ?has been by the Spirit.'

My own corrected version reads as follows:

Yth of certan, a vreder, why the vos luen a dhader hag a skentoleth hag abyl dhe dhesky an eyl y gela. Saw me re screfas dheugh yn hardh yn tylleryow rag dul dheugh perthy cof, rag gras Dew re'm gwrug an menyster a Jesu Cryst dhe'n Jentylys. Ow servys avel pronter yw dhe brogeth awayl Dew may fo an Jentylys offrys avel offryn servabyl ha sacrys der an Sperys Sans.

6.13 Rom. 15:23-8 in Kernowek Kemyn reads as follows:

*Mes lemmyn nyns eus *le dhymm y'n **ranndiryow** ma, ha hwans re'm beu a dhos dhywgh nans yw nebes bledhynyow, pan wrylliv vyajya dhe Spayn. Rag **gwaytyans** a'm beus, pan **dremenav**, a'gas gweles ha genowgh dhe vos spedys war ow fordh wosa my dhe vos lenwys ahanowgh yn rann. Mes lemmyn my a dhe Yerusalem ow menystra dhe'n sens. Rag da o gans **Makedoni** hag Aghaia provia nebes rag an voghosogyon yn mysk an sens yn Yerusalem. Rag da o gansa ha kendonoryon dhedha yns, rag mar kevrenna an **kenedhlow** gansa y'ga **thraow** spyrysek, y tegoedh dhedha ynwedh y'n **traow kigek** menystra dhedha. War-lergh gorfenna hemma ytho ha war-lergh selya dhedha an froeth ma, **yth av dredhowgh** dhe Spayn.*

In the above passage *nyns eus le dhymm* is intended to translate 'I have no place'. In the texts, however, the word *le* 'place' is a bound form. It is used in *yn le* 'instead of', *pup le* 'everywhere', *le may ma* 'where (relative)', *then le na* 'to where', *yn neb le* 'somewhere' and *py le* 'where?'. 'Place' as an unbound form is *tyller*:

> *hag eth 3y* **tyller** *tythy* 'and went to his native place' PA 18a
> *Then* **tyller** *crist re dethye* 'Christ had come to the place' PA 33a
> *yma dev yn* **tyller** *ma* 'God is in this place' OM 1992
> *remmvys the gen* **tyller** 'removed to another place' OM 2045
> *nyns yw thy's* **tyller** *pur es* 'it is not a very easy place for you' PC 86
> *dreugh bys omma thu'm* **tyller** 'bring here to my place' PC 980
> *rak paynys pan na'n gefo* **tyller** *th'y pen* 'so that because of pains he found no place for his head' RD 270
> *iheus arluth cuff colyn the* **teller** *da rum gedya* 'may Jesus dear heart guide me to a good place' BM 628-29
> *kynth yv* **teller** *guyls ha yne* 'though it is a wild and cold place' BM 1145
> *ny a rede in lyas* **tyllar** *in scriptur* 'we read in many places in scripture' TH 6
> *a rella shynya in* **tyllar** *tewlle* 'which would shine in a dark place' TH 18
> *pan vynhy, in* **tellar** *clos* 'when you wish in a concealed place' BK 2977
> *tha gutha in* **tellar** *close* 'to hide in a concealed place' CW 866.

The word *le* here can only mean 'less'. *__Ranndiryow__* is based on Breton *ranndirioù* 'regions' and is unknown in traditional Cornish. It is certainly used in the revived language, but is a modern neologism and would have meant nothing to a speaker of the traditional language. It is out of place in a biblical translation. The word for 'region, district' in traditional Cornish is *cost, costys*:

> *py tyller yma moyses ha py* **cost** *yma trygys* 'in which place is Moses and in which region does he dwell?' OM 1551-52
> *Jhesus a theth then* **costes** *a cesarye philippi* 'Jesus came to the region of Caesarea Philippi' TH 44
> *nena eff a gemeras owne a drega na fella in* **cost** *na* 'then he became afraid to reside any longer in that district' TH 46a
> *Pan nowothou, pan guestlow us genowgh why a'n* **cost** *west?* 'What news have you, what hostages from the western region?' BK 2222-23.

__Gwaytyans__ is unattested in Cornish. The word for 'hope' is *govenek*:

> *rag thy'm yma* **govenek** *cafes the gens tregereth* 'for I have a hope rather of obtaining mercy' OM 453-54
> *ny re duth oma adre in* **govenek** *exaltye meryasek in pur certen* 'we have come here from home in the hope of elevating Meriasek in very truth' BM 2899-901

*Nyn ses thyn naneyll feith, **govenek**, charite, paciens, chastite, na tra vith arell
    ew da* 'We possess neither faith, hope, charity, patience, chastity, nor
    any other good thing' TH 9

*norysshys gans **govenek**, encresshys gans charite, ha confyrmys gans antiquite*
    'nourished by hope, increased by charity and confirmed by
    antiquity' TH 49

*ha **govenak** thym ema* 'and I have hope' BK 1395.

In the traditional language *gweyt* means 'be careful to, take care to', the
unattested word **gwaytyans* would most naturally mean 'carefulness,
circumspection'. As I explain at § 10.12 below, *tremena* without any
qualifying adverb means 'pass over, die'. *Spedya* means 'succeed' rather
than 'send on, dispatch' as is required here. As mentioned at § 4.01
above **traow* is unattested anywhere in Cornish written by Cornishmen. I have discussed the word **kigek* under 'invented words' at § 3.07
above and *froeth* under 'lexical purism' at § 3.04. With all those
observations in mind let us return to Rom. 15:23-28. I assume that a
literate native speaker of Cornish, if he could understand the orthography, would understand the Kernowek Kemyn approximately as
follows:

'But now there is not less to me in these ?share-lands (?gavelkind,
?share-cropping), and I have had a desire of coming to you for a few
years, when I travel to Spain. For I have ?circumspection, when I die, to
see you and with you to be made successful upon my way, after I am
filled with you in share (cf. ?reference to gavelkind above). But now I
shall go to Jerusalem, ministering to the saints. Because *Makedoni* (is this
the same as *Masedonia* elsewhere?) and Achaia thought it good to
provide a little for the poor among the saints in Jerusalem. For they
thought it good and they are debtors to them, for if the generations
?shared with them in their spiritual **traow*, it is fitting for them also to
minister to them in fleshy **traow*. After finishing this therefore and after
sealing this **froeth* to them, I will go through you to Spain.'

The final sentence with its 'I will go through you to Spain' is
particularly unhappy. My own (corrected) version of this passage reads
as follows:

*Saw lemmyn, aban nag ues spas vyth moy dhym y'n costys ma, mal yw genef
dos dheugh nans yw lyes bledhen. Me a dhue dheugh war ow vyaj bys yn
Spayn. Yn gwyr govenek a'm bues agas gweles why war ow vyaj. Why a yll ow
danvon yn rag wosa me dhe vos lowen y'gas cowethas termyn hyr. Saw y'n tor'*

ma yth esof vy ow travalya dhe Jerusalem avel menyster dhe bobel Dew. Plesys vue Macedonia hag Achaia dhe gevranna aga fyth gans an vohosogyon yn mesk pobel Dew yn Jerusalem. Da o gansans gul yndelma hag yn gwyr y cotha dhedhans y wul. Mar tueth an Jentylys ha cafus ran a'ga bennothow sperysek, y tal dhedhans lemmyn gweres pobel Dew ow tuchya taclow an kyg. Rag henna, pan vo an dra ma cowlwres genama ha wosa me dhe dhelyfra dhe bobel Dew pub tra re bue cuntellys, me a vyn dalleth war ow vyaj dhe Spayn. Me a dhue dheugh war an fordh.

I think I have said enough to show that the Kernowek Kemyn translation of this most poetic and profound of all St Paul's epistles is less than wholly successful.

THE SECOND TRANSLATOR

7.00 The second translator was responsible for Acts and 1 and 2 Corinthians. The title of the Acts of the Apostles has been rather imaginatively translated as *Oberow an Abesteli* 'Doings of the Apostles'. The rest of the translation of Acts and of the other two books is less successful, however. In examining the work of this translator, I shall start with a detailed analysis of a single fairly long passage in 2 Corinthians. Thereafter I shall look briefly at all three books one by one.

7.01 In the RSV 2 Cor. 10:1-6 reads as follows:

'I, Paul, myself entreat you, by the meekness and gentleness of Christ— I who am humble when face to face with you, but bold to you when I am away!—I beg of you that when I am present I may not have to show boldness with such confidence as I count on showing against some who suspect us of acting in worldly fashion. For though we live in the world we are not carrying on in a wordly way, for the weapons of our warfare are not worldly but have divine power to destroy strongholds. We destroy arguments and every proud obstacle to the knowledge of God, and take every thought captive to obey Christ, being ready to punish every disobedience, when your obedience is complete.'

This the second translator has rendered:

My ow honan, Powl, a'gas pys dre glorder ha jentylys Krist, my neb yw uvel pan esov orth ganow y'gas mysk mes hardh dhywgh pan esov dhe-ves ahanowgh; lemmyn my a'gas pys, ha my y'gas mysk, na vo edhomm dhymm bos hardh, gans an omgyfyans dredho may prederav bedha bos hardh erbynn an re neb a breder ni dhe gerdhes war-lergh an kig. Rag ni a gerdh mes ni werryn

war-lergh an kig, rag arvow agan gwerryans nyns yns a'n kig mes yma dhedha
nerth Dyw dhe dhomwhel kastylli, ow tomwhel dadhlow ha pub tra woethus
hag a sett orth godhvos Dyw, hag ow talghenna yn keth pub tybyans rag gul
dhodho bos gostyth dhe Grist, ha parys on ni dhe gessydhya pub diwostythter
pan vo kowlwrys agas gostythter.

Although portions of that passage are intelligible, the overall sense is
not clear—without reference to the English. If a literate native speaker
of Cornish from *c.* 1500 read the Kernowek Kemyn just quoted—
assuming that he could make anything of the unhistorical orthography—he would, I suggest, have difficulty in understanding it
completely. He would, I suggest, take the passage to mean something
like the following:

I myself (cf. *my… **ow honan** PC 97*), Paul (cf. *Sent **powl** TH 13*), beseech
you (cf. *arlythy my **agas pys** OM 2347*) through the ?mildness and
graciousness (cf. *Damsel er the **gentylys** OM 2105*) of Christ (*ow cafus **crist***
PC 588), I, who is (cf. *neb yv dev PC 666*) humble (cf. *cortis hag **vvel** yn*
sur BM 182), when I am (cf. *ethesoff ve genowgh TH 17*) ?against ?mouth
(not 'face to face' which would be **orth agas ganow*; cf. *orth **y anov** pan*
govsis BM 1033) among you (cf. *yn **ages mysk** RD 1401*) but bold (cf. *ha*
*pur **hardh** a wovynnys corf Ihesus PA 215b*) to you (cf. *a rys **thyugh** OM*
310) when I am away (cf. *gallas an glaw **the ves** OM 1097*) of you (cf. *onan*
***ahanough** PC 736*), now (*whythyns **lemmyn** pup PC 1242*) I beseech you,
and I among you, that there be not (*na vo marow PC 2446*) need (*esa*
***ethom** the vabden TH 13a*) to me to be bold, with the ?finding ourselves
(*In gulas nef re **omgyffyn** BK 3049*) through whom / which (cf. *dretha may*
hallan bos delyuerys TH 10) I will think (cf. *me ne **brederaf** gwell for OM*
1244) be! / I shall be (cf. *Betha why lawannack Borde & benytha vays ne*
vetha) to be bold against (*erbyn a pyth PC 820*) the ?re who (**an re neb* is
unattested in Cornish) will consider (cf. *why a **preder** a'y passyon* 'you
will consider his passion' *PC 3223*) that we walk (cf. *the gerthes BM*
3345) according to (cf. *warlerth an examplys TH 10*) the flesh (cf. *contrary*
thyn kyge TH 16a). For we will walk in the flesh but we will not make
war (cf. *ha **guerrya** purthyogel BM 3454*) according to the flesh, for the
arms (cf. *in **arvow** rys ew thotha BK 2370*) of our ?making war, they are
not (cf. *nyns yns BM 2045*) of the flesh but they have (cf. *yma thethy aga*
profession TH 32a) the strength (cf. *an principall **nerth** TH 48*) of God (cf.
*pan yv both **dev** OM 1342*) to thwart (cf. *orth ov **domhel** dres an pov*
'thwarting me throughout the country' *BM 2652*) castles (cf. *Pals ew an*
*owr y'th **castylly** BK 1795-96*), thwarting ?dadhlow (**dadhel, *dathel* is
unattested in Cornish) and everything (cf. *ha pub tra ol a vith da BK1020*)
proud (cf. *in gollan del os tha **gothys** CW 284*) which resists (cf. *mata*

orthen ny na set BM 1916) the knowledge of God (cf. *han* **gothfas** *a* **thu** TH 11), and seizing (cf. *me a'n* **dalhen** *fest yn tyn* PC 1131) in the same (cf. **yn keth** *forth na* OM 713) every opinion (cf. *thu'm* **tybyans** *wheth ef ny grys* PC 1213) to make it be obedient (cf. *nefra* **gostyth** *thy gorty* CW 892) to Christ, and ready (cf. **parys** *yw genaf* CW 971) are we (*buthys* **on ny** OM 1705) to ?punish (cf. *ty a berth sure* **gossythyans** 'you will surely endure punishment' CW 1122) every ?disobedience, whenever your ?obedience is complete (cf. *an temple may fe* **coulwreys** OM 2412).

In order to make this clearer, I give here the same with minor adjustments and as a continuous text:

'I myself, Paul, beseech you through the mildness and graciousness of Christ, I, who is humble, when I am ?against ?mouth among you but bold to you when I am away of you, now I beseech you, and I among you, that there be no need to me to be bold, with the ?finding ourselves through whom/which I will think be!/I shall be to be bold against the ?re who will consider that we walk according to the flesh. For we will walk in the flesh but we will not make war according to the flesh, for the arms of our ?making war, they are not of the flesh but they have the strength of God to thwart castles, thwarting ?*dadhlow* and everything proud which resists the knowledge of God, and seizing in the same every opinion to make it be obedient to Christ, and ready are we to ?punish every ?disobedience, whenever your ?obedience is complete.'

It can hardly be claimed, I think, that the Kernowek Kemyn translation is wholly successful in this passage. My own (corrected) version of the same passage reads as follows:

Me, Pawl, me a'gas pys dre glorder ha wharder Cryst—me yw uvel pan esof genough fas dhe fas mes hardh pan esof pell dheworthough—me a'gas pys na wrelleugh ow honstryna dhe vos asper tro ha why pan vedhaf warbarth genough, rag me a vyn cowsel warbyn an re na a laver me dhe wruthyl warlergh brues mab den. Yth yw gwyr ny dhe vos tregys y'n bys, saw ny wren ny gwerrya warlergh squyrys mab den. Ny dhue agan arvow ny dheworth mab den, mes y a's teves nerth Dew hag a yll dystrowy dynasow cref. Yth eson ny ow tyswul argumentys ha pub ancombrynsy prowt drehevys yn ban warbyn an aswonvos a Dhew. Ny a wra prysner a bub preder, may fo va gostyth dhe Gryst. Parys on ny dhe bunsya pub dysobedyens, pan vo collenwys agas obedyens why.

7.02 Predicate wrongly separated from forms of *bos* 'be'

In the first two chapters of Acts we read sentences like the following:

kens lies dyth besydhys gans an Spyrys Sans *vydhough 'before many days you will be baptized by the Holy Spirit' Acts 1:5
kemmerys yn-bann *veu 'he was taken up' Acts 1:9
gwenys y'n golonn *vons 'they were wounded in the heart' Acts 2:37.

The verbs **vydhough, *veu* and **vons* are incorrect. In Middle Cornish a form in *b-* of the verb *bos* 'to be' may appear without the relative particle *a* and with initial lenition, only if such a form *follows the adjective or verbal adjective immediately*, otherwise the verbal particle *y* + mixed mutation is required. Here are some examples from the texts:

gul alter sur da vye 'to make an altar surely would be good' OM 1174
da vye kyns dos sabovt dyswruthyl an fals profes 'it would be good before the sabbath comes to destroy the false prophet' PC 561-62
clewys vyth agas desyr 'your desire will be heard' PC 309
guel vye y gase bev 'it would be better to leave him alive' PC 1592
da vye thy'n mos ganso 'it would be good for us to go with him' PC 1625
guel vye y thylyfrye 'it would be better to free him' PC 1863
kymmys vyth an ponveter 'so great will be the affliction' PC 2655
carrek veryasek holma gelwys vyth wose helma 'this will be called Meriasek's Rock hereafter' BM 1072-73
meryasek ganso lemen helhys vue in kerth heb fael 'Meriasek has been driven away by him now without fail' BM 2248-49
Tregys vue in lestevdar 'He was living in Lysteudar' BM 2284
guel vya dyugh omdenna a dermen 'it would be better for you to withdraw in time' BM 3474-75
megys vue gans boys eleth 'he was nourished by the food of angels' BM 4464
orth ow both gyllys vean gans gorthyb the'n gwelha gowr 'at my desire we would have gone with an answer to the best of men' BK 2092-03
poys vyth ganso 'he will be reluctant [*lit.* it will be heavy with him]' BK 2153.

The translation ought to read *besydhys vydhough gans an Spyrys Sans, kemmerys veu yn-bann* and *gwenys vons.*

7.03 Erroneous initial mutation. At Acts 1:9 we read: *ha kommolenn a'n degemmeras mes a'ga wolok* 'and a cloud took him out of their sight' (RSV). First it should be noticed that the word *comolen* 'cloud' (Kernowek Kemyn *kommolenn*) is unattested in Cornish. The only word attested is *clowdes* 'clouds' at CW 4 and *clowdys* 'clouds' at CW 76. The second point to notice is that *a'ga *wolok* is incorrect. The verbal adjective *aga* is followed by spirant mutation, not lenition. It does affect initial *g*:

> *gans **aga garm*** PA 4b
> ***aga garrow*** PA 45c,
> ***aga gwayn*** PA 114d,
> ***aga gore*** OM 991,
> ***aga gorra*** OM 1694,
> *drok **aga gnas*** PC 1141,
> *th'**aga guythe*** PC 2297,
> ***aga guelas*** RD 899,
> *d'**aga gorre*** RD 2589,
> *h**age goys*** BM 1518,
> *age greff* BM 3136,
> ***aga ganowow*** TH 7a,
> ***aga gwrear*** TH 12,
> ***aga gothfas*** TH 14, *t*
> *h**ega gwetha*** TH 14.

7.04 * *Oll anedha* for *y oll* 'they all'. At Acts 2:4 and 4:31 this version has *hag **oll anedha** a veu lenwys a'n Spyrys Sans* 'and they were all filled with the Holy Spirit'. One also finds *Ha marth o gans **oll anedha*** 'And all of them were amazed' Acts 2:12, ***oll anedha**, byghan ha bras, a goela orto* 'and all of them, great and small, listened to him' Acts 8. 10. I am unhappy about *oll anedha*, since *oll* is an adjective, not a pronoun and indeed *oll anetha* is nowhere attested in Cornish. If one wants to say 'they all, all of them' one says *y oll*:

> *ha kyn fons **y ol** sclandrys* 'and though they all be offended' PC 899
> *thethans **y oll** therag dorne* 'to them all before hand' TH 44a
> *hy a dowlas in offering a Dew moy agis **y oll*** 'she has given as an offering
> to God more than they all' SA 64.

The RSV itself reads 'they all' in each case. 'All of them' is a modern colloquialism in English, which should not be translated literally.

7.05 Mistaken use of *oll* 'all'. The translator's use of the word *oll* 'all' is often questionable. He writes, for example, *hag ev a'n sawyas mes a'**y boenvos oll*** 'and he saved him from all his trouble' Acts 7:10. 'All his' + noun in Cornish is rendered *oll y* + noun, as can be seen from the following examples:

oll y sor may fe gevys 'that all his anger might be forgiven' PA 9a
a ylly neuera **oll y yscren** 'could number all his bones' PA 183c
oll y gorf hay esely 'all his body and limbs' PA 184d
gans **oll y tretury** 'with all his treachery' PA 195d
oll y drok hay anken 'all his hurt and affliction' PA 237d
ol y pobel ymons y 'they are all his people' OM 1687
ef hag **ol y tyskyblon** 'he and all his disciples' PC 636
hag **ol y wythres** *keffrys* 'and all his deeds as well' PC 1443
ol y thyllas 'all his clothes' PC 2842
aleys **ol y wolyov** 'all his wounds spread wide' BM 1848
in mesk **ol y nascon** 'among all his nation' BM 2918
the wull **oll y blonogath** 'to do all his will' TH 23a
oll y Judgment hay oberow 'all his judgement and works' TH 37a
A rug despisia **oll y decreys** 'who despised all his decrees' TH 40a
war **oll y misteris** *omma in bys* 'on all his mysteries here in the world' TH
  52a
ha why **oll ye gowetha** 'and you all his companions' CW 324
oll y gorffe m[ar] pur sembly 'all his body so very seemly' CW 437
oll y joye ythew kellys 'all his joy is lost' CW 1001.

The translation here should have read *oll y boenvos* 'all his trouble'.

Similarly the translation reads ***An dus oll** a'n gwelas ev ow kerdhes* 'All
the people saw him walking' Acts 3:9, *drefenn **an dus oll** dhe ri gordhyans
dhe Dhyw* 'because all the people praised God for what had happened'
Acts 4:31. In Cornish 'all the people' is not ****an dus oll**, but **oll an dus**,
as can be clearly seen from the following examples:

ol an dus ma a leuer 'all these people say' PA 129b
hag **ol an dus** *vas* 'and all the good people' OM 814
ha goky dres **ol an dus** 'and foolish beyond all people' RD 972
the ry laude ha preise the **oll an dus** *da* 'to give laud and praise to all the
  good people' TH 25.

****An dus oll** is not attested in Cornish and cannot be recommended.

7.06 Let us look at Acts 3:9 a little more closely. The text reads: *An dus
oll a'n gwelas ev ow kerdhes ha gormel Dyw*. The only finite verb in that
sentence is *a'n gwelas* 'saw him'. If one uses the verbal noun instead of
a finite form in verbs after the first finite verb, such verbal nouns will
be assumed to have the same subject as the finite verb itself. *An dus oll
a'n gwelas ow kerdhes ha gormel Dyw* can only mean 'All the people saw

him walking and [they] praised God', whereas the translator incorrectly believes it means 'All the people saw him walking and praising God'.

7.07 Incorrect usage with proper names. At Acts 2:7-11 we read:

> *Ha sowdhenys vens, ha marth a's teva, hag i a leveris, 'Otta, a nyns yw oll an re ma neb usi ow kewsel **tus Galila**? Ha fatell glyw pub huni yn y yeth teythyek y honan? **Tus Parthia** ha Medys hag Elamitys, ha **trigoryon Mesopotamia, Yudi ha Kappadosia, Pontus hag Asia, Fryjia ha Pamfylia, Ejyp** ha rannvroyow Libya ryb Syrene, ha godrigoryon a Rom.*

Cornish is a Celtic language and this means that if an indefinite noun is qualified by a definite noun in genitival relationship with it, the indefinite noun itself becomes definite. *Tus* 'people' is indefinite but *tus Galila* is definite and means 'the people of Galilee', not 'people of Galilee'. This feature of Cornish has been disregarded and in consequence we find above such incorrect forms as **tus Galila* 'the Galileans', **Tus Parthia* 'the Parthians' and **trigoryon Mesopotamia, Kappadosia, Pontus hag Asia*, etc. 'the inhabitants of Mesopotamia, Cappadocia, Pontus and Asia, etc.' These forms should have been *tus a Alila, Tus a Barthia* and *trigoryon yn Mesopotamia, Kappadosia, Asia*, etc. Similarly at Acts 8:25 we read *ow pregoth an aweyl yn lies tre an Samaritanys*. As it stands, this can only mean 'preaching the gospel in the many towns of the Samaritans'. And *den Ethiopia* at Acts 8:27 can only mean 'the man of Ethiopia' and *den Tarsus* at Acts 8:11 means 'the man of Tarsus'. At Acts 19:29 we read of *Gayus hag Aristarghus, gwer Masedonia*. This can only mean 'Gaius and Aristarchus, the men of Macedonia'. The translation should have read *Gayus hag Aristarghus, tus a Vasedonia*.

7.08 Unsatisfactory word-order. The word-order in Acts is sometimes less than completely satisfactory. I have space here to look at a few instances only. At Acts 5:9 we read: *Otta, yma treys an re neb re ynkleudhyas dha wour orth an daras*. Here the verb *yma* '(there) is, are' is widely separated from *orth an daras* 'at the door'. As a result, it is natural to read the sentence to mean 'Behold, there are the feet of those who buried your husband at the door'—but, of course, it is the feet that are at the door, not the burial. At first glance one is led to believe that the husband was buried at the threshold.

At Acts 5:20 the translation reads: *Keugh, sevewgh y'n tempel ha leverewgh **dhe'n bobel an geryow** oll a-dro dhe'n bywnans ma*. One naturally takes *oll a-dro* to mean 'all about' and understands the sentence to mean 'Go, stand up in the temple and tell the people all around ?to this life'. In fact, the translation here is intended to translate: 'Go and stand in the temple and speak to the people all the words of this life'.

7.09 Word-order is only one of the problems at Acts 3:2. The text reads as follows:

> *Ha yth esa unn gour, kloppek a-dhia vrys y vamm, ow pos degys, neb a worrens i pub dydh ryb porth an tempel henwys Fethus rag pysi alusen dhiworth an re owth entra y'n tempel.*

At first sight this seems to mean:

> 'And there was a man, having a limp from the womb of his mother, being carried, who they (emphatic) used to ?send by the side of the gate of the temple called Fethus in order to pray alms from the people entering into the temple.'

The vocabulary in this passage is incorrect. *Kloppek* means 'limping', rather than 'lame, unable to walk'. *Pesy* 'to pray' is not normally used of asking for something, which is *govyn*. *An re owth entra* should be *an re na esa owth entra*. *Ow pos degys* 'being carried' might refer most naturally to the *y vamm* 'his mother' immediately preceding. *Gorra* means 'send' or 'put into' rather than simple 'put down', which would better be translated by *settya* 'set'. *Fethus* looks like a personal name, but is intended to translate 'Beautiful', and refers to the gate, not the temple. The word has been respelt from Old Cornish *faidus* 'formosus [beautiful]' but is otherwise unattested. It must be admitted that the multiple infelicities in this passage derive from the way it was translated word for word from the RSV:

> 'And a man lame from birth was being carried, whom they laid daily at that gate of the temple which is called Beautiful, to seek alms of those who entered the temple.'

In my own translation of this verse I attempted to write something that would have been immediately intelligible to a native speaker of Cornish:

Y'n tor' na y fue degys aberth y'n templa den re bya evredhek dhya y enesygeth. Y fedha settys dhe'n dor kenyver jorna orth yet an templa henwys an Porth Teg may halla govyn alusyon orth an re na a vedha owth entra dredho.

7.10 Word-order is also a problem at Acts 28:11, though it is not the only difficulty:

Wosa tri mis ni a voras yn gorhel a Aleksandria re spenas an gwav y'n ynys ha dhodho imaj a-rag a'n Evellyon.

If a good speaker of Cornish heard this verse read aloud, he would take it to mean something like the following:

'After three months we set sail in a ship of Alexandria which has spent the winter in the island and has an image in front of the Twins.'

One should not forget that *re spenas* 'has spent' is perfect rather than pluperfect and that *a-rag* is a preposition meaning 'before, in front of' before it is an adverb. In my own version I attempted to write something that was immediately intelligible:

Try mys warlergh henna ny a voras yn gorhel re bya y'n enys dres an gwaf. Ef o devedhys dhya Alexandria ha'n Evellas o syn y ben arag.

7.11 At Acts 7:12-3 the Kernowek Kemyn reads as follows:

Mes pan glywas Yakob bos ys yn Ejyp, ev a dhannvonas yn-rag agan tasow an **kynsa** **gweyth, ha dhe'n* *nessa *gweyth *Yosep a veu aswonnys gans y vreder* 'But when Jacob heard there was corn in Egypt, he sent our fathers ahead for the first time, and the second time Joseph was recognized by his brothers'.

The first thing to notice here is that **nessa** in Cornish means 'next'; it does not mean 'second' which is always **secund, second**:

yn **secund** *dyth y fynna gruthyl ebron nef hynwys* 'on the second day I shall make a sky called heaven' OM 17-8

an **secund** *feer sur a veth sensys in pov benytha* 'the second fair will be for ever held in the country' BM 2198-99

Arta yma du ow kull an **second** *promys gans an venyn* 'Again God makes the second promise to the woman' TH 13

in **second** *degre y fithe gwryes try order moy yn sertan* 'in the second degree three more orders will indeed be created' CW 51-2 *lebmyn yn second jorna gwraf broster* 'now on the second day I make a firmament' CW 80-81.

Gweyth with the sense 'occasion' is attested nowhere in Cornish. The word for 'time, occasion' required here is *treveth*; cf.

> *ke weth* **tresse treveth** *th'y* 'go still a third time thither' OM 799
> *nena eff a gowsys thotha an* **tryssa trevath** 'then he spoke to him the third time' TH 43
> *arta Crist* **trevath arell** *a leveris then Jewys* 'another time Christ said to the Jews' TH 53.

In all three examples of **treveth / trevath** just quoted the noun + adjective is enough to express 'on the third occasion', 'on another occasion'. One should always remember that Cornish, like the other Celtic languages, dispenses with any preposition when speaking of times, days and occasions. The translation reads *dhe'n nessa gweyth* which I take to be a calque on 'at the second visit' of the RSV. It is not the best Cornish however. It would have been better if the translation had contained the Kernowek Kemyn equivalent of *an second treveth*.

7.12 The ghost-word **dustunier* **'witness'.** Not infrequently in this translation the sense 'witness' is rendered by the word **dustunier*, plural **dustunioryon*, for example:

> *onan a'n re ma dhe dhos ha bos* **dustunier genen ni a'y dhasserghyans* 'one of these [must] become with us a witness of his resurrection' Acts 1:22
> *Dyw a dhrehevis an Yesu ma, ha dhe henna ni oll yw* **dustunioryon* 'God raised up this Jesus, and of that we are all witnesses' Acts 2:32
> *dhe henna* **dustunioryon on ni* 'to that we are witnesses' Acts 3:15
> *hag i a dhros fals* **dhustunioryon, neb a leveris* 'and they brought false witnesses, who said Acts 6:13
> *neb yw lemmyn y* **dhustunioryon dhe'n bobel* 'who are now his witnesses to the people' Acts 13:31

This ghost-word **dustunier* is found in other books in *An Testament Nowydh* also. One should never forget that Cornish *dustuny* means both 'testimony' and 'witness', in the same way that 'witness' in English refers both to the person testifying, and, in the expression 'bear witness', to the testimony given. Here are some instances from the texts of *dustuny* meaning A) 'testimony' and B) 'witness, person testifying':

A **dustuny** 'witness, testimony'

mara kewsys falsury ha na blek genas henna ha fals te dok **dustuny** 'if I have spoken false and that does not please you, and false, do you bear witness' PA 82ab

Ha dew a thuk **dustuny** 'And two bore witness' PA 91a

an eʒewon a gewsys doyn thyn **dustuny** *a wra* 'the Jews spoke: he bears witness to us' PA 111c

ha leas ganso ene doʒo a ʒuk **dustuny** 'and many there with him bore witness to him' PA 208d

ha me a thek **dustyny** *y'n clewys ov leuerel* 'and I bear witness that I heard him say' PC 1313-14

ha the henna me a vyn don **dustuny** *pup termyn* 'and to that I will always bear witness' RD 1052-53.

B **dustuny** 'witness, person testifying'

myns a wruk me a'n avow hag a gyf **dustynyow** *ty the govs er byn laha* 'all that I did, I acknowledge, and I will get witnesses that you spoke against the law' PC 1301-03

hag arte y threheuel yn try-dyth na vye guel the hemma of **dustyny** 'and that he would build it again in three days so that it would never have been better—of that I am a witness' PC 1310-12

pyth yv an ethom gortos na cafus **dustynyow** 'what need is there to wait or to obtain witnesses?' PC 1497-98

sur maria jacobe ha maria salome thy'm **dustyny** 'indeed Mary Jacobi and Mary Salome as my witnesses' RD 1073-75

peys da du thym **dustuny** *nyns off y cafus defry* 'I am not pleased, God is my witness, to get it indeed' BM 3028-29

me an grontse dyogel lowenhe the den arel du **dustuny** 'I would indeed more willingly grant it to another man, God is my witness' BM 3096-98

I can tell you the clen ryght, Du **dustuny** 'I can tell you the clean right, as God is my witness' BK 2525-26.

Dustunier is a solecism and should not have been used.

7.13 ***Babanes* wrongly used to mean 'babies'.** At Acts 7:19 we read *ow kul dhedha gorra aga* **babanes** *yn-mes na na vens gwithys yn few* 'forcing them to expose their infants that they might not be kept alive'. The word ***babanes*** is the unattested plural of *baban* which itself occurs once: *eff a dall deneren nov rag* **baban** *a welogh why* 'it is worth nine pence as a doll, do you see?' BM 3404-05. The Cornish for 'infant, baby, young child' is *flogh* or *flogh byan*, as is apparent from the following instances:

*yn wethen me a welas yn ban vhel worth scoren **flogh byen** nowyth gynys hag ef yn quethow maylys* 'in the tree I saw up high upon a branch a little baby newly born and wrapped in swaddling clothes' OM 804-07

*sav warnough agas honan ha war agas **flehes vyan** ken the ole why a's byth* 'but for yourselves and for your infants you will have cause to weep' PC 2642-44

*erbyn reson yv in beys heb hays gorryth thymo creys bones **flogh** vyth concevijs* 'it is against reason that any baby be conceived in the world without male seed, believe me' BM 844-46

*dugh genavy alemma benen gans the **flogh byen*** 'come hence with me, woman with your baby' BM 1549-50

*Ser emperour dywhy mur grays agys boys mar pytethays orth benenes bohosek rag sawya agen **flehas*** 'Sir emperor, many thanks to you for being so merciful to poor women as to spare our infants' BM 1777-80

thera vi gillyz trei mîz gen 'hlôh; ha lebmen ma dho nei meppig huêg en guili 'I was three months gone with a baby; and now we have a sweet little boy in the bed' JCH

***Flô** vye gennes an mîz Merh* 'A baby born in the month of March' Gwavas

*gworeuh whellaz Seere râg an **Flô** younk* 'look carefully for the young infant [i.e. Jesus]' WRowe

*y a wellaz an **Flô** yonk gen Mareea e Thama* 'they saw the infant with Mary his mother' WRowe

*Pendre vedda why geil rag lednow rag 'as **flo*** 'What will you do for clothes for your baby?' Chygwyn.

Babanes is unattested in Cornish. The singular *baban* means 'doll', not 'baby'. The word for 'baby, infant' in Cornish is always *flogh* or *flogh byan*. *Babanes* should not have been used.

7.14 The Cornish for 'King over Egypt'. At Acts 7:18 the Kernowek Kemyn reads *bys pan sevis ken myghtern **dres** Ejyp, na aswonnis Yosep*. This is a word for word translation of the RSV, ''till there arose over Egypt another king, who had not known Joseph'. Unfortunately the translation cannot be commended. In Cornish the preposition used to connect *mytern* 'king' with the country in which he reigns is not *dres*, but *yn* 'in'. Here are a few examples from the texts:

*Gelwys y 3of conany **mytern yn** bryten vyan* 'I am called Conany, king of Brittany' BM 168-69

*eff an grug **mytern** hag Emperowre **in** norvys* 'he made him king and emperor of the world' TH 2

*Augel, **myghtern in** Scotland* 'Augel king of Scotland' BK1280

*Nyng es **myghtern in** neb gwlas* 'There is no king of any country' BK 1305

*Me ew **myghtern in** Island* 'I am king of Iceland' BK 1540

*Me, Excerces, ew guerror fers, ha **myghtern in** Itury* 'I, Excerces, am a fierce warrior and king of Iturea' BK 2597-99

*ha **myghtern in** Babylon* 'and king of Babylon' BK 2619

me, Mustensar, an tebal-gower, of [leg. ew] ***myghtern in** Affrycans* 'I Mustenar, the evil man, am king of Africa' BK 2654-56

*Bos curunis me a vyn **myghtern in** Bretayn iwys* 'I shall be crowned king of Britain indeed' BK 3075-76

*Me ew **myghtern in** Bretayn* 'I am king of Britain' BK 3120.

The translation should have read: *bys pan devis ken **myghtern yn** Ejyp.*

7.15 The Kernowek Kemyn translation of Acts 8:37-8 reads:

> '*Otta dowr;* **pandr'a'm lett** *rag bos besydhys?*' *Hag yn medh Felip,* '*Mar krysydh gans oll dha golonn,* **ty a yll**.' '"Here is water; what prevents my being baptized?" And Philip said, "If you believe with all your heart, you can."'

This does not seem to make proper sense. The eunuch asks Philip what prevents his being baptized. One would expect Philip to answer *Mar krysydh gans oll dha golonn, tra vydh* 'If you believe with all your heart, nothing' or possibly *Mar krysydh gans oll dha golonn, ty a yll bos besydhys* 'If you believe with all your heart, you may be baptized.' As it stands *ty a yll* 'you can' does not appear to refer to anything previously mentioned. It is quite clear that the English of the RSV has been rendered literally: 'What is to prevent my being baptized? If you believe with all your heart, you may'. The RSV is intelligible. The Kernowek Kemyn translation of it is less so.

7.16 ***Dhe *jydh Sabot** for *dydh Sabot* 'on the Sabbath'. At Acts 13:14 the Kernowek Kemyn reads: *ha **dhe jydh** Sabot i eth y'n synaga* 'on the Sabbath day they went into the synagogue'. Assibilation of *jydh* after the definite article *an* is to be expected; there is, however, no reason to assibilate *dydh > jydh* after the leniting preposition *dhe*. One would expect **dhe dhydh Sabot*. Moreover there is no need for any preposition when using the name of a day adverbially. It would have been more natural to say *i eth y'n synaga dydh an Sabot* 'they entered the synagogue on the Sabbath day.'

7.17 Wrong names for pagan gods. At Acts 14:13 the RSV reads: 'Barnabas they called Zeus, and Paul, because he was the chief speaker, they called Hermes.' (In the Greek the terms are Δία, accusative of Ζεύς, and Ἑρμῆν, accusative of Ἑρμῆς.) In the Kernowek Kemyn version this is rendered: *Ha Barnabas i a henwis **Jovyn**, ha Powl **Hermes**, drefenn y vos an penn-arethor.*The Kernowek Kemyn has thus used one Latin name, *Jovyn*, and one Greek name, *Hermes*. *Jovyn* itself is not really correct, since it does not represent *Jove* 'Jupiter, Zeus' but *Jovinius*, a different name altogether. The correct Latin form of *Jupiter* is attested in the Cornish texts: *golsowugh orth **iubyter*** 'listen to Jupiter' BM 2327. Since a Latin name is used here for Zeus, a Latin name should have been used for Hermes as well, who should have been called 'Mercury'. That name is attested in the Cornish for Wednesday: *kyns ys **dumerher** the nos* 'before Wednesday evening' BM 2254, where *Merher* is from Latin *Mercuris*. The Kernowek Kemyn version ought to have read *Barnabas i a henwis **Jubyter** ha Powl **Mergher***.

7.18 The name 'Ephesians' translated from the RSV not the Greek. At Acts 19:35 the Kernowek Kemyn reads *Tus **Efesus**, piw eus na woer bos sita an **Efesyon** gwithyas tempel an Artemis veur?'* at Acts 19:35. In the Greek there the same word is used for 'men of Ephesus' and 'Ephesians': Ἄνδρες Ἐφέσιοι, τίς γάρ ἐστιν ἀνθρώπων ὅς οὐ γινώσκει τὴν Ἐφεσίων πόλιν νεωκόρον οὖσαν τῆς μεγάλης Ἀρτέμιδος. The RSV, on the other hand, translates the the two differently: 'Men of Ephesus, what man is there who does not know that the city of the Ephesians is temple keeper [sic] of the great Artemis?' This agrees exactly with the present version's two expressions *Tus **Efesus*** 'Men of Ephesus' and *sita **an** Efesyon* 'the city of the Ephesians'. We can, I believe, be fairly certain that this passage has been translated from the RSV, not the Greek.

7.19 Incorrect syntax with *kenyver* 'as many, everyone'. At 1 Cor. 1:2 the Kernowek Kemyn reads: *gans **keniver** yn pub tyller *neb a gri war hanow agan Arloedh* 'all those who in every place call on the name of our Lord' (RSV). The syntax is incorrect. The relative pronoun *neb* is never used with *kenyver* as antecedent pronoun or as an adjective qualifying the antecedent. Here are some examples:

kynyuer den vs yn wlas 'everybody who is in the land' OM 1029
kynyver best vs yn tyr 'every animal that is on the earth' OM 1215
kynyuer dyaul vs yn beys 'every devil that is in the world' PC 3062

kynyuer peyn vs yn beys 'every pain that is in the world' RD 2055

The orth crist y ruk pesy certen desyr eredy the **kenever an gorthya** 'He prayed to Christ for a certain request indeed for everybody who might worship him' BM 4425-27

the **Canevar den** *gwyrrian a vo desyrius e gowis* 'to every righteous man who may be desirous of obtaining it' SA 60

bus openly the **kenever** *a whelha ha vo o sevall rebta* 'but openly to whoever who sees him and is standing near him' SA 60

ha **keneffra** *tra beaw ez a gwayah* 'and every living thing that moves' Keigwin

keneffra *tra ez a cramyhaz wor an beaze* 'everything that crawls upon the earth' Keigwin

drez **keneffra** *tra Vew Ez a quayah wor an beeze* 'over every living thing that moves upon the earth' Keigwin

keneffra *lazoan toane haaz a eze wor enap an Noare* 'every herb bearing seed that is upon the face of the earth' Keigwin

buz gen **kenefra** *geer eze toaze meaze meaza ganaw Deew* 'but by every word which comes out of the mouth of God' Rowe.

The examples come both from Middle and Late Cornish and are widely diverse in date, but in no case is *neb* to be found introducing the relative clause. The translation should have read: *gans* **keniver** *yn pub tyller a gri war hanow agan Arloedh* or *gans* **keniver** *yn pub tyller* **usi ow kria** *war hanow agan Arloedh*.

7.20 The Greek text at 1 Cor. 1:20-1 reads as follows:

Ποῦ σοφός; ποῦ γραμματεύς; ποῦ συνζητητὴς τοῦ αἰῶνος τούτου; οὐχὶ ἐμώρανεν ὁ Θεὸς τὴν σοφίαν τοῦ κόσμου; ἐπειδὴ γὰρ ἐν τῇ σοφίᾳ τοῦ Θεοῦ οὐκ ἔγνω ὁ κόσμος διὰ τῆς σοφίας τὸν Θεόν, εὐδόκησεν ὁ Θεὸς διὰ τῆς μωρίας τοῦ κερύγματος σῶσαι τούς πιστεύοντας 'Where is a wise man? Where is a scribe. Where is a debater of this age? Has not God made foolish the wisdom of the world? For since in God's wisdom the world has not known God by wisdom, God saw fit to save those who believe through the folly of the proclamation.'

The Kernowek Kemyn has apparently not been translated from the Greek. It reads:

Ple'ma'n huni yw skentel? Ple'ma'n skoler? Ple'ma'n dadhlor a'n oes ma? A ny wrug Dyw dhe skentoleth an bys bos fol? Rag yn skentoleth Dyw, a-ban na wrug an bys aswonn Dyw dre skentoleth, Dyw a erviras selwel, dre folneth an pyth a veu pregewthys, an re neb a grys.

This a good speaker of Cornish would naturally understand as follows:

> 'Where is the ?*huni* who is wise? Where is the scholar? Where is the arguer of this age? Did God not make for the wisdom of the world a foolish bush/being? For in the wisdom of God, since the world did not recognize God through wisdom, God decided to save by folly the thing which was preached, the people who will believe?'

The Kernowek Kemyn was apparently based on the RSV:

> 'Where is the wise man? Where is the scribe? Where is the debater of this age? Has not God made foolish the wisdom of the world? For since, in the wisdom of God, the world did not know God through wisdom, it pleased God through the folly of what we preach to save those who believe.'

In my own version I sought to write something that made immediate sense:

> *Ple ma an den fur? Ple ma an scryvynyas? Ple ma arethyor an os ma? A ny wrug Dew gockyneth a furneth an bys? Awos furneth Dew, ny wrug an bys aswon Dew dre furneth. Rag henna Dew a ervyras sylwel an gryjygyon dre wockyneth agan pregoth ny.*

7.21 Incorrect initial mutation and the Cornish for 'generously'. In 1 Corinthians (as in Acts), initial mutations are sometimes incorrectly used. At 1 Cor. 1:8, for example we read *yn *jydh agan Arloedh Yesu Krist.* The initial consonant of *deth, dyth* 'day' is assibilated only after the definite article and there is no article in *yn *jydh.* It should read *yn dydh.*

At 1 Cor. 2:12 the Kernowek Kemyn reads: *may *honvetthyn an *traow res yn hel dhyn ni gans Dyw,* by which is meant 'that we might understand the things bestowed on us by God'. The verb here is *convedhes* 'understand'. The preverbal particle *may* causes mixed mutation. It does not spirantize *c > h; may *honvetthyn* should read *may convetthyn.*

There are further problems in this verse. As we have seen **traow* does not mean 'things' in Cornish, which should always be translated *taclow* or *taclennow.* The translation here uses *yn hel* to mean 'lavishly, generously'. Unfortunately *hel* 'generous' is a respelling of Old Cornish *hail* 'largus [generous]' and is not attested in Middle Cornish. *Hel* in Middle Cornish means 'hall':

Pylat eth yn mes ay **hell** 'Pilate went out of his hall' PA 140a

ha my omma yn ov **hel** 'and I here in my hall' OM 1501

rof thy's ov thour **hel** *ha chammbour* 'I will give thee my tower, my hall and my chamber' OM 2110

wolcom mylwyth yn ow **hel** 'a thousand welcomes to my hall' PC 937

otte dyvythys an guas omma gynen bys y'th **hel** 'behold the fellow has come with us to your hall' PC 1202-03

wolcom kayfas ru'm leaute ty hag ol the gowethe certan y'm **hel** 'welcome, Caiaphas, upon my word and all your companions in my hall' PC 1579-81.

A good speaker, whether reading or hearing the translation at this point, would naturally understand the phrase *res yn hel dhyn ni gans Dyw* to mean 'given in the hall to us by God'. The Cornish for 'generous' is *larch* or *larjy*:

Sul voy ancov a rellogh the **larchya** *preysys fethogh* 'The more deaths you cause, the more generously will you be praised' BM 2351-52

hay bromas y tho **largya** 'and his promise was more generous' CW 780

why as gweall wondrys **largya** 'you will see more lavish wonders' CW 2176

goodly ha **largy** *processe ow tochia thin sacrament ma* 'a goodly and copious discussion about this sacrament' TH 53a.

7.22 1 Cor. 4:6 in the Kernowek Kemyn reads: *My re gewsis an *traow ma, brederedh, adro dhymmo vy *hag Apollos a'gas govis*, which is clearly intended as a translation of 'I have applied all this to myself and to Apollos for your benefit'. Unfortunately the Kernowek Kemyn is incorrect. It says *My re gewsis an *traow ma... adro dhymmo vy* 'I have spoken these things about myself', which is intelligible. Since, however, *adro dhymmo* is a first person singular prepositional pronoun, there is no preposition governing *Apollos*, which in consequence is left hanging. The translation ought to have read: *adro dhymmo vy hag adro dhe Apollos*.

At 1 Cor. 4:7 the Kernowek Kemyn reads as follows:

Rag piw a wel **agas** *bos arbennik? Ha pandr'* **a'gas beus** *na* **dhegemmersowgh**? *Ha mara'n* **degemmersowgh**, *prag y fostyowgh, kepar ha pan na* **dhegemmersowgh**? 'For who sees anything different in you? What have you that you did not receive? If then you received it, why do boast as if it were not a gift?' (RSV).

This has quite patently not been translated from the Greek. It has been wrongly assumed that the 'you' of this verse continued the plural 'you' of verse 6 and in consequence the six references in verse 7 to 'you' are in the second person plural in the Kernowek Kemyn. The references in verse 7, however, are all singular in the Greek:

τίς γάρ σε διακρίνει; τί δὲ ἔχεις ὃ οὐκ ἔλαβες; εἰ δὲ καὶ ἔλαβες, τί καυχᾶσαι ὡς μὴ λαβών [aorist participle, nominative singular masculine] 'for who finds *thee* different? What *dost thou* have which *thou hast* not received? If then *thou* also *hast* received, why *dost thou* boast, as one not having received ?'

In my own freer version, I followed the Greek text:

Pandr' a'th wrug tejy gwell bo uhella es tus erel? Ues tra vyth na wrusta receva yn ro? Mar qurussys y receva, prag yth esta owth omvostya adro dhodho, kepar del na ve va ro?

7.23 At 2 Cor. 1:23 the Kernowek Kemyn reads: *Lemmyn war ow bywnans y halwav orth Dyw avel dustunier* 'Now upon my life I call upon God as witness'. The Greek says Ἐγὼ δὲ μάρτυρα τὸν θεὸν ἐπικαλοῦμαι ἐπὶ τὴν ἐμὴν ψυχήν 'But I call God as witness against my own soul'. We have already seen at § 7.12 that the word **dustunier* is not attested and is inadmissible. The rest of the translation is also open to question as well.

The expression 's God is my witness' is well attested in traditional Cornish:

*a pylat wolcom os fest rak me a'th car **dev yn test*** 'O Pilate, thou art right welcome, for I love thee, as God is my witness!' RD 1811-12 [English by the fifth translator]
*why an prenvyth **du in test*** 'you will pay for it, as God is my witness' BM 3750.

The addition in the Greek of ἐπὶ τὴν ἐμὴν ψυχήν 'against my soul' means 'I forfeit my soul if what I say is untrue.' This is the same sense as the English 'upon my soul', which also occurs widely in Cornish:

*hy yv the wel yn pur wyr **war ov ene*** 'it is for the better right truly on my soul' 'OM 1629-30
*byth ny yllyn tremene an mor ma **war ov ene*** 'never shall we be able to cross this sea, on my soul' OM 1648-49

Na geugh why **war ov ene** *theworthef vy bynythe* 'do not go, on my soul, from me ever' OM 2179-80

my a'n gura **war ov ene** 'I will do it, on my soul' OM 2690

the lee nefra **war ov ena** *me an car in ov bevnans* 'the less ever, upon my soul, will I love him in my life' BM 481-83

Wolcum maseger ylyn oys oma **war ov ena** 'Welcome art thou here, bright messenger, upon my soul' BM 1400-01

gans gras Du, **war ow ena!** 'by the grace of God, upon my soul' BK 60

Why a vyth, **war ow ena!** *stewys fyn ha heb delay* 'You shall be finely bathed and without delay, upon my soul!' BK 1142-4

Le ew gena', **war ow ena!** *gans cletha bos debennys* 'Less of a matter for me is being beheaded with a sword, upon my soul!' BK 2939-41

ny thowtys **war ow ena** *a falsurye* 'I had no fear of treachery, upon my soul' CW 778-79

kemmys gyrryow teake am beff der henna **war ow ena** 'I got so many fair words through that man, upon my soul' CW 1018-19

pandra vyth gwryes me ny won **war ow ena** 'what will be done I do not know upon my soul' CW 1462-63

me an to **war ow ena** *gucky ythoes* 'I swear upon my soul that you are foolish' CW 2302-03.

If one wanted to render the Greek literally as the translator appears to have tried to do, one would say *Dew yn test war ow ena* 'as God is witness upon my soul'. If, one wished to be freer, one would probably say *Dew yn test er ow fyn* 'as God witness against me'. *Lemmyn war ow bywnans y halwav orth Dyw avel dustunier* is not idiomatic Cornish.

7.24 2 Cor. 4:8-9 in the Kernowek Kemyn reads:

yn-dann alar yn pub maner, nyns on ni brewys; ***penndegys,** *nyns eson ny yn desper; arweskys, nyns on ni* ***forsekys;** *gwyskys dhe'n leur nyns on ni distruys* 'we are afflicted in every way but are not crushed; perplexed but not driven to despair; persecuted but not forsaken; struck down but not destroyed' (RSV).

The word **penndegys* is unknown to me. It appears to be a compound of *pen* 'head' and *tegys* 'choked'. The Greek ἀπορούμενοι means 'at a loss, in a quandary, not knowing what to do'. The exact equivalent for that in traditional Cornish is *ameys*:

Ameys of ow predyry pandra allaf the wruthyl an avel orth y dyrry rag ovn genes bones gyl 'I am in a quandary considering what I should do, when plucking the apple, for I fear you are deceitful' OM 193-96

ran in kerth re ruk feya ran ny won pyth ens gyllys mayth ovy **ameys** *oma*
'some [of my companions] have fled away; some, I don't know
where they've gone, so that I am at a loss here' BM 2156-58
Gorthys re bo Du a nef! Gans gweras theworta ef ny rys thymmo bos **ameys**
'Praised be the God of heaven! With help from him there is no need
for me to be at a loss' BK 1176-79.

There is no need for the unattested coinage **penndegys*. Astonishing
also is **forsekys* with *i*-affection. Polysyllabic borrowings of this kind
do not exhibit *i*-affection in the verbal adjective. The verbal adjective of
forsakya certainly has no *i*-affection:

meryasek in certan o thymo pur oges car in kerth galles **forsakis** *y das hay vam
ha ny won pyth eth heb nam* 'Meriasek for certain was a very close relative
of mine; he has gone away, his father and mother forsaken. Indeed I
don't know where he has gone' BM 1939-42.

7.25
There is a very interesting passage at 2 Cor. 8:10-13, where St Paul is
speaking to the Corinthians about generosity in giving to their fellow
Christians. The three verses in Kernowek Kemyn read as follows:

*Hag y'n mater ma kusul a rov vy: rag y telledh dhywgh, neb na dhallathas
warlyna oberi hepken mes keffrys mynnes oberi, lemmyn ynwedh kowlul an
ober, ena kepar dell yw freth agas mynnas, yn kettella bedhes kowlwrys
herwydh agas pygans. Rag mars usi an frethter ena seulabrys, kemmeradow yw
an ro herwydh an pyth a* **biwor, mes nys yw herwydh an pyth na* **biwor.*

Without recourse to an English translation it is impossible to understand the last verse. I suspect that a native speaker of Cornish of *c.* 1500,
if he could make anything of the orthography, would understand the
passage to mean something like the following:

And in this matter I give counsel (*kusul a rov*): for you ought, whoever
did not begin working (*neb na dhallathas oberi*) ?last year without a cause
(*hepken*), but also to want to work, now also to complete the work, there
as your kid-goats are so vigorous (*ena dell yw freth agas mynnas*), in the
same way let them be completed (**bedhes* is not attested in Cornish, for
*bedhens possibly) according to your stabbing (*pygans < pyga* 'to stab').
For if the ?vigour (**frethter* is not attested in Cornish) is there already,
?takeable is the gift according to the thing of **piwor*, but is not according
to that thing *biwor* (*an pyth na biwor*).

The translation was intended to mean:

> 'And in this matter I give my advice: it is best for you now to complete what a year ago you began not only to do but to desire, so that your readiness in desiring it may be matched by your completing it out of what you have. For if the readiness is there, it is acceptable according to what a man has, not according to what he has not.'

The bizarre form *piwor* must be intended as the present autonomous form of the verb *pew* 'owns'. Such a form is unattested anywhere in Cornish. Here are the only forms of the verb known to me:

> *war tu hay vam an* **pewo** *y ben a vynnas synsy* 'towards his mother who owned him he wished to hold his head' PA 207c
>
> *hag ol an tyr a* **bywfy** 'and may you possess all the land' OM 581
>
> *han gvlascor pur yredy me a* **bev** *ol yn tyan* 'and the kingdom in very truth I possess entirely' BM 170-71
>
> *ihesu crist a* **bev** *ry dome* 'Jesus Christ owns the right of giving doom' BM 4007
>
> *Ne ren vry pew a's* **pewa** 'We don't care who may own it' BK100
>
> *te a* **bew** *ol* 'you possess all' BK 1791
>
> *Pobyll abell* **bew** *Castilly* 'People from afar own castles' Scawen MSS
>
> *me a* **pewi** 'I possess' Borlase.

There are no examples in traditional Cornish of any autonomous form of *pew* 'possesses'. *Piwor* is, I fear, not Cornish.

My own translation of this passage is as follows:

> *Hag otomma ow husul y'm mater ma: y tal dheugh gorfenna lemmyn an pyth a wrussough why dalleth warleny. Why a vue an dus kensa dh'y wul ha dhe vennas y wul. Gorfenneugh e lemmyn warlergh agas gallus, may fo haval agas cowlwryans dh'agas bolunjeth. Mar pedhough why whansek dhe weres, plegadow dhe Dhew vydh agas ro warlergh an pyth a'gas bues, kens es warlergh agas dyfyk.*

7.26 2 Cor. 11:1-3 in the Kernowek Kemyn reads:

> *Unnweyth a'm godhaffewgh nebes y'm folneth! mes yn tevri hwi a'm godhav. Gwres a'm beus a'gas govis, gans avy Dyw, drefenn my dh'agas dedhewi dhe unn gour, rag agas profya avel gwyrghes pur dhe Grist, ha par doell doethas an sarf Eva der y felder, yma own dhymm bos agas brysyow dynys yn neb fordh dhiworth lel wonis gwiryon ha pur in Krist.*

If native Cornish speaker of *c.* 1500 either heard or read that, he would probably understand it as follows:

'If only you had endured me somewhat in my foolishness. But indeed you will endure me. I have heat (*gurez* 'heat' Lhuyd) ?on your behalves (**a'gas govys* is unattested in Cornish), with the envy of God, because I promised you to one husband, in order to offer you as a pure virgin, and just as the serpent (feminine) deceived Eve through her distance (**felder* 'cunning is unattested in Cornish; *pelder* 'distance' is attested at least six times in the Middle Cornish texts), I fear that your ?minds / ?wombs (the plural **brysyow* < *brys* 'mind' or 'womb' is unattested) have been sucked (< *dena* 'suck'; *dynnya* 'entice' confined to BM, where it has <nn>) in some way from loyal cultivation (*wonis* < *gonys* 'cultivation, tillage'), honest and pure in Christ.

The following is what was intended:

'I wish you would bear with me in a little foolishness. Do bear with me! I feel a divine jealousy for you, for I betrothed you to Christ to present you as a pure bride to her one husband. But I am afraid that as the serpent deceived Eve by his cunning, your thought will be led astray from a sincere and pure devotion to Christ.'

My own version reads as follows:

Da vya genef why dhe'm perthy tecken y'm gockyneth. Gwreugh ow ferthy! Yth esof vy ragough ow kemeres avy kepar hag avy Dew, rag me a'gas dedhewys yn maryach dhe un gour, may hallen agas presentya why avel vyrjyn heb spot vyth dhe Gryst. Saw dowtys of agas preder dhe vos ledys war stray dheworth devocyon lel ha gwyryon dhe Gryst, kepar del wrug an hager-bref tulla Eva der y sotylta.

I think I have written enough to show that the second translator is on occasion both inaccurate and unidiomatic. His translations can also be shown not to have been based on the Greek.

THE THIRD TRANSLATOR
8.00 The third translator was responsible for Galatians, Philemon and Jude. The Epistle to the Galatians does not begin well: *Powl, abostol nag a dus na dre dhen mes dre Yesu Krist ha Dyw an Tas a'n **difunas** dhiworth an re varow.* In the RSV this reads 'Paul, an apostle—not from men nor through man, but through Jesus Christ and God the Father, who raised him from the dead.' Unfortunately the Kernowek Kemyn does not correspond to that English version, since it means 'Paul, an apostle neither of men nor through man but through Jesus Christ and God

woke him up from the dead'. Not only is there no indication that the verb *a'n difunas* is relative rather than 'abnormal order', but *difunas* is the not the right word anyway. *Dyfuna* only ever means 'wake up' intransitively:

> *wheth ow cufyon* **dyfunough** 'still my beloved ones, wake up' PC 1075
> *Dar, ny ylta* **dyfuna**? 'Hey, can't you wake up?' BK 349.

To be fair, it should be noticed that the Greek uses ἐγείραντος, the genitive of the participle meaning 'having woken', but that does not mean that the word can be literally translated into Cornish.

In Cornish when speaking of rising or being raised from the dead one uses the verb *drehevel* 'rise up, raise up'. Here are two examples from the texts:

> *dun leueryn war anow ay veth del yw* **drehevys** 'come, let us tell [him] face
>   to face that he been raised from the grave' PA 247bc
> *whath yn erna nyn gens war bonas mab du* **drehevys** 'still at that time they
>   were not aware that the Son of God had been raised' PA 252d.

The translation should have read: *dre Yesu Krist ha dre Dhyw an Tas neb a'n* **drehevis** *dhiworth an re varow*.

8.01 At Gal. 1:8 the Kernowek Kemyn reads:

> *mes mar pe pregewthys dhywgh genen ni po gans el dhiworth nev neb aweyl dihaval dhe'n huni a bregewthsyn ni, re bo molla'tyw warnodho* 'but if we or an angel from heaven should preach to you a gospel contrary to that which we preached to you, let him be accursed' RSV.

In the Greek the verb of the protasis is ἐὰν... εὐαγγελίσηται (third person present aorist middle), but ἐὰν + the subjunctive expresses a real condition in future time. The correct translation is therefore 'if either we or an angel from heaven does (at some time in the future)... let him be accursed'. The Kernowek Kemyn has translated with *mar pe* (i.e. *mar* + past subjunctive), which means 'had any gospel been preached', i.e. an unreal condition in past time. Moreover in the Greek and in the RSV the verb is active in sense 'if we or an angel... should preach', but the Kernowek Kemyn is passive *mar pe pregewthys... aweyl*. This means it is not clear to what or to whom the prepositional pronoun in the apodosis refers: does *re bo molla'tyw warnodho* 'may there be God's curse on him/it' refer to the alien gospel or to Paul and/or the angel?

There are further problems here. The term **dyhaval* 'unlike, different' is an invention, being nowhere attested in Cornish; a better word would be **ken** 'different, other' or **contrary**; cf. *han neill ew contrary thy gela* 'and the one is contrary to the other' TH 24a. We have already noted at § 4.02 above that the word *huny* (Kernowek Kemyn **huni*) may not be used, as here, as a noun; this is a further mistake. Perhaps the most serious flaw in the translation here is the expression *re bo molla'tyw warnodho* 'may God's curse be upon him'. *Mollatew* (Kernowek Kemyn *molla'tyw*) < *mollath Dew*, is only ever used in Cornish as a malediction:

gureugh y herthye aperfeth gans **mollat dev** *ha'y eleth ha syns keffrys* 'shove him in with God's curse and the curse of his angels and saints!' RD 2286-88

Ay tevdar ke war the gam **molleth du** *the vapp the vam* 'Hey, Teudar, steady on! God's curse on thy mother's son!' BM 1048-49

gase farwel me a vyn **molleth du** *in cowetheys* 'I will take my leave. God's curse on the company!' BM 1286-87

a **molleth du** *in gegyn* 'Oh! God's curse in the kitchen!' BM 3721

eugh thywhy in le gras ha **mollath Du** *ha'm molath!* 'go off to a place of grace [i.e. hell] and God's curse and my curse on you!' BK 739-40

*Peswara blethan—***mollath Dew** *war ef reeg dry hy uppa* 'Fourth year— God's curse on him who brought her here!' Pryce.

In every instance in that list *mollath Dew* is a colloquial imprecation uttered, often by a low-class character, in anger; *mollath Dew warnodho*, therefore, means something like 'God rot him!' or 'Let him go to hell' and is quite unsuitable for the present context. *Emskemunys* 'excommunicate, anathema' is exactly the right word. My own version of this passage reads as follows:

Mar tuen nyny, bo mar tue el dheworth nef kyn fe, ha progeth awayl contrary dhe'n awayl a wrussyn ny declarya, bedhens emskemunys!

8.02 At Gal. 1:15 the Kernowek Kemyn reads:

Byttegyns pan blesyas *dhe Dhyw a'm apoyntyas a-dhia vrys ow mamm ha'm gelwel der y ras, diskwedhes y Vab ynnov, ma'n pregowthen yn mysk an Jentilys, a-dhesempis ny wrug vy omgusulya gans kig na goes.

This appears to be partially based on the RSV which reads as follows:

> 'But when he, who had set me apart before I was born and called me through his grace, was pleased to reveal his Son to me [*footnote* in me], so that I might preach him among the Gentiles, I did not confer with flesh or blood.'

Unfortunately, the Kernowek Kemyn is not a satisfactory rendering of the English. There is no indication that the verb *a'm appoyntyas* is relative. In consequence a good speaker of Cornish will stumble at *dhe Dhyw a'm apoyntyas*, thinking that a pronoun has been left out and that the text should read *pan blesyas dhe Dhyw, ev a'm apoyntyas* 'when it pleased God, he appointed me'. A further problem is that *diskwedhes* is too far removed from the verb *blesyas* which governs it: 'when it pleased God... to reveal'. The adverb *a-dhesempis* translates εὐθέως 'straightway' (which precedes 'did not consult' in the Greek). It might have been better translated here as *y'n tor' na* 'at that time'.

The most serious deficiency in the Kernowek Kemyn, however, is that the verb *plesya* 'please' is wrongly used. *Plesya* in Cornish takes a direct object, not an indirect one and thus *dhe Dhyw* is mistaken. Here are some examples of the correct usage from the texts:

> *me a garsa crist ʒe **plesya** a newyth hag a henys* 'I should like to please Christ in youth and old-age' BM 165-67
>
> *molothov mur a bobyl rag the **plesya** me rum bue* 'to please you I have got the curses of many people' BM 1579-80
>
> *ihesu pup vr ol ov desyr yv in bysma the **plesia*** 'Jesus, my desire in this world is always to please you' BM 2544-45
>
> *dretha may alsans bewa ha **plesya** du* 'that they might live through it and please God' TH 40
>
> *yma genaf theth **pleycya*** 'I have something to please you' CW 729.

Instead of *pan blesyas *dhe Dhyw* the translation ought to have read *pan veu Dyw plesyes* 'when God was pleased'. The incorrect use of *plesya* with *dhe* at Gal. 1:15 is all the more perplexing when one realizes that it is correctly used in *ow plesya tus* 'pleasing people' twice at Gal. 1:10. The word-order ought also to be re-arranged to make the sentence clearer. This is what I sought to do in my own rendering:

> *Dew a'm settyas adenewan kens es me dhe vos genys hag ef a'm gelwys der y ras. Pan vue va plesys, ef a dhyscudhas dhym y vab may hallen y brogeth ef yn mesk an Jentylys.*

8.03 At Gal. 1:17 the Kernowek Kemyn reads: *na ny wrug vy yskynna bys yn Yerusalem dhe'n re o abesteli kyns es dell *en vy abostol* 'nor did I ascend to Jerusalem to those who were apostles before I was an apostle.' This appears to be based upon the RSV. It cannot be translated from the Greek, because there are no verbs in the second part of the sentence in the Greek original: πρὸς τοὺς πρὸ ἐμοῦ ἀποστόλους '[word for word] to the before-me apostles'. Regrettably the Kernowek Kemyn exhibits the wrong use of tenses here. The others were apostles, while Paul was persecuting the church; their verb is correctly imperfect. The expression 'before I was an apostle', however, really means 'before I became an apostle'. In which case the preterite should have been used. The text ought to read *dhe'n re o abesteli kyns es dell veuv vy abostol.*

At Gal. 1:22 the Kernowek Kemyn cannot have been translated from the Greek which says: ἤμην δὲ ἀγνούμενος τῷ προσώπῳ ταῖς ἐκκλεσίαις τῆς Ἰουδαίας ταῖς ἐν Χριστῷ 'but I was unknown by the face to the churches of Judea, those in Christ'. *Anwothfos* does not refer to lack of acquaintance; it means 'hidden, invisible, unknowable': *Rag henna yma oll an rena vgy ow leverall y bos an catholyk egglos, egglos vnwothfos, ymowns ow kull inivri ha cam the crist* 'Therefore all those who say that the catholic church is a hidden church are guilty of hostility and injury to Christ' TH 17a. *Anwothfas* is quite the wrong word here.

The verbal tense is also mistaken here, though in the opposite direction from the mistake in Gal. 1:17. The text reads: *Mes ow fas a veu anwodhvos dhe eglosyow Yudi esa yn Krist* 'And I was still not known by sight to the churches of Christ in Judea' (RSV). Paul's face was unknown to the churches, but they had heard it said that their persecuter was now proclaiming the gospel. The verb should have been imperfect, not preterite; the text ought to read *Mes ow fas o...* rather than *Mes ow fas a veu.*

In my own version I put things rather differently and said that the churches in Judea had not yet become acquainted with Paul's face: *ha ny aswonas ow fas whath an eglosyow a Gryst yn pow Judy.*

8.04 At Gal. 1:23 the syntax of the Kernowek Kemyn is very odd, but I will leave it for the time being. It should be noted, however, that the Greek τὴν πίστιν ἥν ποτε ἐπόρθει 'the faith that once he was trying to destroy' is rendered *an fydh a *ravnas*. *Rafna* means 'plunder, strip of goods' and is not the right word; moreover the Greek verb is imperfect and this should be made clear in the translation. In my own version I said *an fedh esa va kens ow whelas dystrowy*.

8.05 At Gal. 2:11 the Kernowek Kemyn reads:

> *Mes pan dheuth Peder dhe Antiok, my a sevis ar y bynn orth y fas awos y vos dhe vlamya* 'But when Cephas came to Antioch, I opposed him to his face, because he stood condemned' (RSV).

The translation here contains a rather comic mixed metaphor. What is being said literally translated is 'I stood against his head (*er y byn*) to his face (*orth y fas*).' One or other of the two compound prepositions + possessive adjective should have been differently phrased. In my own version I wrote: *Saw pan dhueth Cefas dhe Antioch, me a gowsas yn apert war y byn rag ef dhe dhampnya y honen*.

8.06 Gal. 2:15 in Kernowek Kemyn reads:

> *Ni yw herwydh **kinda** Yedhewon ha nyns on ni a'n **Jentilys peghadoryon*** 'We ourselves are Jews by birth and not Gentile sinners' (RSV).

In the first place, it is difficult to understand why *kinda* is not spelt **kynda* in Kernowek Kemyn. The word was both *kunde* and *kinde* in Middle English, where the stressed vowel was open *i* or [y], not closed *i*. Indeed the form *unkunda* 'unkind, unnatural' is a variant reading at CW 155. The real problem here, however, is the second part of the sentence. The expression *a'n Jentilys peghadoryon* looks bizarre until one realizes that *peghadoryon* must be understood after *nyns on ni*; cf. the Greek οὐκ ἐξ ἐθνῶν ἁμαρτωλοί '[word for word] not from-Gentiles sinners'. This is by no means clear from the Kernowek Kemyn. The translator ought to have said *nyns on ni peghadoryom mes a'n Jentilys* 'we are not sinners but of the Gentiles' or something similar. In my own translation I attempted to be as natural as possible and wrote: *Me ow honen yw Yedhow warlergh genesygeth. Nyns of onen a behadoryon an Jentylys*.

8.07 Gal. 2:17 in Kernowek Kemyn reads as follows:

> *Mes mars eson ni ow hwilas bos ewnhes yn Krist diskudhys agan honan dhe vos peghadoryon, yw Krist ytho menyster a begh?*

This can only mean 'But if we are seeking to be justified in Christ disclosed—ourselves to be sinners—is Christ a minister of sin then?', which is to say, that the translation does not really make sense. The RSV reads 'But if, in our endeavours to be justified in Christ, we ourselves were found to be sinners, is Christ then an agent of sin?'. It is difficult to see how anything like that sense can be derived from the Kernowek Kemyn as it stands. The word-order is at best very awkward. In my own version I attempted a more intelligible rendering: *Saw mar puen ny agan honen kefys dhe vos pehadoryon awos ny dhe whelas bos justyfyes yn Christ, yw Cryst servont a begh?*

I have discussed only two chapters of Galatians at this point, yet it must already be apparent that the Kernowek Kemyn of this epistle is not without problems. I shall, therefore pass on to the fourth translator.

THE FOURTH TRANSLATOR

9.00 The fourth translator was responsible for Ephesians, Philippians, Colossians , 1 and 2 Thessalonians, 1 and 2 Timothy, Titus, James, 1 and 2 Peter, and Revelation. Uniquely among the six translators the fourth translator writes good, grammatical Cornish. Apart from his questionable orthography, his Cornish is idiomatic and readable. Here is his version of Revelation 12:1-9:

> *Ha tokyn bras a veu gwelys yn nev, benyn gwiskys gans an howl, ha'n loer yn-dann hy threys, ha kurun a dhewdhek sterenn war hy fenn; ha hi gans flogh y'n dorr, a armas yn gloesow, ow lavurya dhe dhineythi. Ha ken tokyn a veu gwelys yn nev, hag otta, dragon rudh meur gans seyth penn ha deg korn ha seyth kurun war hy fennow. Ha'y lost a skubas an tressa rann a'n ster a nev ha'ga thewlel dhe'n dor ha'n dhragon a sevis a-dherag an venyn a vedha ow tineythi, may teppra hy flogh kettell wrella hi y dhineythi. Ha hi a dhineythis mab gorreydh a vedha ow pugelya pub kenedhel gans gwelenn horn: ha'y flogh a veu ravshyes dhe Dhyw, ha dh'y dron. Ha'n venyn a fias dhe'n gwylvos, le may ma dhedhi tyller parys gans Dyw ma's makkens hi ena mil dhydh dew kans ha tri-ugens.*
>
> *Hag yth esa kas yn nev. Mighal ha'y eledh a omladhas erbynn an dhragon; ha'n dhragon a omladhas ha'y eledh hi, ha ny fethsons i; ha ny veu aga thyller kevys namoy yn nev. Ha'n dhragon veur a veu tewlys yn-nans, an hens sarf neb yw gelwys an Jowl, ha Satnas, neb a doell an bys; ev a veu tewlys yn-nans bys y'n dor, ha'y eledh a veu tewlys yn-nans ganso.*

It is such a pity that this translator remains committed to a questionable orthography.

THE FIFTH TRANSLATOR

9.00 The fifth translator was responsible for only one book of the New Testament, the Epistle to the Hebrews. His translation appears largely to have been based on the RSV.

At Heb. 1:2 the Kernowek Kemyn reads:

> *mes y'n dydhyow diwedhes ma ev re gewsis dhyn dre Vab, neb a ordenas an er a buptra, dredho ynwedh may hwrug an oesow.*

The translation is intended to mean, 'but in these recent days he has spoken to us by a Son, whom he ordained the heir of all things, through whom also he made the ages'. Unfortunately the verse is ambiguous: *ev re gewsis dhyn dre Vab, neb a ordenas an er a buptra* might more naturally be taken to mean 'he has spoken to us by a Son, who ordained the heir of all things'.

9.01 At Heb. 2:5 the Kernowek Kemyn reads: *Rag ny veu yn-dann eledh may hworras Dyw an bys dhe dhos, hag anodho dell gewsyn.* This verse is obscure in Kernowek Kemyn even after several readings. The RSV reads here, 'For it was not to angels that God subjected the world to come, of which we are speaking.' The problem in the Kernowek Kemyn is the use of **may** to introduce a relative clause. *May* is used to introduce a relative where the antecedent is governed by a preposition. In the present case, however, this is not the case. The preposition is already present in *yn-dann eledh*. We are not saying 'under which God put the world to come' but 'it was under angels that God placed the world.' A direct relative is required. Moreover, *hag anodho dell gewsyn* is unclear and indeed 'of which we are speaking' (Greek περὶ ἧς λαλοῦμεν) ought be rendered by a continuous present which in Kernowek Kemyn should be introduced by *may*. The translation ought really to have read: *Rag ny veu yn-dann eledh a worras Dyw an bys dhe dhos, mayth eson ni ow kewsel anodho.*

9.02 At Heb. 2:9 the Kernowek Kemyn reads: *kurunys gans golowder hag enor awos godhevel mernans, may *flassa mernans *a-barth pub huni, dre ras Dyw* 'crowned with glory and honour, because of the suffering of death, so that by the grace of God he might taste death for every one'. There are two problems here. The expression is intended to translate *a-barth pub huni* 'for every one' (Greek ὑπὲρ παντὸς 'for the sake of everybody'). Regrettably *a-barth* does not mean 'for, for the sake of' but 'by, in the name of' in oaths:

> *drehevyn ef abarth dev* 'let's lift it, in the name of God' OM 2539
>
> *dus yn mes abarth an ioul* 'come out, in the name of the Devil' OM 2700
>
> *abarth ow thas bynyges th'y thyller arte glenes* 'in the name of my blessed Father, to its place again let it cleave' PC 1152-53 [English by fifth translator]
>
> *dys yn rak abarth iovyn* 'come forward, in Jove's name' PC 1233 [English by fifth translator]
>
> *tormentours abarth a'n iaul fysteneugh th'agas kregy* 'tormentors, in the Devil's name, hurry, hang you!' PC 2045-46 [English by fifth translator]
>
> *hou geiler abarth malan dus yn rag ha'th vaw keffrys* 'Ho, jailor! in the devil's name come forth, and thy boy as well' [English by fifth translator] PC 2235-36
>
> *ha me an benedicconn a ra oma purdyson abarth ov arluth ihesu* 'and I will give the blessing here straightway in the name of Jesus my lord' BM 4532-34
>
> *Ahanan eugh, abarth an Tas* 'Leave us, in the name of the Father!' BK1339-40
>
> *Abarth Christ, an mab gwelha, me a vyn mos gans mer grys* 'By Christ, the best of sons, I shall go very quickly' BK 1282-83
>
> *Me a vyn mos heb gortas, abarth Du in uhelder* 'I will go without waiting, by God in heaven' BK 1330-31
>
> *Py fys abarth Marya?* 'Where were you, in Mary's name?' BK1368.

If one wishes to say 'for the sake of, for the good of' in Cornish one uses the expression *rag kerensa*:

> *Noe rag kerenge orthy's my ny gemere neffre trom dyal war ol an beys* 'Noah, for your sake I will never take harsh vengeance on all the world' OM 1207-09
>
> *fatel fue cryst mertheryys rak kerenge tus a'n beys why a welas yn tyen* 'how Christ was martyred for the sake of the people of the world you have wholly seen' PC 3220-22 [English by fifth translator]
>
> *neb a rug ry y vn vab eff the suffra myrnans rag kerensa y egglos* 'who gave his only Son to suffer death for the sake of his church' TH 31a
>
> *mar sesta worth y wull Rag kerensa an dus* 'if you do it for the sake of the people' TH 48.

The second problem is the expression *may *flassa mernans* 'that he might taste death'. The verb **blasa* 'taste' does not occur in Cornish. 'Taste' is always *tastya*:

> *a dorras an avel tek hag a'n dug thy'm the **dastye** 'who plucked a fair apple and brought it to me to taste' OM 267-68
>
> *pan russys thotho dybry ha **tastye** frut a'n wethen* 'since you made him eat and taste of the fruit of the tree' OM 283-84
>
> *oll an effect, ow **tastya**, ow gwellas, ow predery* 'all the effect, tasting, seeing, thinking' TH 8a
>
> *Judas a ruk **tastia** Corf an arluth* 'Judas tasted the Lord's body' SA 65a
>
> *ef a **tastyas** kigg an arluth Dew* 'he tasted the flesh of the Lord God' SA 65a
>
> *mar pyth y frute hy **tastys** ta a vyth dampnys ractha* 'if its fruit is tasted you will be condemned for it' CW 377-78
>
> *mar gwreth **tastya** an frute ma es oma war an wethan* 'if you taste this fruit which is here on the tree' CW 619-620
>
> *dew a ornas contrary na thefan **tastya** henna* 'God ordered otherwise that we should not taste that' CW 630-31
>
> *genas a peva **tastys** maga fure te a vea yn pub poynt sure avella* 'were it to be tasted by you, you would be as wise as he indeed in every point' CW 641-43
>
> *ny allaf ra pell perthy pan vo reys **tastya** anothy* 'I cannot endure too long since it is necessary to taste of it' CW 690-91
>
> *ha by god nynges ʒym dowte tha **dastya** a[n] keth avall* 'and by God I have no fear of tasting of that same apple' CW 705-06
>
> *mar gwreth **tastya** anotha eve a drayle theʒo tha leas* 'if you taste it, it will turn out to your advantage' CW 738-39
>
> *mar gwrean **tastya** an frut na avell dew ny a vea* 'if we were to taste this fruit, we would be like God' CW 781-82
>
> ***tast** gy part an avallow* 'do you taste some of the apples' CW 831
>
> *hag an dros thym tha **dastya*** 'and brought it to me to taste' CW 880
>
> *mernans ny wressans **tastya*** 'they would not have tasted death' CW 995
>
> *a vs kyek an bestas na na a veast na lodn in beyse ny wressan bythqwath **tastya*** 'of the use of the flesh of those animals nor of animal or beast in the word we never tasted' CW 1470-72
>
> *ny **dastyans** an payne bras* 'they will not taste the great torment' CW 2063.

*May *flassa mernans* 'that he might taste death' looks odd because the verb is wholly unattested in Cornish the form itself, *flassa* in the past subjunctive is less than wholly clear. Notice that *mernans ny wressans tastya* 'they would not have tasted death' is attested in CW. Instead of *may *flassa mernans *a-barth pub huni* the translation would have been better if it had read *may hwrella tastya mernans rag kerensa pub huni.*

9.03 At Heb. 2:10 the Kernowek Kemyn reads: *Rag yth o gwiw ev, *neb ragdho ha *neb ganso y fyw puptra, ow tri lyes mab dhe wolowder, dhe wul awtour aga selwyans perfeyth dre wodhevel.* This bizarre sentence seems at first sight to mean something like: 'For he was worthy, he, ?who for him and ?who with him, everything is alive, bringing many sons to brilliance, to make the author of their perfect saving through suffering'. In fact the translation was intended to mean, 'For it was fitting that he, for whom and by whom all things exist, in bringing many sons to glory, should make the pioneer of their salvation perfect through suffering'. The sentence is not easy, but the translator has made unduly heavy weather of it. The expressions **neb ragtho* and **neb ganso* are unattested anywhere in traditional Cornish and it is difficult to see why the translation did not read: *mayth usi puptra yn fyw ragdho ha ganso.* Since *aga selwyans perfeyth* can only mean 'their perfect saving', the translation should perhaps have read *dhe wul perfeyth dre wodhevel an awtour a'ga selwyans.* My own translation was much freer, but it does, I hope, make immediate sense:

> *Pur ewn o ytho Dew, usy ow formya hag ow sensy pub tra, dhe wul Jesu perfeth dre wodhevyans, may halla va dry lyes mab dhe vos kevrennek ganso a'y glory.*

9.04 At Heb. 2:11 the Kernowek Kemyn reads: *Rag ev neb a *sansha, ha'n re yw *sanshes, yw oll a'n un devedhyans.* First notice that the verb **sanshé* is wholly unattested in traditional Cornish. The only verb in the texts for 'sanctify' (Greek ἁγιάζω) is *sanctyfya*:

> *neb o sanctyfyes* 'who was sanctified' TH 11
> *dre reson y bossy sanctifies ha benegys inweth purchasiis dre mernans agan savyoure Jhesus crist* 'because they are sanctified and blessed, also redeemed by the death of our Saviour Jesus Christ' TH 31.

If the translator found that too English, he could have used *benega* 'to blesss', *dasprena* 'to redeem' or *glanhe* 'cleanse'. The real problem here, however, is not the vocabulary, but the syntax. The clause *ha'n re yw sanshes* can only mean 'and the ?re are made holy'. If the translation was intended to mean 'and those who are sanctified', it should have read: *ha'n re na neb yw sanshes.*

9.05 At Heb. 2:16 the Kernowek Kemyn reads: *Rag yn tevri nyns yw y breder *yn kever an eledh, mes *yn kever has Abraham*. As we have seen *yn kever* is not used with a noun in traditional Cornish and thus **yn kever an eledh* and **yn kever has Abraham* would be meaningless to a native speaker of the language. If such a person were to read the translation here, he would probably understand it to mean: 'For indeed her brothers are not in ? of the angels, but in ? the seed of Abraham'. The translator when he wrote *y breder* meant 'his thought', but *breder* 'brothers' had been mentioned at 2:11 and *fleghes* 'children' at 2:13 and 2:14. The misunderstanding would be most natural.

9.06 At Heb. 3:1 the Kernowek Kemyn reads: *Ytho, breder sans, a *gevrenn galwans nevek, *ombrederewgh Yesu, abostol hag arghoferyas a'gan professyans*. The first part of this verse would naturally be taken to mean 'Therefore, holy brothers, of a share of a heavenly calling.' The second part of the verse is intended to mean 'consider Jesus, the apostle and high priest of our confession'. It is not certain either that *ombredery* is the correct verb here; it is attested once only in traditional Cornish where it means 'think up, devise, invent':

> *ny a vyn **ompredery** forth rag y treyla defry* 'I will devise a way to convert him indeed' BM 2857-78

The word required here should mean 'contemplate, consider, think about'. *Predery a* is the right verb:

> *lemmyn me agis pys oll a baynis crist **predery*** 'now I beg you all to consider the pains of Christ' PA 182c
> *arluth pan dyffy зet pow **predery** ahanaff gura* 'Lord, when you come to your kingdom, consider me' 193b
> *why a **preder** a'y passyon* 'you will consider his passion' RD 3223.

The translation here should read **prederewgh** *a Yesu* rather than **ombrederewgh Yesu*.

9.07 At Heb. 3:3 the Kernowek Kemyn reads:

> *Hogen Yesu re beu reknys gwiw a gemmys moy a wolowder ages Moyses par dell yw neb a dhrehevis an chi moy enorys ages an chi.*

The natural way of construing this verse would be as follows: 'Yet Jesus has been reckoned of as much more glory than Moses, just as is he who built the more honoured house [sic] than the house'. The translation, however, was intended to mean, 'Yet Jesus has been counted worthy of as much more glory than Moses, as a builder of the house has more honour than the house'. It should therefore have read: *Hogen Yesu re beu reknys gwiw a gemmys moy a wolowder ages Moyses, par dell vydh moy enorys henna neb a dhrehevis an chi ages an chi y honen.*

9.08 At Heb. 3:6 the Kernowek Kemyn reads: *mes Krist o len *war ji Dyw avel Mab*, which seems to me to signify 'but Christ was faithful inside— God as Son'. The translation was intended to mean: 'but Christ was faithful over God's house as a son.' In which case it is difficult to see why it did not read: *mes Krist o len **war an chi a Dhyw** avel Mab.*

9.09 At Heb. 3:11 the Kernowek Kemyn reads: *Dell des yn ow sorr 'Ny wrons entra dhe'm powesva.* This verse is a quotation from Psalm 95 and someone who was familiar with neither the psalm nor this passage would have great difficulty in understanding the present translation. The word *des* is the lenited form of **tes*, the first person singular of the preterite of *ty* 'swear'. This form is unattested in traditional Cornish. As far as I am aware the only finite form of the verb *ty* 'to swear' anywhere in our surviving texts is as follows:

*y'n naghen ef a'm guarnyas rak henna me a sorras hag a **tos** na wren neffre* 'he warned me that I would deny him; therefore I grew angry and swore that I never would' PC 1420-22

It would have been more sensible here to have used an auxiliary verb, e.g. *Dell wrugavy ti y'm sorr*, for example.

The whole verse here reads in the Greek: ὡς ὤμοσα ἐν τῇ ὀργῇ μου, Εἰ εἰσελεύσονται εἰς τὴν κατάπαυσίν μου 'so that I swore in my anger That they would not enter into my rest'. As we have seen this has been rendered in Kernowek Kemyn as *Dell des yn ow sorr 'Ny wrons entra dhe'm powesva.* Exactly the same quotation from Psalm 95 is repeated at Heb. 4.3: Ὡς ὤμοσα ἐν τῇ ὀργῇ μου, Εἰ εἰσελεύσονται εἰς τὴν κατάπαυσίν μου. In the second case, however, the words have been translated into Kernowek Kemyn as: *Dell des y'm sorr, nevra ny dhons a-ji dhe'm powesva.* Exactly the same Greek words, then, have been translated into Kernowek in two different ways in Kernowek Kemyn. The only reason for the two versions' being different is that they have not been translated from the Greek but from an English version. In all modern English translations that I have consulted the two verses are translated identically. In the Authorized Version of 1611, however, the two are different:

Heb. 3.11
'So I sware in my wrath, They shall not enter into my rest' AV

Heb. 4.3
'As I have sworn in my wrath, if they shall enter into my rest' AV

It seems probable that the dissimilarity in the Authorized Version between the two verses, meant that their identical wording in the original Greek was overlooked and they were in consequence translated differently in the Kernowek Kemyn. It seems highly likely, therefore, that these verses were not translated from the Greek but from the Authorized Version of 1611.

9.10 At Heb. 5:11-14 the Kernowek Kemyn reads:

Gwarnyans rag *Negedhses

*Yn kever hemma ni a'gan beus meur dhe leverel yw kales dhe styrya a-ban dheuthewgh ha bos poes agas klywes. Rag kyn tegoedh dhywgh bos dykadoryon erbynn an termynn ma, edhomm a'gas beus nebonan dhe dhyski dhywgh kynsa elvennow a lavarow Dyw. Edhomm a'gas beus a leth, yn le boes kales, rag pubonan a vyw orth leth yw heb prevyans y'n ger a wiryonedh, rag ev yw fleghik. Mes boes kales yw rag an *devisigyon, rag an re a's teves kowses dyskys dre usadow *dhe dhissernya yntra da a dhrog.

The English of the RSV (from which the above seems to have been translated) reads as follows:

'About this we have much to say which is hard to explain, since you have become dull of hearing. For though by this time you ought to be teachers, you need some one to teach you the first principles of God's word. You need milk, not solid food; for everyone who lives on milk is unskilled in the word of righteousness, for he is a child. But solid food is for the mature, for those who have their faculties trained by practice to distinguish good from evil.'

The English makes excellent sense. The Kernowek Kemyn is difficult to construe, however. Let us look at the passage in detail, starting with the heading: *Gwarnyans rag *Negedhses*. I have already pointed out at § 3.07

above, that *negedhses* is unnecessary. The syntax is also problematic. I can find only one example of *gwarnya rag* in traditional Cornish: *ha pelha agys hemma, pan ve den **gwarnys** aragdorne **rag omwetha** theworth peryll ha danger ara cotha warnotha* 'and further than that, when someone has been warned beforehand to keep himself from peril and danger, which will fall upon him' TH 4. Here *gwarnya... rag omwetha* means 'to warn someone to keep' not 'to warn someone against keeping'. *Gwarnyans rag *Negedhses*, then, if it means anything, signifies 'Warning to Apostasize'—the very opposite of what was intended.

We have already seen that expressions like *yn kever hemma* not attested in Cornish. It is also apparent that *a-ban dheuthewgh ha bos poes agas klywes* '[literally] since you have become dull as to your hearing' has been translated directly from the English. It is a pity the translation used such an unidiomatic rendering. 'Since you have become dull of hearing' means the same thing as 'since your hearing is now dulled'. It would have been equally possible to write *aban yw agas klywes gyllys poes* 'since your hearing has become dulled', which would have been simpler, more succinct and better Cornish (though the spellings *klywes* and *poes* are both inauthentic).

The translator's expression *Rag kyn tegoedh dhywgh bos dyskadoryon* is also questionable. It means 'For, though it behoves you to be teachers'. What was intended, however, was 'you ought to have been teachers'— which is not the same thing. It would have been better to have written *kyn talvia dhywgh bos dyskadoryon*. I am also unhappy about *kynsa elvennow a lavarow Dyw* 'first elements of the words of God'. In the first place the article is required here. The translation ought to have read *an kynsa elvennow a lavarow Dyw* 'the first elements of the words of God'. *Elven* is not the correct word here, either. It is attested only in Cornish dialect as *elvan* meaning 'porphyritic rock' and the Cornish word could only have meant 'spark, atom'. It does not mean 'rudiments, basics, first steps' (Greek στοιχεῖα τῆς ἀρχῆς 'the first elements').

The term *tevisigyon* 'adults' is also invented and is based on the verbal adjective *tevys* 'grown'. The word in the Greek is τελείων, the genitive plural of τέλειος 'perfect, grown, mature'. I do not understand why the translation did not use here some periphrasis like *an re athves* 'the mature ones' or *tus athves* 'mature people'.

The most serious problem in the Kernowek Kemyn translation of this passage, however, is the expression *dhe dhissernya yntra da a dhrog*. The translations seems to be conflating two quite separate idioms: A) to discern good from evil and B) to discern between good and evil. He ought to have written either A) *dhe dhissernya yntra da ha drog* 'to discern between good and evil' or B) *dhe dhissernya an da dhiworth an drog* 'to distinguish the good from the evil.' The expression *dhe dhissernya yntra da a dhrog*, as it stands, can only mean 'to discern between good of evil'. It is curious that the translation is mistaken here, since the correct expression is to be found in Middle Cornish:

> A das ha mam ov megyans yv bos gorrys ȝe ȝyskans rag attendie an scryptur gothvos ynweth **decernya** omma **ynter drok ha da** yv ov ewnadow pur vr 'Father and mother, my upbringing is to be put to learning to study the scripture. To be able also to discern in this world between good is ever my longing' BM 25-30.

My own translation of this passage reads as follows:

> Ow tuchya an mater ma, ny a'gan bues lowr dhe leverel hag yma cales dhe glerhe, rag why yw gyllys talsogh y'gas convedhes. Y talvya dheugh warbyn omma bos descajoryon, saw yma othem dheugh a dhescajor a alla declarya dheugh an penrewlys kensa a oraclys Dew. Othem a'gas bues a leth, adar sosten cales. Rag neb a'n jeffa leth avel bos yw flogh munys ha dygreft ow tuchya an ger a ewnder. Saw y teseth sosten cales dhe'n dus athves, dhe'n re na a's teves an gallus dhe dhecernya ynter drog ha da.

THE SIXTH TRANSLATOR

10.00 This translator is also the general editor. He was responsible for the Gospels of Luke and John and for revising published versions of Matthew and Mark. I shall concentrate on his rendering of the two gospels that he translated *de novo*, those of Luke and John.

10.01 Inconsistent plurals. At Matt. 2:11 we read *hag owth igeri aga* **thresorow** 'and opening their treasures' but at Matt. 6:19 *Na guntellewgh dhywgh agas honan* **tresorys** *war an nor* 'Do not collect for yourselves treasures upon earth'. In Greek the same word θησαυρούς 'treasures' (both in the accusative plural) is used in both passages. It is not clear why there are two different plurals in Kernowek Kemyn of the same Greek word in the same gospel.

At Matt. 6. 28 we find *lili an* **parkow** 'the lilies of the fields' but at Matt. 6:30 the text reads: *gwels an* **gwelyow** 'the grass of the fields'. It is difficult to understand why two different words have been used in the Kernowek Kemyn, when the Greek word is the same in both cases: τὰ κρίνα τοῦ ἀγροῦ 'the lilies of the field' and τὸν χόρτον τοῦ ἀγροῦ 'the grass of the field'. It should be noticed, moreover, that the expression 'flowers of the field' is attested in traditional Cornish where the word used is neither *parcow* nor *gwelyow*, but *prasow*: *kepar ha flowres in prasow* 'like flowers in the fields' TH 7.

10.02 The erroneous plural of *chy* 'house'. At Matt. 10 27 the Kernowek Kemyn reads: *war bennow an chiow* 'on the roofs of the houses', at Luke 20:47 we read *neb a gowllenk chiow an gwedhwesow* 'who devour widows' houses' and at Luke 16:4 *rag ma'm degemmerrons y'ga chiow* 'so that they may receive me in their houses'. The plural **chyow* (KK **chiow*) is nowhere attested in traditional Cornish. The word for 'houses' is *treven*. There are three examples in the texts:

> *Neb a garra y das po y vam, y vab po y virth, chy, **trevyn** po tyrryow, moy agesa ve* 'Whoever loves his father or his mother, his son or his daughter, house, houses or lands more than me' TH 21a
> *Ny dale dien* [leg. *dieu*] *gwile **treven** war an treath* 'you should not build houses on the sand' James Jenkins
> *An house, a lodging, a dwelling, C[ornish] Tshyi [plur **Treven**]* AB: 55c.

*Chiow is unwarranted and should not have been used.

10.03 The Authorized Version as source. The editor of *An Testament Nowydh*, who tells us on page xii of his introduction that each translator produced his first draft "straight from the Greek text". The editor also is the translator of St Luke's Gospel, parts of which, at least, have clearly not been translated from the Greek. At Luke 2:9 in the Kernowek Kemyn reads:

> *Hag **ott**, el an Arloedh a sevis a-dheragdha, ha golowder an Arloedh a splannas a-dro dhedha, hag own bras a's teva* 'And behold, the angel of the Lord stood before them, and the brilliance of the Lord shone round about them, and they were very afraid.'

The Greek text reads:

> καὶ ἄγγελος Κυρίου ἐπέστη αὐτοῖς καὶ δόξα Κυρίου περιέλαμψεν αὐτούς, καὶ ἐφοβήθησαν φόβον μέγαν 'and an angel of the Lord stood near them, and the glory of the Lord shone around them, and they feared with great fear'.

In the Greek text there is no word corresponding to the *ott* 'behold' in *Hag ott* 'And behold' of the Kernowek Kemyn. 'Behold' is also absent from all modern English translations. The Authorized Version, however, reads:

> 'And, lo, the angel of the Lord came upon them, and the glory of the Lord shone about them: and they were sore afraid'

Far from being directly from the Greek, the version in Kernowek Kemyn seems here to have been based on the Authorized Version of AD 1611.

10.04 In Luke 4:16-30 we read how Jesus preached in the synagogue of his own home town and so outraged its inhabitants by his claims to be God's Anointed that they forcibly expelled him. When at verse 27 Jesus has finished speaking, verses 28-29 in the Greek texts continue: καὶ ἐπλήσθησαν πάντες θυμοῦ ἐν τῇ συναγωγῇ ἀκούοντες παῦτα, καὶ ἀναστάντες ἐξέβαλον αὐτὸν ἔξω τῆς πόλεως 'and everybody in the synagogue was filled with wrath hearing these things, and getting up on their feet they threw him out of the city'. The Greek verb ἐπλήσθησαν... θυμοῦ in the first clause is in the aorist passive and means 'they were [thereupon] filled'. The Kernowek Kemyn version reads: *Hag oll an dus y'n synaga *o lenwys a sorr pan glywsons hemma, hag i a sevis yn-bann ha'y jasya yn mes a'n sita.* The imperfect **o lenwys*, rather than the preterite *a veu lenwys*, is incorrect. *Oll an dus... o lenwys* means that the people were already filled with anger, whereas the Greek tells us (as does common sense) that they were outraged only on hearing Christ's sermon.

Notice also that the Greek says 'hearing these things', whereas the Kernowek Kemyn version says *pan glywsons hemma* 'when they heard this'. It seems clear that this sentence has not been translated from the Greek, but from the TEV, which here reads: 'When the people in the synagogue heard this, they were filled with anger'. The Kernowek Kemyn has been translated word for word from the TEV here.

10.05 At Luke 5:19 the Kernowek Kemyn reads: *Ha rag na gavsons fordh dh'y dri a-ji awos an routh, i a yskynnas dhe benn an chi ha'y iselhe der an prileghennow gans an gravath *y'n mysk a-dherag Yesu* 'And because they did not find a way to bring him inside because of the crowd, they went up to the roof of the house and lowered him through the tiles with the stretcher into the midst before Jesus.' Similarly at Luke 6:8 the

Kernowek Kemyn reads: *Sav, ha deus y'n mysk* 'Stand, and come into the middle'. In both cases the Kernowek Kemyn phrase **y'n mysk* 'in(to) the middle' has been used to render the Greek εἰς τὸ μέσον.

Unfortunately the expression **y'n mysk* cannot be used in this way. In traditional Cornish *yn mysk* is a compound preposition. It is used both with possessive adjectives, e.g.

> *yn agan mysk* PC 1374
> *in agan myske* TH 21a
> *in agis mysk* PA 75a
> *in ages mysk* RD 1401
> *in age meske* BM 2368
> *in aga mysk y* TH 33
> *mesk angy* NBoson

and with nouns, e.g.

> *yn mesk fleghys ysrael* OM 1553
> *yn myske y tus* PC 967
> *yn mysk pryues* RD 2011
> *yn mysk arlyჳy* BM 8
> *yn myske an Jewys* TH 26a
> *yn mysk cansaw* BK 1329
> *in myske bestas* CW 1481
> *amisk an Gweeth an Looar* Rowe
> *mesk an Boble* Rowe
> *amesk an poble* John Tonkin.

It is never used as a noun by itself. In the first example should have been translated as *aberth yn cres an chy* (cf. *yn cres a'n chy* OM 2481). The second example should have been translated as *saf yn ban, ha dues yn rag omma*. The adverbial use of the phrase *y'n mysk* 'in the midst, in the middle' is inadmissible.

10.06 Luke 6:12-16 tells how Jesus chose his twelve apostles. The Kernowek Kemyn version of 6:13 reads: *Ha devedhys an jydh, ev a elwis y dhyskyblon dhodho, ha dewis dewdhek dhiworta, **neb a henwis** abesteli*. This appears to have been translated from the TEV: 'When day came, he called his disciples to him, and chose twelve of them, whom he named apostles.' Unfortunately the Kernewek Kemyn is ambiguous. The antecedent of the relative *neb* could perfectly easily be *dewdhek dhiworta* and the sentence could be understood to mean: 'And when day came,

197

he called his disciples to him, and chose twelve of them, who named apostles.' The same problem occurs again at 6:13: *Simon, neb a henwis ynwedh Peder*. The intended sense here is 'Simon whom he also named Peter', but it could equally well mean 'Simon who also named Peter'. This ambiguity ought to have been avoided.

10.07 At Luke 11:5-8 the Kernowek Kemyn reads as follows:

> *Hag ev a leveris dhedha, 'Piw ahanowgh a'n jevydh koweth ha mos dhodho *dhe hanternos ha leverel dhodho, "Koweth, ro *kendon dhym a *dri thorth, rag ow hothman re dheuth dhymm a vyaj ha nyns eus genev travydh dhe ri dhodho." Hag ev a worthyp *a'n tu a-bervedh ha leverel, "Na wra ow throbla; an daras yw deges, hag yma ow fleghes genv y'n gweli, ny allav sevel dhe ri dhis." Me a lever dhywgh, kyn na vynn sevel ha ri dhodho awos y vos y gothman, awos y *ynniadow ev a sev ha ri dhodho puptra a'n jevydh edhomm anodho.*

This passage in Kernowek Kemyn is both inaccurate from the grammatical point of view and also contains rather unidiomatic Cornish. Let us examine the problems one by one.

First notice that μεσονυκτίον 'in the middle of the night' has been rendered as **dhe hanternos*. Such an expression is unknown in Cornish. The correct phrase is seen in: *gansa y an hombronkyas* **yn prys hanternos** *heb wow bys yn aga fryns annas* 'with them they took him in the middle of the night without doubt to their prince Annas' PA 77c.

Secondly, it should be noted that 'lend me' has been translated *ro *kendon dhym*. The word *kendon* means 'debt' in a general sense and is confined to Lhuyd: *Ne vedn e nevra doz vês a* **gyndan** 'He'll never get out of debt' AB: 230c. There is no evidence that the word was ever used in the sense of 'thing lent' or 'thing borrowed'. If one does not wish to use an unattested neologism, like **prestya* (Nance) or **lendya* one might say *ro dhym rag prys* 'give me for a while'.

Thirdly it should be noted that the word *torth* 'loaf' is only ever used in conjunction with the word *bara* 'bread':

> *athyrageugh me a ter* **torth a vara** 'before you I will break a loaf of bread'
> RD 1313-14
> *an arluth ihesu guella athyragon* **torth vara** 'Jesus the best lord broke a loaf of bread before us' RD 1489-90.

It should also be noticed that *vara* is lenited after *torth*, which implies that Cornish *torth* is feminine. This view is reinforced by Welsh *torth* 'loaf' which is feminine and Breton *torzh* 'tourte, miche' which is also feminine. The expression, therefore, of *a *dri *thorth* ought to have been *a deyr thorth vara*. It is remarkable that *torth* is mistakenly masculine here, since the Kernowek Kemyn dictionary (GKK) cites *torth* as FN, i.e. a 'feminine noun'.

Undoubtedly the most problematic expression in the whole passage is *Hag ev a worthyp a'n tu a-bervedh* 'And he will answer from the inside'. 'Inside' means 'in the house' and 'inside' here ought to have been translated as 'from inside the house'. For the use in Cornish of *chy* with the sense 'inside, within' cf. the following:

> *rag mar a tuefe yn **chy** ef a's gor theworthy'n ny yn kettep pol* 'for if he comes inside, he will take them from us, every one of them' [Satan talking about the souls in hell] RD 3052
>
> *mara keller y wythe a **chy** na alla yntre the'n darasow* 'in case it is possible to keep him from entering within the doors' [of hell] PC 3060
>
> *mes y aswon ev a wra der a' planantis mes ha **chy*** 'but he will know it through the planets outside and in' CW 1409.

The word *ynnyadow* (Kernowek Kemyn) is attested once: *ythaf hep ynnyadow the wonys a dro thotho* 'I am going without prompting to be busy about it' OM 999-1000. *Ynniadow* is too weak to translate the Greek διά τὴν ἀναιδίαν αὐτοῦ 'because of his shamelessness/effrontery/shameless persistence'.

My own version of this passage reads as follows:

> *Ef a leverys dhedhans, "Pyw ahanough a vensa dos y'n nos dhe onen a'y gothmens ha leverel, 'A vroder, gwra prestya dhym teyr thorth a vara, rag coweth re dhueva dhym dheworth an fordh ha ny'm bues tra vyth dhe settya dheragtho?' Nena an den y'n chy a vyn gortheby ha leverel, 'Na wra ow throbla. Yma an daras deges solabrys ha'm flehes genef vy y'm gwely. Ny allama sevel ha ry dhys.' Me a laver dheugh kyn na vensa sevel ha ry dhodho tra vyth dre reson y vos y gothman, dhe'n lyha ef a vensa sevel yn ban ha ry dhodho pynag oll tra a wrussa desyrya awos y dhuryans hyr."*

10.08 At Luke 11:27-8 the Kernowek Kemyn reads as follows:

> **Hag ev ow leverel hemma, unn venyn y'n routh a dhrehevis hy lev ha leverel dhodho, *'Gwynnvys an torr a'th tug ha'n *dhiwronn a'th vagas.' Mes *ynmedh ev, 'Kyns, *gwynnvys seul a *glyw ger Dyw ha'y witha'* 'And as he

was saying this, a woman in the crowd lifted up her voice and said to him "Blessed is the woman that bore you and the breasts that fed you.' But he said "Rather, blessed is whoever hears the word of God and keeps it".'

No speaker of traditional Cornish would, I think, have written the above, since it is neither correct gramatically nor idiomatic—to say nothing of the unhistoric orthography. Let us look at the two verses in greater detail.

The use of *ha(g)* to introduce a subordinate clause without a main verb is permissible in Cornish, but not at the head of its sentence. Here are some examples from the texts:

> *ʒe worte vn lam beghan y ʒeth pesy may halle ʒy ʒas yn weth vgy a van* **hag ef rag own ow crenne** 'from them he went a short distance to pray also to his Father who is above and he trembling in fear' PA 52cd
>
> *tresse gwyth* **hag ef yn cren** *y pesys du delyr vy* 'a third time and him a-tremble he prayed "God deliver me"' PA 57c
>
> *pedyr sur a omdennas yn vrna del rebeghse ow nagha du leun a ras* **hag ef gwarnyys** *del vye* 'Peter indeed withdrew then as he had sinned denying God full of grace, and he warned how it would be' PA 86cd
>
> *A vyne gwarʒe y ben war y gorff bys yn y droys squardijs oll o y grohen* **hag ef cuʒys yn y woys** 'From the topmost crown of his head to his feet on his body all his skin was torn and he covered in his blood' PA 135ab
>
> *gans y vam y fye guris* **hag ef gensy ow tene** 'by his mother it had been made while he was being breastfed by her' PA 161c
>
> *gweʒe goʒyans aga meyn orth Ihesus a omgame* **hag ef moygha yn y beyn** 'the worst they could they twisted their faces at Jesus and him in his greatest agony' PA 196bc
>
> *En eʒewon skyntyll keth resteffo mur vylyny ʒe veras worth crist y eth* **hag ef yn crous ow cregy** 'The clever wretched Jews, may they have much shame, went to look at Christ and him hanging on the cross' PA 216ab
>
> *In corff Ihesus y ʒese* **hag ef yn crows ow cregy** *pymp myll strekis del iove ha pedergwyth cans goly* 'In Christ's body there were, and him hanging on the cross, five thousand weals as j'oué [I have heard] and four times a hundred wounds' PA 227ab
>
> *A myleges y'th ober ty re'n lathes ru'm lowte* **hag ef ahanan mar ger** 'O accursed in your deeds, you have killed him upon my honour and him so beloved of us' OM 610-12

yn wethen me a welas yn ban vhel worth scoren flogh byen nowyth gynys **hag**
ef yn quethow maylys 'in the tree I saw up high upon a bough a little
child newly born and him wrapped in swaddling clothes' OM 804-07

yn ov colon asyw bern pan welaf ov map ihesu a dro th'y pen curyn spern **hag**
ef map dev a vertu 'how grieved am I in my heart when I see my son
Jesus with a crown of thorns about his head and him the son of
mighty God' PC 2932-35

An trubut pan ve tochys, e worthyb o tyn ha freth **hag ef garaw, hag owth**
avowa forsoyth *a'y wlascor trubut na goyth* 'When the tribute was
mentioned, his answer was sharp and bold, and he was rough, and
he claimed that no tribute is due from his kingdom' BK 2262-66.

Ha(g) is a coordinating conjunction which connects a phrase or clause
to something which precedes it. It cannot be used when nothing comes
before it. The translators **Hag ev ow leverel hemma* '[literally] And him
saying this' at the beginning of a sentence without anything before it, is
inadmissible in Cornish.

We meet a second problem in the use of the idiom *gwyn bys*
(Kernowek Kemyn **gwynn bys*). This literally means 'blessed the world
(of)', i.e. 'happy is he who'. It is used only with a personal subject:

pup vrol oberet da **guyn bys** *kymmys an gvrello* 'happy are those who at all
times do good works' OM 604-05

guyn ov bys *kafus cummyas the wothfos pyth vo ena* 'how lucky I am to get
permission to know what may be there' OM 750-51

bos cummyas thy'm **guyn ov bys** 'how lucky I am that I have permission'
OM

a dev lemyn **guyn ov bys** *gothfos guyr ol yredy* 'O God, now I am lucky to
know all the truth indeed' OM 791-92

guyn bys *bones thy'm fethys lafur ha duwon a'n bys* 'happy am I that I have
vanquished the toil and sorrow of the world' OM 850-51

guyn beys *ha quellen an gyth may fe yrhys thy'm hethy* 'happy would I be
were I to see the day when I should be bidden to cease' OM 1013-14

guyn y vys *pan ve gynys a allo gul thy's servys* 'happy is the man who can
do thee service when he is born' OM 1476-77.

Although the womb which bore Christ and the breasts which suckled
him were human, they cannot class as a human subject and *gwyn bys*
is therefore unsuitable in the present instance. The correct word to be
used here with a non-person subject is *benegys* 'blessed'. This is
particularly clear from the following example, where wombs and
breasts are being called 'blessed':

en deʒyow a vyth guelys hag a ʒe sur yntreʒon may fyth **torrow benegis** *bythqueth na allas eʒon ha benenas kekyffrys na ve ʒeʒe* **denys bron** 'the days will be seen and are surely coming among us when wombs will be blessed that never could bear and women also whose breasts were never sucked' PA 169b-d.

The translation should have contained **benegys yw** rather than **gwynnvys*.

The Kernowek Kemyn form **dhiwronn* 'breasts' is also without any justification. From the time of the earliest Middle Cornish texts the distinction between the masculine and feminine dual prefixes **dew-* and **dyw-* had been lost. In fact the only attested instance of the Cornish for 'two breasts' is: *me a weall vn mayteth wheake ow setha in pur sertan hag in y* **devran** *flogh teake* 'I see a sweet maiden sitting indeed and on her breasts a fair child' CW 1835-37, where the prefix *dew* (not **dyw*, and certainly not **diw* as in Kernowek Kemyn) has become fused with the initial of *vron*.

A further problem is to be seen in the unidiomatic use of *yn-medh* in *Mes* **yn-medh** *ev* 'But he said'. The English is 'But he said, "Blessed rather are… "'. There is a contrast between the words of the woman and Jesus' reply. In English one would naturally stress the pronoun 'he' in 'But *he* said'. Cornish is a Celtic language and it shares with all its sister languages the inability to emphasize by the use of intonation. In no Celtic language can one say the equivalent of 'But *he* said'. Such emphasis in Cornish can be indicated in verbs only by the use of abnormal word order. Unfortunately the form *yn medh* (< *y'n medh* 'he says/said it) must always be in normal order, i.e. particle + verb. There cannot be any emphasis of the subject when *yn medh* is used. In order to emphasize 'he' in 'But *he* said' one needs to use abnormal order, where the emphasized personal pronoun stands at the head of its clause: *Mes ef a leverys*, where the emphasis is naturally on the *ef* (since *ef a leverys* actually means 'it was he who said'). *Yn medh ev* cannot receive emphasizing intonation and is therefore inadequate. In this respect the translation is defective.

The translation *Kyns, *gwynnvys seul a *glyw* is also mistaken. In the first place, as we have seen, *gwynnvys* is not the right word. A further problem involves the verb after *seul* 'whoever'. This is an indefinite subject meaning 'whoever', i.e. 'blessed is whoever hears the word of God and does it'. As such it requires a subjunctive verb. This is clear from the following examples:

Suel a vynno bos sylwys golsowens ow lauarow 'Whoever wishes to be saved, let him listen to my words' PA 2a

Pur apert hag yn golow y leueris ow dyskas ow lahys haw lauarow suel a vynna y clewas 'Very publicly and in daylight I gave my teaching, my laws and my sayings, whoever wished to hear it' PA 79ab.

The same use of the subjunctive is found with other indefinite pronouns, e.g. *kenyver, pynag oll* and *neb*

ny fynnaf certan gase onan vyth-ol the vewe pynag a wharfo an cas 'I will certainly not allow any one of them to live, whatever happens in the matter' OM 1696-98

my a vyn aga threhy pepynag ol a wharfo 'I will cut them, whatever happens' OM 1735-36

neb a'n gothfo gorthybes kyn fo mar stout a'y golon 'whoever knows it, let him answer, though he be stout in heart' PC 775-76

neb a vo yn moghya gre a vyth an brassa henwys 'whoever is in the highest degree shall be called the greatest' PC 777-78

The orth crist y ruk pesy certen desyr eredy the kenever an gorthya 'From Christ he prayed for a certain wish for whomsoever should worship him' BK 4425-27

bus openly the kenever a whelha ha vo o sevall rebta 'but openly to whoever sees and is standing near' SA 60.

The translation should have read *Benegis yw seul a glywo*. As it stands, it is less than perfect.

10.09 At Luke 12:4 in the Kernowek Kemyn there is a heading which reads: *Neb yw Res y Owna*. This is clearly intended to mean 'He who it is necessary to fear'. Since in *y owna* 'to fear him' the *y* 'his' refers to the antecedent *Neb* 'He who', the relative clause is itself indirect. The translation ought therefore to have contained an indirect relative clause, rather than a direct one. It should have read: *Neb mayth yw res y owna*; cf. *neb may fe moghya geffys a gar moghye yn pup le* 'he to whom is most forgiven loves most everywhere' PC 513-14.

There is a much more serious fault in the semantics of the heading, however. The word *owna* 'to fear' is not, as far as I am aware, attested anywhere in Middle Cornish. The equivalent of 'to fear' in English is expressed in Cornish by the noun *own* 'fear' together with one of the verbs *perthy* 'bear', *kemeres* 'take', *y'm bues* 'have' or *bos the* 'have'. Here are some examples from the texts:

ovn a'm bus vy 'I am afraid' OM 1452

na porth ovn vyth na veth trest 'do not fear at all, do not be sorrowful' OM 1467

na bertheugh ovn a henna 'do not be afraid of that' OM 2518

mar thues ovn bones knoukys 'if you fear being struck' PC 2245

ny'm bues ovn vyth annotho 'I am not afraid of him at all' RD 385

na gymmer ovn vyth dremays 'do not be afraid at all, good man' BM 1112

ha na berthuth ovn in cays 'and do not fear in the matter' BM 1376

nena eff a gemeras owne a drega na fella 'then he feared to dwell any longer' TH 46a

nu'm bues owne a gows orto 'I am afraid of speaking to him' BK 559

nyng es owne thym ahanas 'I am not afraid of you' CW 562

owne ahanas rag neffra dean an gevyth prest pub preis 'fear of you a person will have always for ever' CW 910-11

owne yma thym a bub dean 'I am afraid of everybody' CW 1527

ha na gymar owne in bys 'and do not be afraid at all' CW 1785.

Owna 'fear' is attested in Late Cornish:

Ouna Dêu Matern 'Fear God the king' Pryce

Cara, gorthya ha ouna Dew An Mateyrn ha'n lahez en guz plew Ouna Dêw, parthy Mateyrn 'Love, worship and fear God, the king and the laws of your parish. Fear God, obey the king' Gwavas.

Unfortunately *owna* in Late Cornish also means 'mend, repair':

Mar kressa an Dean deskez feer na gwellaz hemma [ev] a venga kavaz fraga e ouna en skreefa-composter 'If that wise and learned man were to see this, he would find reason to correct it in orthography' NBoson

Gwra ouna guz furu 'Mend your ways' Gwavas.

The heading *Neb yw Res y Owna* at Luke 12:1 might make no sense to a Cornish speaker of the sixteenth century. Or more probably, he would understand it to mean 'He who must be repaired'. A better translation would have been *Henna mayth yw Res Kemeres Own Anodho*.

10.10 At Luke 15:16, in the story of the Prodigal Son, we read in the Kernowek Kemyn: *hag ewl a'n jevo a dhybri y walgh a'n plisk-karob a wre an mogh aga dybri, mes *denvydh a's ri dhodho* 'and he desired to fill his belly from the locust-tree fruits which the pigs were eating, but nobody actually gave [Greek ἐδίδου, "vivid" imperfect] any to him.' *Denvyth* in Cornish means 'anybody':

ple ma haneth a wor **den vyth** 'where is he tonight—does anybody know?'
RD 849

Mar teffa **den vith** *ha pregoth thyn kythsame barbarus nacions ma in aga eyth y aga honyn* 'If anybody were to come and preach to these same barbarous nations in their own languge' TH 19

Mar pith **den vith** *ioynys the chear pedyr* 'If anybody is attached to the see of Peter' TH 49

pan dra ill **den vith** *leverell, fatell rug Du apperia in flam a dan* 'what can anybody say, that God appeared in a fiery flame' TH 55a

Mars ues **den vith** *a vyn cows* 'If anybody wishes to speak' BK 1496

prag e tevons heb **den vith** *th'aga gonys* 'why they grow without anybody's tending them' BK 2133-34.

Den vyth means 'nobody' only if there is also a negative particle, *ny(ns)* or *na(g)* before the verb. The following selection of examples from the texts makes the syntax clear:

ny yl **den vyth** *amontye myns a gollas yn chyffar* 'nobody can calculate how much he lost by the deal' PA 40b

den vyth *ny yl amontye na leuerell war anow oll myns peynys an geve* 'nobody can estimate or describe in words all the extent of the torments he suffered' PA 59cd

Rag the verkye my a gura yn bys **den vyth** *na'th latho* 'For I shall mark thee so that nobody in the world shall kill thee' OM 602-03

ow spyrys **ny** *dryc nefre yn corf map* **den vyth** *yn beys* 'my spirit shall dwell for ever in the body of no man in the world' OM 925-26

ny yl **den vyth** *gorthyby* 'nobody can answer' PC 821

the **den vyth** *ny wruk trespys* 'he did wrong to nobody' PC 2458

nynsus **den vyth** *yn powma a whytho guel* 'there is nobody in this land who will blow better' PC 2710-11

byth **ny** *yl awos an bys* **den vyth** *bones dasserhys wose merwel* 'for all the world nobody can ever have risen again after death' RD 938-40

ny'n saw **den vyth** 'nobody will save him' RD 1988

Nyns yv the **denvyth** *guertha ov map grays du war an beys* 'my son, it is for nobody to sell the grace of God in this world' BM 2482-83

ha me **ny** *won* **den vyth** *wel* 'and I know nobody better' BM 2713

nynses **den vith** *abill the wothfas mas dre speciall revelacion* 'nobody is able to know except by special revelation' TH 17

nena **ny** *russa* **den vith** *resak in heresy* 'then nobody would have rushed into heresy' TH 19a

nan geffo **den vith** *wosa hemma Just cawse rag pretendia igorans* 'so that nobody hereafter may have just cause to claim ignorance' TH 20a

na rens ef examnya den vith arell, mas y golan y honyn 'let him examine
nobody else, but his own heart' TH 23a

ny *rug* **den vith** *govyn pew a rug hemma na henna* 'nobody asked who did
this or that' TH 57

ny *vynsa* **den vyth** *gwaya na styrrya warbyn an bredereth a crist* 'nobody
would have moved or stirred against the brothers of Christ' TH 48a

Ny yl **den vith** *don ow sor* 'Nobody can withstand my wrath' BK 1264.

This a universal Celtic syntagm. Welsh *neb* means 'nobody' only when
used with a negative particle. The same is true of Irish *duine ar bith* or
aon duine 'anybody'. In *mes denvydh *a's ri dhodho* there is no negative
particle, the sentence can only mean 'but anyone was giving them to
him.' It is remarkable the translation was allowed to contain such an
elementary error.

10.11 At Luke 16:4 in the parable of the Unjust Steward we read: *My a
woer pand' a wrav* **pan ov remevys** *a'm soedh, rag ma'm degemmerrons y'ga
chiow* 'I know what I shall do, when I lose my job, so that they will
receive me into their houses'. The clause beginnning *pan *ov remevys*
(literally 'when I am removed') has apparently been based on the
English 'when I am removed from my job'. In Cornish, however, when
referring to the future after *pan* 'when', the present of *bos* may not be
used—since the present of *bos* refers to present time, not the indefinite
future. Cornish in such cases uses the subjunctive, as can be seen from
the following examples:

> *ha'n el thy'm a leuerys* **pan vo** *tryddyth tremenys* 'and the angel told me
> when three days are past' OM 844-45
>
> **pan ven** *ny sur coth ha gwan gvreth agan revlys tek* 'when we are indeed
> old and feeble you will keep our goodly rules' BM 68-9
>
> *ke ha dus* **pan vy** *plesyes* 'come and go whenever you are happy to' BM 139
>
> *mar myn ov descans servya genogh* **pan ven** *apposijs* 'if my education is
> sufficient, when I am examined by you' BM 524-25
>
> *the peyn yfern sur ytha the torment* **pan vo** *marov* 'to the pain of hell he will
> go certainly when he is dead' BM 1214-15
>
> **pan vegh** *in henna golhys yth egh gvyn avel crystel* 'when you are washed
> in that, you will become as clear as crystal' BM 1520-21
>
> **pan vo** *an rema marov wegennov ny a ra moy* 'when these are dead, we'll
> make more little darlings' BM 1564-65
>
> *Ha* **pan vesta** *sav ha glaan gueyt dustruya in tyan ol templys an falge dewov*
> 'And when you are cured and clear, be sure to destroy completely all
> the temples of the false gods' BM 1719-21

pan veste epscop worthy iiij cans puns gyllyth speyna 'when you are a respected bishop you can spend four hundred pounds' BM 2819-20

an iovle agis acectour rebo **pan vowhy** *marrov* 'may the devil be your follower when you are dead' BM 3523-24

pan vo *an dewetha gyrryow clowis a onen a vo in y gwely marnance* 'when the last words are heard from someone on his death-bed' SA 59

ha **pan vova** *recevis (g)enas, kee thath tre* 'and when he is accepted by you, go home' SA 60a

pan vo *an kigg gulhis, an nenaf a veth glanhis* 'and when the flesh is washed, the sould will be cleansed' SA 60a

Me a'm byth drog neun hanath gans Teuthar **pan vo** *clowys* 'I shall have dreadful hunger tonight, when it is heard by Teudar' BK 488-89

Ow holan a vyth in cren **pan vo** *kowsys a'y hanow* 'My heart will shudder when his name is mentioned' BK 2317-18

nebas lowre a vyt[h] an gwayne **pan vo** *genas cowle comptys* 'small enough will the profit be when it is all added up by you' CW 793-94

Ha **po** *[< pan vo] tî ha dha urêg an moiha lûan uarbarh* 'And when you and your wife are happiest together' JCH § 12.

The translation ought to have contained the Kernowek Kemyn equivalent of *pan vyf remuvys* or *pan ven remuvys*. As it stands, the tense is mistaken and the translation is thus defective.

10.12 At Luke 18:37 the Kernowek Kemyn reads: *I a leveris dhodho, 'Yesu a Nasara* **a dremen'** 'They said to him "Jesus of Nazareth is passing"'. In traditional Cornish, when used with a qualifying adverb or adverbial phrase, the verb *tremena* can mean 'pass, go':

kyns ys y the **tremene** *an mor ruyth sur* 'before they pass over the Red Sea indeed' OM 1634-35

byth ny yllyn **tremene** *an mor ma war ov ene* 'never will we be able to pass over this sea upon my soul' OM 1648-49

gesough ov thus vs gene the ves quyt the **tremene** 'allow my people who are with me to depart freely' PC 1120-21

rag me a'n guelas dufvn dresof ef a **tremenas** 'for I saw him wide awake— he passed over me' RD 524-25.

More often, however, *tremena* means 'pass over, die', particularly when it not accompanied by any adverb or adverbial phrase:

ha pan wryllyf **tremene** *an bys ru'm gorre th'y wlas* 'and when I pass from the world may he bring me to his kingdom' OM 530-31 *ov tas fest lowenek vyth mar scon a'n bys* **tremene** 'my father will be very happy so soon to pass from the world' OM 833-34

res yv porrys an sprus ma pan **dremenna** *an bys ma yn y anow bos gorrys* 'it is very necessary that these pips be put in his mouth when he pass from this world' OM 874-76

kepar del fue thy'n yrhys gans y das kyns **tremene** 'just as was commanded us by his father before he passed away' OM 2375-76

ha gans myyn gureugh hy knoukye er na wrello **tremene** 'and pelt her with stones until she die' OM 2694-95

saw y ober hay thyskes pup ol a wra **tremene** 'but for his work and his teaching all will die' PC 57-8

kergh thy's ov ene gans el pan wraf a'n beys **tremene** 'fetch to thee my soul by an angel when I pass from the world' PC 429-30

ef a'n pren kyns **tremene** 'he will pay for it before he dies' PC1470

awos kemmys drok a wren a'n beys ny fyn **tremene** 'after all the evil we do he will not pass from the world' PC 2113-14a

kymeres corf ihesu yv yn pren crous **tremenys** 'to take the body of Jesus who is dead upon the cross' PC 3113-14

nynsyv ihesu **tremenys** 'Jesus is not dead' PC 3118

pan fy a'n bys **tremenys** *gans cryst y fythyth trygys* 'when you have passed from the world you shall dwell with Christ' PC 3232-33

pan fo a'n beys **tremenys** *yth a the'n nef* 'when he has passed from the world we will go to heaven' RD 287-88

dovtyogh drok thagis eneff pan **dremennogh** *an bysme* 'fear evil for your souls when you depart from this world' BM 1891-92

pur thefry kyns **tremena** *ahanan y a perth coff* 'truly before they die they will remember us' BM 2485-86

meryasek an den worthy del glowa yv **tremenis** 'Meriasek, the worthy man, as I hear, has passed on' BM 4369-70

tremenys *yv meryasek* 'Meriasek has passed on' BM 4383

yv meryasek **tremenis** 'has Meriasek passed on?' BM 4409

Arluth eff yv **tremenys** 'Lord, he has passed on' BM 4413

Te a'n ser kyn **tremena** 'You will be angry for it before you die' BM 3085

yeth esaf ow **tremena** 'I am dying' CW 1696

ena adam **tremenys** 'Adam's soul [has] passed on' CW 2011.

In the light of the above, we can see that in the Kernowek Kemyn sentence *Yesu a Nasara **a dremen*** the verb would naturally be understood to mean 'pass over, die'. The tense is the present-future and the whole would therefore mean 'Jesus of Nazareth will die'. For 'Jesus of Nazareth is passing by' Cornish would say something like *Yma Jesu a Nazara ow passya* or *Yma Jesu a Nazara ow kerdhes dreson ny*.

10.13 'On the Sabbath day' wrongly translated. Notice the following in the Kernowek Kemyn of St Luke's Gospel:

orth aga dyski y'n Sabot 'teaching them on the Sabbath' Luke 4:31
ow kerdhes der an ysegi y'n Sabot Luke 6:1
an pyth nag yw lafyl y'n Sabot Luke 6:2
mar mynna yaghhe y'n Sabot Luke 6:7
pyneyl yw lafyl y'n Sabot Luke 6:9
ow tyski yn onan a'n synagys y'n Sabot Luke 13:10
ader y'n Sabot Luke 13:14
yw lafyl yaghhe y'n Sabot po a nyns yw Luke 14:3
Hag i a bowesas y'n Sabot herwydh an gorhemmyn Luke 23:56.

It is quite clear that in this translation *y'n Sabot* is considered a legitimate way to render 'on the Sabbath'. I am not so sure. Before I discuss my reasons for my scepticism, I should like make a further point. At Luke 13:15 the Greek text reads:

Ὑποκριταί, ἕκαστος ὑμῶν **τῷ σαββάτῳ** οὐ λύει τὸν βοῦν αὐτοῦ ἢ τὸν ὄνον ἀπὸ τῆς φάτνης καὶ ἀπαγαγὼν ποτίζει; 'Hypocrites, does not each one of you **on the Sabbath** loose his ox or his ass from the stall and leading it away give it to drink?'

The same verse in the Kernowek Kemyn reads:

Falswesyon, a ny wra pubonan ahanowgh digelmi y ojyon po y asyn a'n presep ha'y hembronk dhe ves rag gul dhodho eva? 'False one, does not everyone of you untie his ox or his ass from the manger and lead it away to make it drink?'

In the Kernowek Kemyn version the mention of the Sabbath has been acidentally omitted. This is regrettable, since the Sabbath is the topic of interest.

Let us return to the expression *y'n Sabot*. In traditional Cornish (as in other Celtic languages) when using the names of the days of the week or feast days adverbially it is not necessary to use any preposition, though with days of the week and some festivals the prefix *de, du* is prefixed to the name of the day:

*kergh a'n fenten thy'm dour cler the thygh[t]ye bos thy'nny ny erbyn soper kepar del yv an vaner **duyow hamlos*** 'fetch from the well for me clean water to prepare supper as is the custom on Maundy Thursday' PC 650-55 *drefen na fynnyth crygy an arluth the thasserghy* **du pask** *vyttyn* 'since you will not believe that the Lord rose again on Easter Day in the morning' RD 1106-08

arta me a thue **deth yov** 'I will come again on Thursday' BM 1472

me a vyn mones **deyow** *prest the helghya* 'I shall go on Thursday indeed to hunt' BM 3159-60

an peath eggee e lal tha ni **da zeel** 'what he tells us on Sunday' JTonkin.

The another syntax involves using the preposition *war* 'upon' in imitation of English:

maner o ʒen eʒewon **war dyth pasch** *worth an Iustis an preson govyn onon ha bos henna delyffrys* 'the Jews had a custom on Easter Day to request someone from prison from the Justice and to have that one released' PA 124cd

bythqueth re bue vs geneugh **war pask** *my the ase theugh vn prysner ha'y thelyffre* 'you have always had a custom that at Easter I should allow you one prisoner and set him free' RD 2034-36

the gowse in aga hanow y oll then bobyll **war du fencost** *myttyn* 'to talk in all their names to the people on Pentecost Sundary in the morning' TH 44a

ma An mab leean ni E gana terwitheyaw **war an zeell** 'our parson sometimes sings it on Sunday' Thomas Boson.

In Cornish 'Sabbath' is *sabot* at PC 1504, 2557 and *dyth Sabbat, an Sabbath* JKeigwin. We do not know how traditional Cornish said 'on the Sabbath day' or 'on the Sabbath'. The most likely translation is **dedh Sabot** (cf. Tonkin's **da zeel** 'on Sunday'). There is no warrant for the **y'n Sabot* that is used here.

10.14 There are a great many problems in the translation of St Luke's gospel. I should like to mention just one more. At Luke 16:19-21 in the Kernowek Kemyn we read as follows:

Yth esa den ***golusek**, *neb a omwiska yn purpur ha sendal, ow kevywya yn splann pub dydh oll. Hag yth esa unn den boghosek,* ***Lasarus** *y hanow, neb* ***re bia gorrys** *orth y yet,* ***podrek**, *hag ev hwansek dhe dhybri y walgh a'n brewyon a goedha a voes an den golusek. Mes an keun keffrys a* ***dheuth** *ha lapya y* ***wenennow** 'There was a rich man, who was dressed in purple and fine silk, feasting lavishly every single day. And there was a poor man, Lazarus by name, who had been laid at his gate, rotten, and he desirous to eat his fill of the crumbs which fell from the table of the rich man. But the dogs also came and licked his sores'.

The first thing to notice is that the 'updated' *golusek from Old Cornish has been used in preference to the more genuine rych of the Middle Cornish texts. The second point to notice is that the name of the poor man is *Lasarus, which is neither Greek, English nor Cornish (see § 2.06 above). The Greek ἐβέβλητο πρὸς τὸν πυλῶνα αὐτοῦ 'he had been placed at his gate' is also translated too literally as *neb re bia gorrys orth y yet 'who had been sent at his gate' when the Greek means simply that Lazarus was lying at the rich man's door. More unfortunately the translation juxtaposes yet 'gate' and podrek 'rotten', separating them only by a comma. Someone reading the text quickly might be forgiven for thinking that the poor man had been put at the rich man's rotten gate.

What is really curious about the Kernowek Kemyn version is that, apart from re bia gorrys, the verbs are imperfect: yth esa... neb a omwiska... yth esa... a goedha, until suddenly an keun keffrys a dheuth. The passage therefore means: 'There was a rich man... who was dressed... and there was a poor man... anxious to eat the fragment that used to fall... And the dogs came [once] and licked his sores'. The Greek says οἱ κύνες ἐρχόμενοι ἐπέλειχον τὰ ἕλκη αὐτοῦ 'the dogs coming used to lick his ulcers'. The verb a dheuth in the Kernowek Kemyn, however, implies that they came but once.

In fact, the dogs did not lick his ulcers at all, for the word used here is *gwenennow, an unattested plural of Lhuyd's guenan glossing pustula 'a blister' AB: 132c (where the Irish equivalents given by Lhuyd are bolg 'bladder', fearb 'weal', spuaic 'blister', puchóid 'pustule' and goirín 'pimple'). The Greek word used by Luke is ἕλκη 'ulcers', which is not what is meant by gwenennow. Lazarus in Greek and in English is covered in the sores of skin-disease and / or malnutrition. *Lasarus in the Kernowek Kemyn version seems to suffer from small-pox or just blisters.

10.15 The Sixth Translator and St John's Gospel. The translator of St Luke also translated St John's Gospel, which in language is probably the simplest book of the New Testament. There are, nonetheless, many problems in the Kernowek Kemyn translation of the fourth gospel. I shall here examine a few of them.

10.16 The Greek at John 1:12 here reads: ὅσοι δὲ ἔλαβον αὐτόν, ἔδωκεν αὐτοῖς ἐξουσίαν τέκνα Θεοῦ γενέσθαι 'but as many as received him, to them he gave power to become the children of God.' The Kernowek

Kemyn, however, reads: *Mes seul a'n degemmeras, *dhedha y ros ev galloes dhe vos fleghys Dew*. The indefinite pronoun *suel* (Kernowek Kemyn **seul*—a form unattested in traditional Cornish) is singular and is referred to by singular verbs and singular pronouns:

> *alemma bys mayth ello sul a the'n nef* 'until departs from here everyone who will go to heaven' RD 135-36
> *Suel a'n gorth ef, a'n geveth nef* 'Who worships him will get heaven' BK 655
> *A'y lavarow sul ew stowt, my a'n gwra clor* 'Who is stout in his words, him I will render mild' BK 2790-91.

The translation wrongly refers to *seul a'n degemmeras* 'as many as received him' by **dhedha* 'to them', when it should have read *dhodho* 'to him'.

10.17 The Greek text at John 1:14 reads: καὶ ἐθεασάμεθα τὴν δόξαν αὐτοῦ, δόξαν ὡς μονογενοῦς παρὰ Πατρός '[literally] and we gazed upon the glory of him, glory as of one-begotten from Father'. This is rendered into Kernowek Kemyn: *ha ni a welas y wolowder, golowder avel dhe *unnik-gennys y Das*. *Genys* (Kernowek Kemyn *gennys*) means 'born', but the Greek μονογενής, in the genitive μονογενοῦς here, means 'only-begotten', speaking of the begetting of the Second Person of the Trinity from all eternity. It is not a reference to the birth of Christ. The neologism **unnik-gennys* 'only born' is therefore inaccurate. It should also be remembered that *unyk* (Kernowek Kemyn *unnik*) is attested only in Late Cornish (*idnack* Gwavas MSS, *ednak* Lhuyd) and may in fact be a borrowing from Welsh. The correct Cornish term to be used here is *un vab* 'only son', which is well attested in traditional Cornish:

> *ihesus crist the vn vap ker* 'Jesus Christ thy only son' PC 160
> *cryst guyr vn vap dev a nef* 'true Christ the only son of the God of heaven' PC 1577
> *genys a vaghtyth glan vn vap certan os the'n das du* 'of a pure virgin thou art the only son of God the Father' PC 3026-28
> *eff appoyntias thean dalleth an bys y vn vab eff, an second person in dryngys, the vos savyowre an bys* 'He appointed from the beginning of the world his only Son, the Second Person of the Trinity, to be the saviour of the world' TH 12a

*eff a rug agan redemya dre an pascion han myrnans ay **vnvab** eff Jhesu crist agan savyour ny* 'he redeemed us by the passion and death of his only son Jesus Christ our saviour' TH 16

*du golosek, neb a rug ry y **vn vab** eff the suffra myrnans rag kerensa y egglos* 'mighty God, who gave his only son to suffer death for the sake of his church' TH 31a.

The translation ought to have read: *golowder avel dhe **un vab** y Das.*

10.18 At John 1: 21 we read how John the Baptist was baptizing in the Jordan and the leaders of the Jews sent priests and Levites to enquire whether he was the Messiah. John denied it. The Kernowek Kemyn text then reads: *Hag i a wovynnas orto, 'Piw ytho? Osta Elias?' Yn-medh ev, '*Nyns ov vy'* 'And they asked him "Who then? Are you Elijah? He said 'I am not'". This is ungrammatical. When answering a question with a tag-verb in Cornish, one uses the particle *na*, not *ny(ns)*. This can be seen from the following examples:

> *ny won us methegyeth am gruelle sav der lyfryov.* **Nag us** *arluth rum lovta* 'I wonder whether there is any salve that would by books heal me. There is not, lord, upon my loyalty [Constantine and Episcopus Poli talking] BM 1487-79
>
> *ha nagh Christ, an casadow, a'th vewnans may fyge suer.* **Na nahaf**, *a bur woky!* 'And deny Christ, the hateful one, so you may be sure of your life. I will not, you utter fool!' [Teutharus and St Kea talking] BK 575-77
>
> *Rys ew gwelas orth an wel nag ota ge mowas lows.* **Nag of**, *ou arluth, defry* 'It is necessary by sight to see that you are not a slack girl' 'I am not, my lord, indeed' [Teutharus and Oubra talking] BK 1115-17
>
> *marsew an oyle a vercy dres genas omma theth tas pur lowan me a vea.* **nag ew** *whath ow thaes forsothe* 'if the oil of mercy has been brought here by you to your father, I should be very happy. It has not yet indeed, O my father' [Adam and Seth talking] CW 1887-90.

The translation should have read: **Yn medh ev, 'Nag ov vy'.** The translation is wrong here, though we find the correct form, *nag ov* correctly later in the same verse.

10.19 At John 1:38 in the Kernowek Kemyn we read: *Yn-medhons dhodho 'Rabbi' (styr *henna *treylys yw Dyskador, *ple trigydh?* The expression *styr henna treylys yw Dyskador* is intended as a translation of the Greek ὃ λέγεται μεθερμηνευόμενον Διδάσκαλε, literally 'which is said when

213

translated, O Teacher'. The Kernowek Kemyn, unfortunately, is not correct.

In the first place one cannot in Cornish use *styr henna to mean 'the meaning of that', since henna is never used in this way. If henna is used genitivally one must use a henna 'of that':

> yn **dysquythyens a henna** ny a bowes desempys 'in demonstration of that I shall rest immediately' OM 147-78
>
> dre an **koll a henna** cothes in extreme miseri 'through the loss of that fallen into extreme misery' TH 3
>
> mas an **blonogeth a henna** neb a rug ow denvon 'but the will of that one who sent me' TH 22a.

As it stands styr henna would either mean 'interpret that!' or more probably, 'stir that!'

In the second place the basic meaning of treylya is not 'translate', but 'turn' and the verb is often used of 'turning away, perverting':

> ol an cyte ow **trylye** theworth mahomm 'turning all the city away from Mahound' PC 578-79
>
> me re'n cafas ov **treylye** agan tus yn lyes le yn mes a grygyans 'I have found him in many places turning our people away from faith' PC 1570-72
>
> ef re **trylyas** lyes cans yn mes a'n fey 'he has turned many away from the faith' PC 1995-96.

As a consequence styr [a] henna treylys might most naturally be taken by a native speaker of Cornish to mean 'the sense of that perverted'. The attempt to adhere closely to the Greek has produced ambiguous and poor Cornish. The correct expression to use here would have been hem yw dhe styrya 'that is to say, that means', a phrase used by Tregear when he is turning into Cornish a preceding passage of Latin:

> **hemma ew the styrrya,** I wysce ath face te a thebbyr the vara 'that is to say, in the sweat of thy brow wilt thou eat thy bread' TH 6
>
> **hemma ew the Styrrya,** mabden genys a venyn 'that is to say, man born of woman' TH 7
>
> **hemma ew the styrrya,** neb a rug benega 'that is to say, he who blessed' TH 13
>
> **Hemma ew the styrrya.** In mar ver dell ew lymmyn infancy passys 'That is to say, Inasmuch as infancy is past' TH 28
>
> **hemmew the styrrya,** Na in tyller arell 'that is to say, Neither in another place' TH 42a

There is a also problem with *ple trigydh?* 'where do you live?' since the present-future of *trega* (Kernowek Kemyn *triga*) is not used in this way. This difficulty has become apparent since the publication of *An Testament Nowydh*, and on the on-line errata page *pleth esosta trigys* 'where are you living' is recommended as a substitute for *ple trigydh*. From the syntactic point of view *pleth esosta trigys* is more correct than *ple trigydh* (see the discussion at § 6.09 above). It is still inadmissible, nonetheless, since *esosta* is nowhere attested in traditional Cornish. The form is invariably *esta*.

10.20 There are problems again when translating 'that means, that is to be interpreted' at John 1:42. The final portion of the verse in Kernowek Kemyn reads: *Ty a vydh henwys Kefas (yw treylys, Karrek)*. This is intended to mean 'You will be called Cephas (which is translated, Rock)'. Unfortunately, the Cornish cannot bear this sense. There is no indication that *yw trelys* is relative, since it is not preceded by either a relative pronoun or any antecedent. *Yw* at the head of its clause is most naturally understood as interrogative, e.g.

> *spencer yv parys pub tra* 'spencer, is everything ready?' BM 268
> *Te javal, ew henna gwyr?* 'You scoundrel, is that true?' BK 78
> *what ew hena tha thevyse* 'what? is that your plan?' CW 625.

The expression *yw treylys Karrek* would, therefore, be most naturally understood to mean 'Has a rock been turned?' A better translation would have been *Hem yw dhe styrya "Carrek"* 'That is to say "Rock".'

10.21 The word-order in this translation has not always been given sufficient thought. At John 1:45 we read: *ni re'n kavas neb a skrifas Moyses anodho y'n lagha, hag ynwedh an brofoesi*. This is intended to mean 'we have found him about whom Moses in the law and also the prophets wrote'. Unfortunately the word-order is unclear and the Kernowek Kemyn would more naturally be construed as 'we have found someone that Moses wrote about in the law, and also [we have found] the prophets.'

In my own version I avoided the ambiguity by using a passive verb: *Ny re gafas henna may fue screfys anodha gans Moyses y'n laha ha gans an profettys*.

10.22 At John 1:46 we read: *A yll *neppyth da dos *dhiworth Nasara?* which is intended as a translation of 'Can any good thing come from

Nazareth?' Unfortunately the Cornish is inaccurate. *A yll neppyth da dos* does not mean 'Can *anything* good come?' but 'Can *something* good come?'. 'Anything' in questions is *tra vyth*, not *neppyth*. In the second place *dheworth* (Kernowek Kemyn *dhiworth*) is the wrong preposition. Jesus lived *in* Nazareth, which means he came **out of** Nazareth. The translation should have contained *mes a* 'out of', rather than *dhiworth*. Compare the following examples from the texts:

> *ty a gam wruk yn tor ma **mes a egip** agan dry* 'you did wrong now bringing us out of Egypt' OM 1646-47
>
> *hy re ruk ov delyfrya **mes a preson*** 'she has delivered me from prison' BM 3758-59
>
> *Pegh o an pith a rug then tas a neff humbrak mabden **in mes a baradise*** 'Sin was what brought mankind out of paradise' TH 3
>
> *the Rosewa **in mes a Gooddron*** 'to Rosewa from Godren' BK 1105.

In my own version I wrote: *A yll tra vyth 'vas dos mes a Nazara?*

10.23 At John 2:7 the translation reads: *Hag i a's lenwis *bys dhe'n topp* 'And they filled them to the top'. We have seen at § 6.05 that *bys dhe* cannot be used with common nouns, but only when *dhe* is part of a prepositional pronoun; in consequence *bys dhe'n topp* is mistaken. It should have read *bys y'n topp*.

10.24 At John 2:9 the translation reads: *ha ny *wodhva a ble feu* for 'and he did not know from where it came'. *Ny *wodhva* is the preterite of *godhvos*. It is unattested in traditional Cornish, although it was hypothetically reconstructed by Lhuyd. The verb here has presumably been based on the English 'knew' and has thus been translated as past. The attested imperfect would have been the correct tense to use: *ny wodhya*. The same mistake has been made again at John 16:19: *Yesus a *wodhva i dhe vynnas govynn orta* 'Jesus knew that they wished to ask him'.

10.25 At John 2:15 the translation reads: *ev a's tewlis *oll anedha mes a'n tempel* 'he threw them, all of them out of the temple'. We have already seen at § 7.04 above, that the expression *oll anedha* is inadmissible in Cornish. At John 2:15 the text ought to have read *ev a's tewlis oll mes a'n tempel* 'he threw them all out of the temple.' The contemporary use in English of 'all of them' is the origin of this mistake in Cornish. One should remember that from the historical point of view 'all' in English is an adjective, not a pronoun. If in English one said 'them all', rather than 'all of them', one would not be tempted to write the "Cornish" phrase *oll anedha.

10.26 The Kernowek Kemyn translation of John 2:16 reads as follows: *ha leverel dhe *neb a wertha an *kolommes, 'Kemmerewgh an taklow ma *alemma; na *wrewgh chi ow Thas yn marghatti.'* 'and said to those who were selling doves, "Take these things hence; do not make a marketplace of my Father's house"' There are several problems here. Let us look at them one by one.

In the first place we notice that 'to those who were selling' is rendered *dhe *neb a wertha*. In traditional Cornish *the neb* 'to whom' refers to a singular antecedent only:

> *Iudas ow ry ty a vyn dre ȝe vay a reyth mar whek ȝe neb am tormont mar dyn* 'Judas, by your kiss which you give me so sweetly, you will deliver me to him who will torment me so bitterly' PA 66ab
>
> *mercy yw scos the nep a'n pys puppenag ol a vo ef* 'mercy is a shield for him who prays for it, whoever he may be' PC 22-3
>
> *vengyans the nep a'n sparryo* 'vengeance on him who spares him' PC 2078
>
> *o salve sancta parens the nep yv ioy ow colon* 'O hail holy parent, to whom is the joy of my heart' RD 455-56
>
> *mahum darber hardygrath ȝe neb a ruk ov throbla* 'Mahound inflict misfortune on him who troubled me' BM 948-49
>
> *Leverough both ages brys, ow arluth, the neb na fyll* 'Speak the wish of your mind, my lord, to him who fails not' BK 392-93.

Jesus addresses the money-changers in the plural. The translation ought therefore have read either *ha leverel dhe'n re na neb a wertha* or *ha leverel dhe'n dus a wertha* 'and spoke to those people who sold'. In my own version I wrote *dhe'n re na esa ow quertha* 'to those who were selling.'

The translator writes *kolommes* (i.e. *colomas*) 'doves' and in my own version I similarly wrote *colomas*. It has subsequently become apparent, however, that the plural of *colom* 'dove' in Cornish is *kelemmy*:

> *deaw gopyl a gelemmy, dof gans pluf gwyn, rag an vyghternes real* 'two pairs of doves, tame with white feathers, for the royal queen' BK 2045-47.

Kelemmy might well have been used here.

In the Kernowek Kemyn version Jesus tells the money-changers to take their wares *alemma* 'hence', but the wares are in the temple and should be taken 'out', rather than just 'away'. This is clear from the relevant passage in *Passio Christi*:

> *why guycoryon eugh **yn mes** y thesough ov kuthyl ges a thu hag e sans eglos* 'you merchants go out; you are making mockery of God and his holy church' PC 331-2.

In my own version I wrote: *Kemereugh an taclow ma **mes** alemma.*

The Kernowek Kemyn version says: *na wrewgh chi ow Thas yn marghatti* 'do not make my Father's house into a market-house'. This is an idiom for which I can find no parallel in traditional Cornish. The more natural way of expressing the idea of making X of Y, would have been to say *na wrewgh marghatti a ji ow Thas* 'do not make a market-house of my Father's house'. Compare the following examples from traditional Cornish:

> *Dyllas crist a ve rynnys **pedar ran guris a neȝe*** 'Christ's raiment was divided; four parts made of it'
>
> *fas ihesu gynef yma yn **hyuelep gurys a'y whys*** 'I have with me the face of Jesus in a likeness made of his sweat' RD1704-05
>
> *yscar ha canfas garow, an pith **a vetha gwrys syehar anotha*** 'tow cloth and rough canvas, that from which sacks used to be made' TH 6a
>
> *kyn rellyn ny signifia **bara gwrys a eys** in agan commyn eyth* 'though in our common speech we mean bread made from corn' TH 57a.

In my own version I wrote *na wreugh marhasva a jy ow Thas* 'do not make a market-place of my Father's house'.

10.27 At John 2:17 the translation reads: *Diwysekter *a-barth dha ji a'm devor* as a translation for 'Zeal for thy house devours me'. We have already seen at § 9.02 above that *a-barth, abarth* does not mean 'for, for the sake of', but rather 'in the name of' in oaths. The translation here ought to have read: *diwysekter rag dha ji*.

10.28 At John 2:23 we read: *Ytho pan esa ev yn Yerusalem *y'n Pask, *y'n dy'goel* for 'Thus when he was in Jerusalem during the Passover festival'. We have already seen, when discussing **y'n Sabot* at § 10.13 above, that the Cornish for 'at Easter' is *war Pask*. **Y'n Pask* is not Cornish, and neither is **y'n dy'goel*.

10.29 At John 2:25 we read: *ev a aswonni pandr' *a veu yn den* 'he knew what was in a man'. The verb *aswonni* is imperfect. The verb in the subordinate clause should therefore also be in the imperfect. The translation should have read: *pandr' esa yn dyn.* The expression *pandr' a *veu yn den* with the preterite instead of the long imperfect cannot be defended.

10.30 At John 3:7 the translator writes: *Na vedhes* marth dhis my dhe leverel dhis* 'Do not be astonished that I say to you'. **Na vedhes* (an invented form in Kernowek Kemyn, recte *na vedhens*) *marth dhe* is unattested in Cornish. If in Cornish one wishes to say 'Do not be astonished' one says *Na gemer marth.* This can be seen from the following examples:

> *A'm dyrryvas **na gemer marth** 'Do not be astonished by what I say' BK 141-42
> **na gymmar marth** vyth benynvas* 'do not be astonished, madam' CW 554
> **na gymar marth** anotha* 'do not be astonished by it' CW 560
> *ow hothman **na gybmar marthe** 'my friend, do not be astonished' CW 2304.

Not only is the form **vedhes*, **bedhes* unwarranted in this verse, the syntax is unwarranted as well.

10.31 The Kernowek Kemyn translation of John 3:20 reads as follows: *Rag *pub den neb a wra *drog a gas an golow, ha ny dheu *bys dhe'n golow, *rag ma na vo diskudhys y oberow* 'And everyone who does wrong hates the light and does not come to the light, so that his works are not discovered'. Unfortunately there are at least four problems in the translation of this verse. We will examine them in turn.

The first problem involves the expression **pub den neb a wra* 'everybody who does'. *Pub den neb* + relative verb is unattested in traditional Cornish. *Pub den* is used directly before the relative particle without *neb*:

> *hen yw dyth a bowesva the **pup den a vo** sylwys* 'that is a day of rest for everyone who will be saved' OM 145-46
> *mas **pub den a vo** sufficient instructys ha diskys a yll, dre folya an dyscans na, dos thin bewnans heb deweth* 'but everyone who may be sufficiently instructed and educated may, by following this teaching attain everylasting life' TH 20.

In fact 'everybody who' is more frequently translated *suel a*, e.g.

> **Suel a vynno** *bos sylwys golsowens ow lauarow* 'Everybody who wishes to be saved' PA 2a
>
> **suel a vynna** *y clewas* 'everybody who wished to hear it' PA 79b
>
> **suel a wressa** *both y das* 'everybody who would do his Father's will' PA 213b
>
> *Lowena thu'm arluth stowt gallosak drys* **suel a ve!** 'Greetings to my stalwart lord, powerful above everyobody who ever was!' BK 2546-47
>
> *rag own bonas kerethis gans* **suel a ugar** *ganow* 'for fear of being rebuked by everyone who opens his mouth' BK 3093-94.

or *kenyver (den) a*, e.g.

> **kynyuer den** *vs yn wlas* 'everybody who is in the country' OM 1029
>
> *the* **kenever an** *gorthya* 'to everybody who may worship him' BM 4427
>
> *the* **Canevar den** *gwyrrian a vo desyrius e gowis* 'to everybody righteous who will be desirous of getting it' SA 60
>
> *bus openly the* **kenever a whelha** 'but openly to everybody who sees' SA 60
>
> *drys* **kenever us** *in wlas* 'beyond everybody who is in the country' BK 3046.

*Pub den neb is not correct.

The second problem here involves the expression *a wra* **drog a gas** *an golow*. The translation here was intended to render 'who does evil hates the light' where the (incorrectly used) relative pronoun *neb* is followed by two different verbs. This is rather awkward and, more unfortunately, is ambiguous. A native speaker of Cornish would not expect two relative verbs one after the other, and would naturally take *a wra* **drog a gas** *an golow* to contain one verb only. He would understand the clause to mean 'who does/will do evil of the case of the light', or possibly 'who does/will do evil of the battle of the light'. The sense intended by the translator would, I believe, be less likely to occur to him.

The third problem in this verse involves the expression *ny dheu *bys dhe'n golow*. This is intended to mean 'does not come to the light'. As we have seen at § 6.05 above *bys dhe* is used only with pronouns, e.g. *bys dhym, bys dhodho*. With common nouns, *golow* here, for example, one must use *bys yn*. The translation should have read: *ny dheu bys y'n golow*. Notice that the same mistake is made again in the next verse (John 3:21) where we read *a dheu *bys dhe'n golow* 'comes to the light' instead of the correct *a dheu bys y'n golow*.

The fourth problem involves the expression **rag ma na vo diskudhys y oberow* 'so that his works be not disclosed'. We have already seen at § 4.09 above that **rag ma na* is not used in Cornish. One says *ma na* 'in order that... not'.

In my own version I translated this verse as follows: *Rag suel a wrella drog, cas yw an golow dhodho, ha ny vyn ef dos dhe'n golow ma na vo rebukys y oberow*. It will be seen that I have avoided all the problems encountered in the Kernowek Kemyn version.

10.32 The Kernowek Kemyn version at John 3:26 reads:

Hag i a dheuth dhe Yowann ha leverel dhodho, 'Rabbi, ev neb a *veu genes *an tu arall dhe Yordan, a neb te re *dhustunias, ott, yma ev ow pesydhya, ha pub den oll a *dheu dhodho.' 'And they came to John and said to him, "Rabbi, he who was with you on the other side of Jordan, of whom you have borne witness, beyond, he is baptizing, and everybody is going to him."'

There are a number of difficulties here. Let us look at them one by one.

The first problem involves the verb *a *veu genes* 'who was with you'. Jesus had been with John for a while beyond the Jordan. The verb required is the imperfect, not the preterite. The translation should have contained *esa* 'was' rather than *veu*. Moreover, because *esa* cannot stand at the beginning of a clause unless it is relative, the relative pronoun and relative particle are unnecessary, when *esa* is used. Instead of the rather awkward (and incorrect) *ev neb a *veu genes*, the translation should have read: *henna esa genes* 'that man who was with you'; cf. *ha in aga myske y thesa henna esa crist pub vr ow kull mer anotha, henno S Johan* 'and among them was that man of whom Christ continually mentioned, namely St John' TH 43.

The second difficulty here is the expression **an tu arall dhe Yordan* translating the Greek πέραν τοῦ Ἰορδάνου 'beyond the Jordan'. 'On the other side of' is a way of saying 'beyond'; there is no parallel in traditional Cornish for **an tu arall dhe* with such a meaning. *Dres an Jordan* 'across the Jordan' could have been used. There are further problems with an *tu arall dhe Yordan*, however, the name of the river might be expected to be preceded by either the definite article or by the word *dowr* or *ryver* 'river'; cf. the following:

A

yn trok horn y fyth teulys **yn tyber** *yn dour pur dovn* 'in an iron coffin he will be thrown into the Tiber into very deep water' RD 2166-67

B

yn dour tyber *ef a sef* 'he will stay in the river Tiber' RD 2137

teuleugh ef yn trok a horn yn **dour tyber** *yn nep corn may fo buthys* 'throw him in the coffin of iron into the rivr Tiber in some corner so he may be drowned' RD 2162-64

den dreys **dour tyber** *nyns a yn certan na vo marow* 'no man goes across the river Tiber without dying' RD 2214-15

yn **dour tyber** *ef a fue yn geler horn gorrys dovn* 'in the river Tiber he was put deep in an iron coffin' RD 2319-20

rag e laver ol an tyr a **Thowr Hombyr** *the Scotland* 'for his labour all the land from the River Humber to Scotland' BK 3236-37

hag orth **an ryuer** *surly* **a josselyne** *chapel guthel me a vyn* 'and indeed on the river of Josseline I shall build a chapel' BM 1141-43.

Even if we accept that *an tu arall* 'beyond' is admissible, the syntax used, *an tu arall dhe Yordan*, is odd. *An tu arall* is a noun phrase and would more naturally be attached to the name of the river by the preposition *a* 'from, of'. Moreover, *an tu arall* itself is not introduced by any preposition. It would have been better Cornish had the translation read: *war an tu arall a dhowr Yordan* 'on the other side of the river Jordan'. The present **an tu arall dhe Yordan* is much less satisfactory.

The expression *a neb te re *dhustunias* is also problematic. In the first place the verb **dustunya* (Kernowek Kemyn **dustunia*) is unattested in traditional Cornish. If one wishes to say 'bear witness' one says either *don dustuny* or *desta*. I have already cited examples of *don dustuny* at § 7.12 above. Here are some examples of *desta* 'bear witness' from the texts:

duen the'n myghtern the **thysta** *an gyst na vyn dos the squyr* 'let us go to the king to bear witness that the beam will not fit the desired length' OM 2543-44

dun ny the **thesta** *in scon d'agan epscop del yv gureys* 'come, let us bear witness immediately to our bishop that it is done' OM 2749-50.

There is no need to use an unattested verb here.

The final problem in this verse involves the verb *a dheu* 'comes'. The phrase in the Greek πάντες ἔρχονται is best translated 'all are going'. But the translation here reads: *ha pub den oll a *dheu dhodho* 'and

222

everybody will come to him'. It would have been better to have written *yma pub den oll ow tos dhodho* 'everybody is coming to him, everybody comes to him'.

10.33 At John 4:37 the Kernowek Kemyn reads: *Rag yndella gwir yw an lavar, "*Unn den a *wonis, ha *den arall a *vys"*. This is intended to mean: 'Thus true is the saying, "One man sows and another man reaps"'. There are, however, a number of difficulties in the translation.

In the first place the most natural way in Cornish to translate 'One man... another' is *an eyl... y gela* and it is difficult to see why 'one... another' was not here translated in this, the most obvious way. The second problem involves the word *gonys* (Kernowek Kemyn *gonis*). The Greek here is unambigous, σπείρων 'sowing', but *gonys* means 'cultivate, plough', rather than merely 'sow (seed)'. This can be seen from the following examples:

eugh the wonys guel ha ton 'go to cultivate field and lea' OM 1164

pandra amount thy'n gonys mar serryth orth den hep wow 'what use is it to us to cultivate if you are angry with man indeed?' OM 1233-34

ha me a's gor the wonys gans weras Christ lun a ras 'and I will set them to plough with the help of Christ full of grace' BK 856-57

A dyr bryntyn the wonys teurant re bo confoundys 'Of fine land for cultivation a tyrant has been confounded' BK 1180-81.

The last problem is with the verbal form *a vys*, which is intended to mean 'reaps'. The Cornish for 'reap' is attested in Late Cornish only in the following sentence from Pryce:

Whelas megouzion tha medge an îsse 'Look reapers to reap the corn'.

It would seem that the Middle Cornish for 'reap' was either **mesy* or **megy* and it is quite possible, therefore, that the third singular present-future was indeed **mys* (cf. *pegy ~ pys, cregy ~ crys*). Since, however, **mys* is unattested, it would have been sensible to avoid it. Moreover **mys* would have meant 'will reap' as much as 'reaps'. Furthermore the expressions *unn den a wonys* and *den arall a vys* might well have suggested to a native speaker of Cornish something like 'one man of cultivation' and 'another man of a world/of a finger.' It will be admitted, I think, that the present translation of this verse is not without difficulties.

In my own translation of the New Testament into Cornish I translated the whole verse as follows: *Yndelma gwyr yw an lavar coth, 'Yma an eyl ow conys ha'y gela ow mejy'*.

BACK MATTER AND MAPS

11.00 At the end of the book there is a table of neotestamentary weights and measures, followed by maps of St Paul's four journeys, the Holy Land in the time of the New Testament, a map showing the churches mentioned in Revelation and a map of Jerusalem in New Testament times. It is not clear in the table of money and weights why coins are called *Bathow* **grek** 'Greek coins' whereas the weights are referred to simply as *Greka* 'Greek'. This seems to be another example of the hesitation between *Grek/Greka* noted at § 2.10 above.

As has been noted above, at Acts 28:1 (and heading) 'Malta' is called *Malta* in Kernowek Kemyn. On the map on page 424, however, the island is clearly labelled *MELITA*.

CONCLUSION

12.00 *An Testament Nowydh* was launched with much public fanfare in 2004 by the Cornish Language Board. Any expectations that the work would be of a very high standard, however, have been disappointed. The deficiencies of the translation might be summarized as follows:

i)   The orthography used for *An Testament Nowydh* is often claimed to be easier to use than any other spelling system for revived Cornish. Yet the translation of *An Testament Nowydh* is not spelt consistently within the chosen orthography, for all its beng 'fit for purpose'. There is also considerable hesitation in the translation about when and where to capitalize proper names.

ii)   the translation into Kernowek Kemyn of personal names and place-names is also inconsistent. Sometimes names are respelt to make them conform to the conventions of Kernowek Kemyn. Sometimes pre-existing Cornish forms of names are adopted. At other times pre-existing Cornish forms of names (*Mathew, Erod,* for example) are ignored English names are used instead. At other times, although Cornish names exists, forms are invented that are neither Cornish nor English (e.g. **Aramat, *Lasarus*). Furthermore the use of nomenclature is inconsistent in *An Testament Nowydh*, and the same name is not infrequently spelt in two different ways (e.g. *Lukius/Lusius Abraham/Abram, Makedoni/Masedonia, Kyrene/Syrene*) for no apparent reason.

iii) names of Hebrew and Greek origin, which in Cornish were undoubtedly pronounced with initial <J>, are written here with <Y>, though the name *Jamys* escapes this reshaping. This means that the two disciples are known throughout as *Jamys ha Yowann*. Even with Old Testament names, however, the translation is inconsistent, since one finds *Yesse* 'Jesse', and *Yosafat* 'Jehosaphat', for example, but *Job* 'Job'.

iv) the translation uses invented words rather than items actually occurring in traditional Cornish, e.g. **denel* 'human', **eskarogeth* 'hostility', **hevelder* 'likeness', **mebyoneth* 'sonship', **negedhses* 'apostasy', **pervedhel* 'internal', etc. Even here, however, the policy is inconsistent, since one finds at one point in *An Testament Nowydh* the form *trodreghya* 'circumcise', for example, but the attested *circkumcisya* 'circumcise' at another.

v) the translation is not infrequently unsure of Cornish inflection and syntax. Indeed, as I have cited extensively, there are many places in *An Testament Nowydh* where the translation can be described as grammatically incorrect.

vi) Parts of *An Testament Nowydh* are written in good idiomatic Cornish—although the orthography throughout is inauthentic. There are many other parts, and I have recorded a great number, where the language is less idiomatic. Indeed is frequently difficult to make much sense of the translation as it stands.

vii) It is claimed that *An Testament Nowydh* has been based largely on the Greek—a claim which is difficult to sustain. A close analysis of the translation indicates that it owes as much to English versions, the RSV, the TEV and the Authorized Version, for example, as it does to the Greek *koinē*.

I have had space above to deal with only a fraction of the errors and inconsistencies in *An Testament Nowydh*. In consequence I have not really given an adequate impression of this version of the New Testament. If one wanted to write a full analysis of all the problems in *An Testament Nowydh*, it would take a very long time indeed. In the introduction to the Kernowek Kemyn version of the New Testament we are told that the book is intended for "both public and private use". Regrettably it is not really suitable for either.

REFERENCES

BM = Whitley Stokes (ed.), *Beunans Meriasek: the life of St Meriasek, Bishop and confessor, a Cornish drama* (London: Trübner and Co. 1872)

CT = Nicholas Williams, *Cornish Today: an examination of the revived language*, first and second editions (Sutton Coldfield: Kernewek dre Lyther 1995)

CT3 = Nicholas Williams, *Cornish Today: an examination of the revived language*, third edition (Westport: Evertype 2006, ISBN 978-1-904808-07-7)

CW = Whitley Stokes (ed.), *Gwreans an Bys: the Creation of the World*, (London: Williams & Norgate 1864 [reprinted Kessinger Publishing 1987, ISBN 0-7661-8009-3])

KKC21 = *Kernewek Kemmyn: Cornish for the Twenty-First Century*, Paul Dunbar and Ken George ([s.l.], Cornish Language Board 1997) ISBN 0-907064-71-X

OCV = "Old Cornish Vocabulary" [quoted from Norris 1859 ii: 311-435 and Campanile 1974]

OM = "Origo Mundi" in Norris (1859) i: 1-219

Nance 1952 = R. Morton Nance, *An English-Cornish Dictionary* (Marazion 1952) [reprinted 1978]

Nance 1955 = R. Morton Nance, *A Cornish-English Dictionary* (Marazion 1955) [reprinted 1978]

Norris 1859 = Edwin Norris, *The Ancient Cornish Drama* i-ii (London [reprinted New York/London: Benjamin Blom 1968])

PC = "Passio Domini Nostri Jhesu Christi" in Norris 1859 i 221-479

TH = John Tregear, *Homelyes xiii in Cornysche* (British Library Additional MS 46, 397) [text from a cyclostyled text published by Christopher Bice ([s.l.] 1969)]

Wijk 1959 = Axel Wijk, *Regularized English: An Investigation into the English Spelling Reform Problem with a New, Detailed Plan for a Possible Solution.* (Acta Universitatis Stockholmiensis: Stockholm Studies in English; 7) Stockholm: Almqvist & Wiksell, 1959.

Williams 1997 = Nicholas Williams, *Clappya Kernowek: an introduction to Unified Cornish Revised* (Agan Tavas, Portreath 1997, ISBN 1-901409-01-5)

HKΔ = British and Foreign Bible Society. 1958. *Η Καινή Διαθήκη.* Second edition with revised critical apparatus. London: British and Foreign Bible Society.

Lightning Source UK Ltd.
Milton Keynes UK
UKOW04f1851020316

269499UK00001B/68/P